PRAISE FOR *A HEART FOR FREEDOM*

As a foremost student leader of the Chinese democracy movement, Chai Ling gives us a deeply touching firsthand account of what really happened in China that eventually led to the Tiananmen Square massacre on June 4, 1989. By preserving memories of this epoch-making event and its aftermath from oblivion, *A Heart for Freedom* not only makes an important contribution to history but also helps keep alive China's ever-increasing hope for freedom and democracy.

YU YING-SHIH

Professor emeritus, Princeton University, and recipient of the John W. Kluge Prize (2006), Library of Congress

Chai Ling is one of the most courageous women I know, and always has been—from her early days as a self-possessed student thrust suddenly onto the worldwide stage to her current role as a fierce defender of women and girls. Her conviction that every person should have a voice has informed her whole life and made her a powerful role model to *Glamour*'s 12 million readers and to women worldwide of every political persuasion. Quite honestly, she awes me!

CINDI LEIVE

Editor in chief, Glamour *magazine*

I am delighted that Chai Ling, who has promoted and sought freedom all of her life, has found the greatest freedom of all in Christ. And I pray for God's blessing on her in the coming years as she discovers new ways to serve and minister in the world in the power of the gospel.

TIM KELLER

Senior pastor, Redeemer Presbyterian Church, New York City, and author of The Reason for God

Chai Ling bravely fought for democracy in China but found something even more transformational—grace. This memoir is not just for people interested in a compelling first-person account of politics and history. It is for all of us seekers who search for true meaning and purpose while battling our private fears and regrets. It is about that liberating discovery when we learn that there is nothing we can do that will make God love us any more, and nothing we can do that will make God love us any less.

MICHEAL FLAHERTY
Cofounder and president of Walden Media

What was it like to be at the center of the Tiananmen democracy movement in Beijing in 1989? Chai Ling, who was the commander in chief of the students, tells the story in a gripping and moving way. She shares her insights into the student movement and the personal narrative of her dramatic escape from China and experience as an immigrant in the United States. If you want to read one book about China's student democracy movement and what happened to its activists, *A Heart for Freedom* will keep you completely engrossed.

DAVID AIKMAN
Former TIME *magazine Beijing bureau chief, eyewitness to the Tiananmen massacre, and author of* Jesus in Beijing

Chai Ling has a dramatic story to tell of God's transforming power—from radical dissident to radical Christ-follower, now changing China and the world in ways she never dreamed possible. Her book, *A Heart for Freedom*, will inspire you to pursue great things for a great God!

DR. BRYAN WILKERSON
Senior pastor, Grace Chapel, Lexington, Massachusetts

A HEART FOR
FREEDOM

THE REMARKABLE JOURNEY OF A YOUNG DISSIDENT,
HER DARING ESCAPE, AND HER QUEST
TO FREE CHINA'S DAUGHTERS

CHAI LING

TYNDALE™
MOMENTUM

*An Imprint of
Tyndale House Publishers, Inc.*

Visit Tyndale online at www.tyndale.com.

Visit Tyndale Momentum online at www.tyndalemomentum.com.

TYNDALE is a registered trademark of Tyndale House Publishers, Inc. *Tyndale Momentum* and the Tyndale Momentum logo are trademarks of Tyndale House Publishers, Inc. Tyndale Momentum is an imprint of Tyndale House Publishers, Inc.

A Heart for Freedom: The Remarkable Journey of a Young Dissident, Her Daring Escape, and Her Quest to Free China's Daughters

Designed by Erik M. Peterson

Edited by Dave Lindstedt

Library of Congress Cataloging-in-Publication Data

Ling, Chai.
    A heart for freedom : the remarkable journey of a young dissident, her daring escape, and her quest to free China's daughters / Chai Ling.
        p. cm.
    Includes bibliographical references (p.   ).
    ISBN 978-1-4143-6246-5 (hc)
1. Ling, Chai. 2. Christian converts—China—Biography. 3. China—Politics and government—2002-
4. China—Politics and government—1976-2002. I. Title.
    BV4935.L525A3 2011
    248.2′46092—dc23
    [B]   2011024188

ISBN 978-1-4143-6485-8 (International Trade Paper Edition)
ISBN 978-1-4143-6247-2 (sc)

Printed in the United States of America

18   17   16   15   14   13   12
7   6   5   4   3   2   1

To all the people who courageously sacrificed and fought for
a freer China, including the Tiananmen generation.
May the day of eternal freedom come soon!

———

When they walk through the Valley of Weeping, it will become a place of
refreshing springs. The autumn rains will clothe it with blessings.

PSALM 84:6, NLT

TABLE OF CONTENTS

PREFACE

As EARLY AS MAY 27, 1989, I felt the need to bear witness to the events unfolding in Tiananmen Square and to record my experience there for posterity. I've long felt there was a much deeper meaning and reason for what happened at Tiananmen, but for twenty-two years I had been unable to articulate it. In 1995 and early 1996, I wrote more than two hundred pages of an initial draft but could not finish it. I sensed there was a precious story and truth to be told, but for the past two decades, I could not capture the essence of it. It was like a free bird—I could hear it singing and feel its presence and heartbeat, but I could not quite grab hold of it. Like the sparkle of sunlight on a river, I could not capture it and put it down on paper. But for all these years, I have never given up my pursuit of this truth.

I searched in many places: in democracy work on Capitol Hill and at the UN; in a Princeton and Harvard education; in the fast-paced, high-pressure investment banking and consulting industries; in self-help books and leadership seminars; even in founding an Internet company and starting a foundation. But I couldn't find the answer that would quench my thirst.

Then, on December 4, 2009, my heart was profoundly changed and my eyes were opened to all the dramatic events of my life. For the first time, everything started to make sense. I now see that the thirst I had is the longing for freedom placed in our hearts by God. Only when I came to know God could I truly begin to comprehend his unique purpose for my life. I've since been given renewed strength, healing, and insight to explain my perspective on China's past, the meaning of the Tiananmen movement, and God's future plan. I've come to realize this is not a book I could write on my own; rather, it's a book that could only be written *through* me.

By May 2011, I finally was able to write about the events of my life in their entirety. I used to feel hurt and betrayed by so many; now I've been healed from most of the pain, and God has given me the strength to finish the story.

Over the past twenty-two years, many reports have been written about Tiananmen Square, and no doubt most have mentioned my role there. I have not read them all, nor would I be able to even if I wanted. This book is *my* story, a story of youth, passion, sacrifice, and triumph in the search for freedom and justice against great evil. And it is a story of the ultimate truth that sets us free.

PRELUDE

"WE'RE NOT GOING ALONG WITH YOU THIS TIME!" my father said out of the blue. He looked especially frail and upset as he stood in the entryway of my home with his hand on the doorknob, ready to storm out. "Twenty years ago," he said sternly, "you were young and brave and full of hope. You were so lucky to survive. We are fortunate to have half our family intact. You know how much we miss your mom and Grandma. . . ."

He paused, and we became silent. In 1991, we had lost both my mother and my grandmother, and it was still painful enough that we didn't talk about it often.

After an awkward silence, Dad continued at a slower pace: "Things are different now. We are older. We are tired. We can't do this again. . . . And you—can you do this again? You are no longer young and naive; you are a wife and a mother now. Getting involved in the movement again, after all you went through—what kind of consequences will you bring to us as a family? What kind of grief will you bring to your children?"

This was my father, the most amazing dad, who had been a devoted and talented doctor in the Chinese army, and later the head of a hospital, but who had given up everything he had worked for his entire life to be with us in America. Now in his seventies, he had stood by me, his eldest daughter, in the midst of the most difficult period of our family's life, with no resentment and no complaint. But this time he was putting his foot down.

"Why can't you be like your sister and your other friends and try to live a normal and common life?" Dad looked at me, shook his head, and walked out the door. A nice Sunday brunch ended abruptly.

All I had said was that, in a few days' time, I would be on a plane to Washington, DC, to celebrate with Fang Zheng, a fellow survivor of Tiananmen Square, who had lost his legs during the massacre and who was now going to be able to walk—and dance—for the first time on prosthetic legs he received after coming to the United States. It seemed my father was making a bigger deal of it than was necessary. Yet, at the same time, I knew all too well his concerns could be well founded.

"What do you think, Bob?" I turned to my husband, hoping for some perspective. "Should I still go to DC?" I knew the impact on him might be the same as it was on my dad. He had seen the consequences of my involvement in the Chinese democracy movement.

Bob, in the middle of watching a Sunday football game, shot back a quick reply. "Of course you should go," he said. "It's fun. It will be great." To my husband, a typical American, politics are as simple as a sporting event. You win or you lose, but you don't die.

The situation, of course, is much different in China. There, trying to live a common life can lead one to become a revolutionary or a wanted criminal. And even if one leaves the country, the persecution doesn't end. Recently, my dad was given a severe warning by some leaders from China: "If Chai Ling continues to join the movement, there will not be any good consequences for all of you," they said. "China is different now; we are stronger and more powerful. A lot of things could happen . . ."

What was left unsaid made a big impression on my dad, but it isn't something the average American can understand. Life in America is hectic and stressful, with concerns about money, bills, and a shortage of time. But the stakes are much higher in China, where you can lose your freedom or your life for merely trying to express yourself.

In the spring of 1989, the simple act of bringing water and bread to fellow students at Tiananmen Square led me to the top steps of the Monument to the People's Heroes—center stage in the student protests for government reform and greater freedom. Later, in the face of oncoming tanks and troops, I would have to make a choice between life and belief. Now, after all these years of sweat and tears to rebuild my life in America, could a simple trip to Washington, DC, lead my family and me into another Valley of Weeping?

But how could I not go? How could I give up what we stood for? What if this were the very work I was kept alive to finish?

On the morning of October 7, 2009, I woke up early, knowing this would be a big day. Just four months earlier, on June 4, we had marked the twentieth anniversary of China's Tiananmen movement and the Beijing Massacre; today we would celebrate a major victory in the life of one of the survivors.

Two decades had passed so quickly. In my mind, I was still the same young woman who had escaped from China, after months in hiding, as one of the "21 Most Wanted" student leaders at Tiananmen Square, not knowing if I would live or die. Now I live in the Cradle of Liberty— Boston, Massachusetts—the site of another historic massacre in the cause of freedom and democracy (though only five people died in Boston, compared to hundreds or thousands in Beijing).

Twenty years ago, I was a lonely immigrant—in exile—who barely spoke English. Now I am the mother of three young children, the wife of a loving American husband, and a successful business entrepreneur with a nice home—to many, perhaps, a poster child for freedom and the American Dream.

Even in my wildest dreams, I could not have imagined my life would turn out this way. What I have experienced is far beyond what any country girl from a fishing village in China could ever have expected. Often when I'm at an expensive country club or a fancy fund-raising event, I still feel a bit out of place, like I'm living in a fairy-tale world. Sometimes I wonder, *Who am I now? Is this my true destiny?*

I said good-bye to my husband and my girls and settled into the taxi that would take me to Logan Airport. The light of the morning sun dappled the colorful leaves of the majestic oaks that give our home the feel of an old English estate. As we drove along the gleaming Charles River, which winds past the ivy-covered brick buildings of Harvard Business School, my alma mater, the morning turned into a glorious New England fall day. The air was fresh and crisp, the sky a sapphire blue.

Aboard the plane, as I squeezed into a middle seat between two large passengers, I reflected on the twenty-year anniversary of Tiananmen Square. An article in *The Chronicle of Higher Education* had called it "The Great Forgetting."[1] Few students inside China today would recognize the iconic picture from 1989 of a lone young man standing in front of a line of tanks. And many middle-aged Chinese no longer talk about the reform movement. In a more prosperous China, they no longer are interested in discussing politics or think it is relevant to their busy lives of raising their families and getting on with their jobs. I was deeply saddened by this.

That's why the day's event was so special. While the rest of the world tried to forget Tiananmen, a few still chose to remember. That's why it was important for me to drop my daily duties to be with Fang Zheng, to celebrate and be a witness to his amazing triumph, and to thank the people who continued to do the right thing by offering love and support to the oppressed.

My dad's voice still rang in my ears. I wished I could tell him that I had to do the right thing, especially when the rest of the world remained silent. If I became afraid and caved in to the pressure, I would deny the very person I am.

Maybe Dad was just overreacting. Maybe I'm just imagining things.

My stomach started hurting again. How much I hated this kind of conflict! What would it be like to live like a common person, never having to confront or experience this kind of pain or mental anguish?

The steady noise and motion of the aircraft dulled my senses and lulled me to sleep.

I awoke to an awful sensation of suffocation, as if someone were choking me. I opened my mouth as wide as I could, but I could not breathe. My arms and legs seemed to be losing strength. If this is not what it's like to die, then I don't know what dying will be like. I tried to shout, but the noise of the plane drowned me out. The two giants on either side of me must surely have heard my cries, but for some reason, they kept looking straight ahead—as if I were crazy and their best response was to pretend I wasn't there.

Finally, I tapped the arm of the person sitting to my left, closest to the aisle. "I can't breathe," I said. "Please get someone to help me."

A few minutes later, a flight attendant arrived and escorted me to the front of the cabin. She gave me a cup of water and a bag to breathe into, which helped a little. My face must have looked as pale as a sheet. A doctor traveling on the plane checked me and asked me a number of questions.

"You are having an attack," he said. "Are you anxious? Are you nervous?"

"I don't think so," I replied, a bit confused. I had never experienced this kind of debilitating emotion, even at the height of the Tiananmen crisis or throughout my underground escape.

"It seems you are suffering an anxiety attack," he said. "Have some more water. You should get better." He told me to call my physician when we landed, and he went back to his seat.

Anxiety attack? I couldn't believe it. I didn't know that what was happening in my subconscious could have the power to create such a powerful reaction in my body. On this day of joy and triumph, my past journey and my future destiny decisively collided.

Like Abraham going up to the mountain to offer his most beloved son, I felt as if I were climbing the mountain for a second time, to again face the anxiety of possibly losing everything most near and dear to my heart. The first time happened in the last hours at Tiananmen, as the tanks and soldiers converged on the Square. Then, we were young, passionate, and with a big dream to reform China. And though our dreams were crushed and my heart was broken, our lives were spared, like the life of Abraham's son. But now I had real children, beautiful and innocent children, who knew nothing about the cruelty of evil. How could I rejoin a battle that could not be won and in the process sacrifice my most precious loved ones? Who was I, a common individual, to take on a battle against an entire regime with enormous resources and networks, against the backdrop of a world that seemed to have forgotten—or at least was unaware of—the situation in China? I felt the wind being sucked from my sails. I could not move forward, and I could not move back. I was stuck in an ocean of anxiety.

———————

A year later, in June 2010, I caught the same flight from Boston to DC—this time to announce the beginning of a movement called All Girls Allowed, whose mission is to end China's one-child policy and stop the world's largest gendercide against women and girls, a massive crime against humanity that has taken more than four hundred million innocent lives. This new battle seems so much larger than Tiananmen, yet I no longer live in fear and conflict. My life is truly filled with peace, and I overflow with joy and laughter.

If someone had told me in 2009 that my panic attack would be the beginning of a beautiful chapter in my long, arduous—yet splendid—journey; or that shortly after my return to Boston, God would meet me and lead me to the summit of a tall mountain from which I could look down upon the torturous path of my life with new understanding, I would not have believed it. Nor, perhaps, would you. This book, which started out as a simple memoir for my American-born children to know their mother's history of coming to freedom, has become an audacious hope to record and reveal what might have been the mind of God all along—to free China and to free girls and women under oppression around the world. But for you to see and believe, we will have to start at the beginning of the journey. . . .

DAUGHTER
OF CHINA

1

GROWING UP IN THE CITY OF SUNSHINE

I WENT TO BEIJING for the first time when I was seventeen—a young girl on the threshold of life. So much would happen during the short span of time between that ride, in 1983, and the one I would take *out* of Beijing in June 1989 that decades could well have passed since the morning I traveled through the Chinese countryside to begin my university studies.

On the bus from Rizhao, my father sat beside me in great spirits. He didn't say much, but every so often he let out a sigh to show me how happy he was that his firstborn child was on her way to Peking University—or Beida, as we fondly call our school—the most prestigious institute of higher learning in all of China. He was relieved, because he knew things could have turned out differently. For a father who valued Chinese tradition, I—his firstborn, but not a son—was once a big disappointment. Still, as a young girl determined to overcome her "gender deficiency," I had brought home the prize, which gave my father a profound sense of pride and contentment.

"Ling Ling," he said as we settled in for the seven-hour trip from our village in Shandong Province, "you are leaving your home now. You know, I also was seventeen when I left home to join the army."

Like most Chinese names, my father's name, Chai Jingjin, which literally means "Going to Beijing," embodied a cherished family wish. My grandfather had fervently hoped his son would grow up, leave the countryside, and go to the capital city to find a better life in serving the emperor, perhaps as a scholar. Dad never got to seek his fortune in Beijing, but he did leave the countryside to pursue a career as an army doctor.

Now he and I were headed for Beijing on a crowded bus, which bucked and jolted along a winding road through the Eastern Mountains on its way from our seaside village to the vast interior of the Chinese heartland. A perilous abyss yawned below us on one side, and the sun seemed to scorch the sheer rock walls rising sharply above us on the other. Every so often, we'd pass a pitiful collection of little straw huts shaded by a lone tree. I saw rags set out to dry on the hot rocks and small children scampering about in open-slit shorts that exposed their tiny backsides as they shouted and chased their goats in a haze of dust. On a far mountain ridge, a man with a bare, dark-brown torso moved in and out of view as he toiled behind an ox and plow, swaying in perfect rhythm under the broiling sun.

Along the roadside, women and children would stop whatever they were doing and stand motionless, their mouths agape and faces blank, staring at the bus and its passengers as we drove past them into a distance they couldn't reach and a future they could not even imagine. I was deeply saddened by the sight of these people on the mountainside, trapped in the suffering landscape with no way to make life better and no hope for the future of their children.

It reminded me of the time when I was five years old and was left in the foster care of a peasant family while my parents were sent on a military mission. I lived with these people in their mud-brick hut, with its central platform that served as a place to eat meals, sit during the day, and sleep at night. I remember the smell of smoke coming into the room when the bed was warmed by burning hay on winter nights. Now I was leaving behind these villages filled with helpless poverty, illiteracy, and boredom, but my heart ached for them. I felt they were a part of me—the earthy, hardy places where I came from and the roots that gave me the foundation and strength in my life.

"Bye, now," I said silently as my view of the people faded behind the bus. "I am going away to learn, but I will be back someday when I am older and stronger. I will help you, bring you hope, freedom, and more. Someday!"

———

The sight of those poor peasants reminded me of my dear grandma—and thinking of her made my heart ache even more. Grandma, who had come to live with us and who had raised me, was the stable parenting figure in my early years when Mom and Dad were constantly sent on military missions. Her face had many wrinkles, and her tiny body had withered with age, but hidden within her small frame was the heart of a hardworking, enduring, tireless woman. The veins that stood out like blue ropes on the backs of her hands were a testimony to her years of manual labor in the fields, in every season and right up to the last hour each time she gave birth. She had married Grandpa at a young age and gave birth to seven surviving children, often returning to the fields within days of delivery.

As with many traditional Chinese women, the years of hard labor and subsistence living left Grandma with a strong set of values and traditions. Because Grandpa had died of starvation during the three-year famine in the late 1950s, Grandma was extremely careful not to waste food. She never started a meal when we did, but would wait for us to finish and then eat our leftovers. She got up early every morning, at five o'clock when my parents did their calisthenics, and began to make breakfast, wash clothes, and straighten up the house. She often went tottering about on her bound feet to gather twigs and leaves for kindling. On bone-chilling winter mornings, we would see her form rising and falling in the gray mist; and when she returned with an armful of sticks, her silvery-gray hair, which normally was combed neatly and coiled up into a bun, was blown down all over her forehead. My dad, a young officer with great potential and always concerned with appearances, forbade Grandma to go out, lest one of his army comrades see her and wonder why an officer of his rank had his mother out gathering sticks. But Grandma would say, "I'm no good anymore anyway. What's wrong with helping you save a little money on kindling so I'm not just freeloading all the time?"

When Dad still strictly forbade her, my siblings and I inherited Grandma's job. We quickly learned that she believed in Master Chan's saying: "If you don't work, you don't eat." Though Grandma was illiterate and uncultured, the virtue of hard work was deeply rooted in her life—and now in mine.

Hard times did not keep Grandma from having a big heart full of mercy and kindness to people and creatures in worse situations than hers. One time I bought a number of little chicks, and Grandma helped me raise them. One of the chicks was crippled and could not completely stand up. A neighbor suggested we make a nice chicken soup, but Grandma felt a special compassion for the poor chick and always gave her more food and care because of her illness. Later the chick grew into a hen and laid many eggs. Grandma always said that hen worked extra hard to thank her owners for showing mercy and kindness.

When I told Grandma I was going to Peking University, her ancient, wrinkled face lit up with joy. In that moment, all the years of toil and strife fell away, and she was transformed into a young girl again, radiant, with a glimpse of sparkle in her eyes. I couldn't remember ever seeing her so happy. She beamed and laughed and showed her missing teeth. All her long-buried memories rushed up, vivid and beautiful, and burst out in a flurry of words.

"In the old days," she began, "when a student passed the exam and made the emperor's list, the imperial palace sent a messenger by horseback to the village to deliver the news to the family. Can you imagine? The whole village came out to celebrate. They banged drums and performed dragon dances. That was a lot of fun, I can tell you. If the student happened to make the number one list, he won a chance to marry the emperor's daughter and live in a palace in Beijing. Sometimes he'd bring his bride back home to visit the village and see his parents. Then the whole road would be strewn with flowers and brightly colored paper, and soon a team of horses, palace guards, flags, carriages, and sedan chairs—each one carried by eight people—would arrive. It was the greatest honor a son could possibly bring to his family."

Grandma went on and on, as if she had just returned from a voyage to another century—the century before 1911, when the last emperor in a series of dynasties was abolished. In Grandma's generation, those stories had been kept alive through folk music and plays, but my parents' generation and mine—those who grew up in the "new society"—never saw such a thing.

"That's why we named your father 'Going to Beijing,'" Grandma said. "It's too bad that when your father was growing up, China was in a different time. They didn't have those exams anymore, or that kind of fun. But now my granddaughter is going to Beijing!" She clapped her aged, weatherworn hands. "At last, somehow, that Chai family wish has come true. How wonderful is that?"

Usually when Grandma got going on all the good things she missed about the "old society," as the Communists called it, my dad would tell her to stop talking. He worried someone would overhear what she said and report that our family didn't like the "new society"—a crime that could lead to death or a life sentence in a forced labor camp. This time, though, I guess she touched a soft spot in Dad's heart. Instead of stopping her, he joined in with his own rhapsody.

"Today's exam is no less competitive than in the old days," he said. "It may even be harder. Only fifty spots for this university are permitted for our province, with millions of bright kids competing."

Dad and Grandma were grinning, and my mother beamed with joy as well. She could clearly recall the day she passed the exams and entered medical school. She remembered what joy she'd brought to her mother and what pride she'd given her family. I couldn't tell whether Grandma heard what my father had said, but this much was clear: The whole family was overjoyed that a family dream had finally come true after three generations. As it sank in, the realization that I was going to Beijing had a different meaning for everyone, but the whole family agreed that a bright future awaited me, and they acknowledged the luster and glory I had brought to the family. I loved the idea that I had done something to give my mother and grandmother such joy. What made me even happier was the thought that, by leaving, I would get out from beneath my father's thumb.

I love my father, but I was intimidated by him when I was growing up. Our relationship became better when I started doing well in school, but less than a year before my acceptance at Beida, he and I got into a major conflict when I told him I didn't plan to join the Communist Youth League. I felt so hurt by his reaction that I did not speak to him for some time. I decided to skip a class in order to test for university. Surprisingly, he later went to talk to the school principal, who agreed to establish an accelerated program for a few students, and some of us went on to college.

My dad saw college as the next step on a set pathway to success within Chinese society. I saw it as the gateway to freedom and happiness. Though focused on different destinies, we agreed on one thing: Beida was the culmination of the fairy-tale dreams of three generations of Chais.

2

CHILD OF THE TIGER DAD

My father was born in 1935, the third child among seven siblings. My grandfather, whom I knew only through a faded photograph, was a hardworking and remarkably capable man. He farmed a few acres and occasionally hired some help during harvesttime. During the less busy times, he took fresh peanuts and home-raised pigs and chickens to the farmers' market in the nearby city of Qingdao. Grandpa also knew how to turn animal skins into leather using a unique softening process that today he might be able to patent or use to open a factory. But this was 1930s China, and he was busy supporting his large family.

In 1937, Japan invaded China, and their troops swept down from the north and occupied Grandpa's hometown, making his business and farming enterprise no longer possible. The Japanese army often came to the villages to seize supplies, food, and livestock—and sometimes to arrest people. My dad remembers a time when he and his family had to run to the mountains to hide. He remembers seeing Japanese soldiers ransack the town, taking livestock and emptying food containers. Surprisingly, my dad did not seem frightened or upset by all this. But he was a kid, after all. Though feeding a family of nine during the turbulent war years was no easy task for Grandpa, he made sure the kids had enough to eat and that they learned to read and study.

After Japan was defeated and withdrew from China in 1945, civil war broke out across the country as the Nationalists and Communists battled for control. By 1949, the Communists had secured their victory.

When Dad turned twenty-one, he joined the People's Liberation Army (PLA). The new China had a shortage of people who were educated and skilled. Because Grandpa had enabled my dad to finish high school, Dad became a valuable asset to the army. He was a handsome, smart, diligent, humble, and sensible young man, well liked by his army bosses, peers, and colleagues.

In 1960, among the choices of medical colleges, engineering colleges, and military academies for future officers, Dad was sent to the medical school to be trained as an army doctor. To this day, he is grateful for this. At school Dad became a leader in the student government, and he had a few female admirers who would come by from time to time to ask him to dance or visit. "In those days," he said, "life was simple and upbeat."

My mother also grew up in a peasant family, but in a different county of Shandong. Her family did not emphasize education—especially for a young girl—but Mom loved school nevertheless. Whenever her mother wanted to pull her out of school to help in the fields, Mom begged to stay in class and promised to finish her chores right away when she got home. From a young age, my mom went immediately into the fields after school to feed the animals and clean up the yard. When all the work was done, she ate her dinner quickly and went on to her homework under the light of a small lamp. She often told me how fortunate my siblings and I were because we were spared from all the work so we could focus on our studies.

When my mom finished high school, she tested and got into the Medical School of Cheeloo University (now part of Shandong University School of Medicine, the same university my sister later attended). Mom was not only beautiful, smart, and diligent, she also loved the performing arts and was quite talented at singing the traditional Chinese operas. Naturally she became a leader in the student government's culture and art department and the Youth League.

Because my mother possessed all the attributes of a successful modern woman (intelligence, talent, and a future career as a highly respected medical doctor) yet also maintained all the virtues of a traditional Chinese woman (beauty, tenderness, kindness, and tolerance), she had many eager suitors. Her pure mind, childlike love for singing, and joy for life attracted a wide range of men, from high-ranking military officers, to classmates, to doctors and professors. Mom kept her preferences close to her heart, which made my dad work even harder to win her over. She never told us how Dad managed to beat out the other competitors, but we're thankful he won.

At the beginning of the 1960s, just as a new China was emerging, their young lives were ready to blossom, and their view of the future was full of hope and happiness. Mom graduated a year ahead of Dad, and when the army came to recruit among the recent college graduates, she applied. After inspection and review, this Cinderella from a peasant family, who'd had to finish all her chores in order to stay in school, became a bona fide army doctor. Upon her enlistment, she had a picture taken in her crisp, new uniform, and she looked radiant. When my siblings and I were growing up, Mom often teased us by asking who wore the uniform better, Dad or Mom. Of course, we always said both, but Mom was simply gorgeous.

Six months after Dad's graduation, they married. Assigned to separate units, stationed on opposite sides of Jinan, Mom and Dad were able to see each other only on weekends and occasional evenings. When Dad was assigned to another location to help build a new army hospital to serve the local peasants, Mom volunteered to leave her comfortable city assignment to be with him in the countryside. The army higher-ups quickly approved the change. So, in 1965, Mom and Dad were reunited and were able to start their family. At that time, Chairman Mao was encouraging families to have many children. Some women who had seven or eight kids were deemed to be Mothers of Glory. Mom regretted that between military training and her medical practice, all she could handle was three. With both my parents working full-time as doctors, Grandma was brought out to take care of me and my two siblings.

China in the late 1950s, '60s, and early '70s was filled with massive political storms and tragedies. When the anticorruption and anticapitalist movements initiated by Chairman Mao led millions of peasants to suffer in a devastating famine, the military became a place of refuge. The leaders made sure the People's Liberation Army had enough food. When my dad was courting my mom, he saved some of his food coupons to make sure she had enough to eat. Soon the Cultural Revolution swept the entire country, but the military structure remained virtually untouched, except for a few higher-up leadership conflicts. My parents survived this period of unrest without harm, except that their promised promotions were frozen.

During the Cultural Revolution, a time when education and knowledge were condemned as useless or as something that could actually bring harm, my father quietly maintained the conviction that education is good. As soon as the new reforms began, Dad delayed purchasing any luxury goods, such as a television or new furniture, and instead used an entire month's salary to buy me a thirty-volume set of reference books to invest in my education. Those books were effective in supplementing my schoolwork, and today I would have to say my father's vision paid off. Grandpa's and Dad's unfinished dreams came to fruition in my generation, half a century later.

Even though my family did not suffer many of the hardships others faced during the Cultural Revolution, life in the military had its own price for parents and families. Because Mom and Dad were two young army doctors who devoted their lives to caring for the sick and the poor, my earliest memories are of separation from them. I remember as a young child standing with my grandma at the gate of the army compound, waving good-bye to my mother and father as they marched with a group of soldiers to a row of trucks that would take them to faraway places. And that was just the beginning.

When I was five, Grandma declared she couldn't take care of three children at once, lest something awful happen to one of us. So I was sent to live with a peasant family while my parents were off tending the poor and the sick, delivering the great leader Chairman Mao's love and care.

The night before my dad was to leave again with the troops, he dropped me off in the countryside, along with a bag of grain and some food coupons, and told me to be a good girl while he was away.

I went to the village school with the sons of my foster family, ate salty fish and homemade cornbread, sang songs to provide entertainment for the family, and slept with them all on the same mud-brick bed. I don't remember how long it went on like this (it felt like a century), but one night, after laughing and dancing and pretending to be happy, I woke up in tears and the truth came out: "I want to go home. Please take me back home!"

I begged and begged until the father took me home on the backseat of his bike. It was a thirty-minute ride in the darkness, and to a child, it was like coming back from another world. The man was not happy, but I could not endure my own misery any longer to please him and his family.

When we arrived at the military compound, the man knocked on our neighbor's door and woke them up to open our house for me. The home that had been filled with warmth and people when I left was now dark and empty; everyone was gone. A curious neighbor saw the open door and stopped by to ask if I'd like to stay with her family. When I said no, she asked why I wanted to stay in the house when my family was all gone. I forced a smile and said, "Just being in my own room already makes me feel better." She shook her head with confusion and tucked me into bed. As I was lying in the dark, I heard the neighbor say to someone else, "That poor child. She feels better by just looking at her room." Tears came to my eyes as I held my pillow close to my chest and clutched my favorite blanket. The familiar smell and feel of the fabric comforted me. I missed my parents terribly.

When my father came home a few days later, he was understandably upset. "You are such an irresponsible kid! How could you quit like this? If you were in the army, you could be kicked out and locked up for punishment. Don't you know your mom and I go out to help the poor and the peasants? It is a very important job, and it is our duty as military doctors. That's why we can't stay with you all the time. You are not just anyone's daughter; you are the daughter of two PLA doctors. If you don't ask yourself to behave better than other kids, how can I trust you and give you more responsibilities in the future? What a hopeless thing. You will not amount to anything worthwhile!"

Dad's words of disappointment crushed me. How I wished I could be a good little trouper and please him. But I was only five. Later, my dad said, "What a shame. We just gave them a whole bag of grain," which in those days was like a bag of gold.

"Can we ask for it back?" I asked carefully.

"Of course not!"

Now I felt even worse. As a PLA kid, I bore special responsibilities. There was no place for personal sentiment or emotion. My parents' work was more important than my needs, and my irresponsibility had caused a terrible waste. But what was done was done. I could only try harder to redeem myself in the future to earn my father's trust and respect.

That opportunity arrived five years later, at the time of the Tangshan earthquake, which struck in the early morning hours of July 28, 1976, measuring 7.5 on the Richter scale and killing or injuring more than 240,000 people. That night after dinner, when I slipped out to play with my friends, I overheard an announcement on the military base: "Emergency! Assembling! Ready to move out."

When I came home and casually mentioned to my dad what I had heard, his countenance fell and he became serious. Dropping the dinner dishes he had been washing, he dried his hands and went outside. When he returned a few minutes later, he told my mom, "Pack up; the army is being sent on a rescue mission."

Within half an hour, my parents emerged in full uniform with supply belts, water bottles—the whole package. After giving me a few instructions about how to use our ration cards to buy flour, rice, and cooking oil; where to take my siblings to kindergarten; and how to send letters to update them on family affairs, my parents walked out the front door and joined the assembling troops in the darkness.

After watching them march out the front gate and disappear into the night, I walked home slowly. There, in the dim candlelight—there was no electricity that night—I saw my six-year-old sister, my four-year-old brother, and my ancient grandma, who was terrified by the responsibility of caring for three children. In all the chaos, my little brother had managed to drink some of my dad's alcohol and was now burning with a high fever. There I was, barely ten years old and fully in charge.

By the time my parents came back from Tangshan one year later, my childhood was over. I knew how to care for my siblings, purchase and cook all our food, write regular letters to my parents to report on family news, and comfort Grandma. With some determination, I learned how to build a chicken coop, bought some little chicks from a nearby farm, and raised them to lay eggs. With Grandma's help, I also farmed a little piece of land and planted vegetables. I sent my brother to day care and took my sister to school with me. During this important time of transition into being a grown-up, my bond with Grandma grew even stronger.

3

"MAKE ME AN EXTRAORDINARY CHILD!"

ONE DAY DURING MATH CLASS, the teacher assigned us some exercises to work on independently and then walked out of the room. I finished the assignment quickly and began looking around for something to occupy my attention. In the pencil box of a boy seated nearby, I saw a dried sea horse with a big, round belly and an almost perfectly round tail curling down. I asked the boy to hand it over so I could play with it, but he wanted a pencil in return. Just as we were haggling over the trade, the teacher opened the door and came back in.

"Who has broken the discipline?" he shouted. "Stand up, come up to the lectern, and talk if you have something to say!"

I immediately bowed my head, not daring to move an inch.

Seeing we weren't responding, the teacher burst out like a fire doused with gasoline. Dragging my classmate out of his seat, he kicked him up to the lectern. As the boy struggled to his feet, the teacher punched and kicked him down again. I was scared out of my wits; I couldn't imagine how this teacher was going to deal with me next. By this point, all the kids had stopped their exercises and were looking on. Between the teacher's explosions of fury, there was utter silence in the room. I wanted to slip through a crack in the floor. Thankfully, the teacher didn't raise a hand against me. Instead, he gave me a furious glare and turned his attention back to my cowering classmate, who was still lying on the floor at the front of the room.

In a sharp, shrill voice, the teacher hollered at the boy, "You'll never amount to anything, you dog! You're up to your tricks all day, and you won't listen, no matter what! There's a saying that goes, 'You can teach first-class people with your eyes; with second-class people, you need the lips; but with third-class people, only a whip will work.' You remember that! Now go!"

With that, he kicked the boy again and sent him scrambling back to his seat.

Though I was glad to have escaped such humiliation, I was shocked by what the teacher had said. In my heart, I swore to myself, *I'm not going to wait for someone to use a whip to teach me like that!*

On my way to school the next day, the air was thick and oppressive, as it usually is before a storm. At the horizon, I couldn't distinguish the sky from the earth. As I walked alone on the empty, quiet road, the phrase "You'll never amount to anything" swirled about in my head. Gradually, an idea came into my mind: *You must become someone extraordinary!*

At that moment my muddy thoughts became clean and bright, as if a magic force between the earth and the sky had brought me a revelation. As I continued on my way, I silently recited my new mantra: "Be an extraordinary person!"

That day in language class, I wrote a long essay as soon as I picked up my pen. When I turned it in, the teacher sighed happily and told all the students to put down their pens and listen as he read my essay aloud. Then, without saying a word, he gazed at me deeply. I was embarrassed and bashful at this sudden glory, but after that long stare from the teacher, I understood the meaning of "teaching with the eyes." In his gaze, there was nurturing, hope, praise, delight, and expectation—and it planted an aspiration deep in my heart.

That night, after dinner, I took advantage of the general chaos in the house to sneak into my parents' bedroom and latch the door behind me. Kneeling in front of the big mirror on the wall, I closed my eyes, pressed my hands together, and prayed, "Dear God, please help me to be an extraordinary child. Thank you!" I had never been to church, or seen a Bible, or prayed before; I had only read the word *God* in a foreign novel. We had been taught religion was poison, but the people in the novel prayed, so I decided to try it too. I was a little embarrassed. When I was done, I saw in the mirror the face of a pious and sincere child.

That year, I put a lot of effort into making other people treat me as a "first-class person who can be taught with the eyes." By working hard, I earned the Three Merits Student honor, which was awarded to students who excelled in academics, athletics, and morals. I also made it into a Jenza class—the class for the best and the brightest—which was the top-level junior high school class, in which the best students from the entire county were gathered into one school.

The Three Merits Student award brought surprising attention to our army compound. Each year before the winter break, the teachers and students marched in a parade, banging on drums and gongs, while the Three Merits Student award certificates were brought into the military unit's courtyard and pasted on the wall of the little convenience store. The year I got the certificate, all the military aunts and uncles came to have a look, clicking their tongues in admiration, praising Old Chai's family for having a kid with potential. I didn't think it was anything special, but there were some kids in the army compound who used to bully me, and none of them got the award, so I did feel quietly vindicated.

In the crowd, I saw my dad's face redden happily with pride as he muttered, "Ayah, it's all just a kid thing, no big deal." He searched the sea of faces for me and said loudly, "Ling Ling, where have you gone off to? Come home and eat!"

When his eyes met mine, I saw that the ferocity I had feared so much as a girl was gone, replaced by tenderness, pride, and respect for my having outstripped his expectations. On our way home, for the first time I was not walking behind my dad but side by side with him, and in my heart I let out a long sigh of relief.

By the beginning of the 1980s, the publishing world in China was filled with new vitality. The days of printing only *Selected Works of Chairman Mao* were over, and many publications appeared to encourage individuality, which was a departure from those that talked only about the Party line. I began to read with so much excitement that I forgot about sleeping and eating.

At a young age, I was impressed by Thomas Edison. His inventions and devotion to discovery made a big impression on my mind. As I grew into a young woman, I began to relate more and more to Madame Curie. I was inspired by the resolute and diligent exploration and experimentation that had led her to achieve extraordinary results, including two Nobel Prizes. Before long I was studying day and night, hoping to emulate Madame Curie's success.

The first day of ninth-grade physics, I encountered someone who would change my thinking about science and politics forever. As the students settled into their seats, a middle-aged woman walked into the classroom. She stopped at the lectern and looked at us with a concentrated, keen gaze before she spoke, her angular face filled with resolution. She had a robust, vigorous air, entirely different from any other teacher I knew. Her name was Mrs. Qian, and she soon became my best friend, mentor, and enlightened instructor. It was she who helped me learn to think for myself. A few afternoons each week, I stopped by her house after school for a heart-to-heart talk. Gradually, I came to know her unusual life story, how she had fallen from a prestigious family in Beijing to our remote village in Shandong.

Before the Communist victory in 1949, Mrs. Qian's family was one of the few great capitalist families in Beijing, specializing in the silk trade. Among their enterprises were the silk shops that even today populate the commercial area near Tiananmen Square. In her youth, she lived a life of luxury, with servants attending to her and four younger sisters in the family's two-story estate. After World War II, when the Nationalists took over, Beijing became a den of iniquity and corruption that was eventually smashed by the Communist Party. As the People's Liberation Army marched into the capital, Chairman Mao stood on the Gate of

Heavenly Peace in Tiananmen Square and declared to the world, "The people of China have now stood up!" Mrs. Qian and her family were among the crowd in the Square that boiled with enthusiasm at Mao's words.

Not long after liberation, the Communist Party initiated a policy of cooperation between public and private management. The Qian family's capital was completely nationalized, leaving them only their house. They were just grateful to be part of the exciting new society, which offered so much hope and promise. Little did they know that in 1966, at the beginning of the Cultural Revolution, their house would be ransacked at night, sealed off, and confiscated because of their capitalist background. The Red Guards subsequently sent Mrs. Qian's mother to the countryside, on a train filled with so-called rich imperialists and counterrevolutionaries, who for the most part were a bunch of old men and women. To express their hatred for class enemies, the Red Guards commanded the old men and women to kneel on the floor and crawl from one car to the next, while the guards brandished their belts and mercilessly whipped anyone who crawled too slowly.

While Mrs. Qian's mother was humiliated on the way to the countryside, Mrs. Qian herself was struggling with tuberculosis. She had been accepted into the architecture department of Tsinghua University (equivalent to MIT in the United States), but because she was from a capitalist family, she was not allowed to join the Communist Party at school, nor was she allowed to pursue the study of physics and follow in the footsteps of Madame Curie. Eventually she transferred to the hydraulics department and later married a young air force pilot who had fallen in love with her while she was in the hospital.

One afternoon when I entered Mrs. Qian's courtyard gate, I ran into a man dressed like a peasant, his dark face wrinkled like a walnut. He was not quite standing and not quite sitting outside the house, smoking a cigarette. He reminded me of the country people I often saw at the bus stop, the ones the city people made fun of for their backward ways and appearance.

After the man had left, Mrs. Qian said to me, somewhat uncomfortably, "That is the father of my children. He fixed a tractor for the production team today and stopped by to see the kids because he was in the neighborhood. Don't pay attention to what he looks like now; twenty years ago, when he was an air force pilot, he was really handsome and had a great spirit!"

Dumbfounded, I watched the stooped-over man hobble off into the distance. I couldn't for the life of me relate him to the Mrs. Qian I knew. I'll never forget the image of that man; it was as if life had squeezed him dry of the spirit and vigor of youth. What kind of force could do such a frightening thing?

Mrs. Qian told me that soon after their marriage her husband had been relieved of all his assignments and accused of committing some political error by aligning with the traitor Lin Biao, who was a vice chairman of the Communist Party and one of Chairman Mao's closest friends. One day Lin Biao's plans for a coup against Mao were discovered, and he and his family were forced to flee. They tried to escape to Russia, but their plane either was shot down or crashed in Mongolia, and all on board were killed.

After Lin's death, his subordinates in the air force were investigated, punished, and sent home. Mrs. Qian and her family were sent to her husband's hometown—my village of Rizhao. And because they came back with the shame of expulsion, no one in the village, including her husband's family, dared pay attention to them. Upon arriving in the village, Mrs. Qian was confronted with an earthen house without a courtyard wall. She found a basket and went to the riverbank, a half mile away, to bring back stones as big as her fist, one basket at a time, to build a knee-high courtyard wall.

The village head at the time was a force to be reckoned with. Even though Mrs. Qian was a woman, he assigned her the work of a man. This pampered young woman from Beijing was sent up the mountain to gather wood. She gave it her all, swallowing her pride and not complaining. When she got home at night, one shoulder would be an inch higher than the other, swollen from the heavy loads she was forced to carry all day. She had trouble getting her clothes off because the dried blood held the fabric fast to her flesh. After a year, however, she had become accustomed to the hardest work our remote village had to offer.

An even greater torture for this refined lady from the capital was the monotony of village life. She built herself a desk out of packed earth, pasting several layers of newspaper on top to make a smooth surface. In the winter, when there was little farmwork to do and the peasant men and women sat around smoking their pipes, nursing their children, and gossiping, Mrs. Qian was at her desk working out physics problems. Copying from a portrait in a book, she made a pencil sketch of Madame Curie and put it on her desk to encourage herself.

When the Cultural Revolution finally ended, the education system was reformed and the selection of talented teachers through testing was allowed. Mrs. Qian was the first to register, and she was placed in the best junior high school because of her extraordinary performance on the test. For a little town in the countryside to have a Tsinghua-educated, college-level teacher was a great blessing. When she became my physics teacher, I became the best student in her class; but even more valuable was what she taught me outside the classroom. She had a profound effect on my young mind and life.

4

TOUGH LOVE AT HOME

AFTER CHAIRMAN MAO'S DEATH IN 1976, people began actively debating and discussing his achievements and mistakes, reflecting on and exploring the country's values and ideals. Ordinary people, especially younger people like me, began to think more critically about the society we lived in. At the same time, within the government and intellectual circles, an equally robust debate about the principles of government was underway.

I began to form my opinions about whether to enter the Communist Youth League, which was the first step toward becoming a Communist Party member. The Youth League was an organization for good students who had a flawless family background and great potential. About a third of my friends were members. Youth League members were given a special place in Party activities, leading call-and-response chants while holding up their red scarves with one hand at each corner:

Beloved revolutionary martyrs, may you rest in peace,
The Young Pioneers will remember you!
The People will remember you!

The Motherland will remember you!
Let our brilliant red scarves serve as our pledge.
We love the Chinese Communist Party!
We love the Socialist Motherland!
We love the People's Liberation Army!
We will carry on the cause of Communism!

For years my father had urged me to apply for membership in the Communist Youth League, but I had managed to evade the issue. One night, however, I lost my patience and told him the truth.

"I'm not sure I want to be a Youth Leaguer or a Party member! What's so great about them? Some aren't even as good as ordinary people. Look at Mrs. Qian; she's not in the Party, but she's a hundred times better than a lot of Party members."

I saw that my father's face had become grave. He grabbed me by the arm and shoved me into his room, yelling, "If we don't straighten out this problem today, you're staying here! Don't think of going to school. Once we've cleared this up, then you can go. A little kid who's been reading books for a few days doesn't know everything in heaven and earth. What gives you the right to say something like that—'What's so great about the Communist Party?' How many Party members do you know? All day you study everything but the good stuff, and the more you study the more confused you are. I've gone to all this trouble to give you an education, and what do you do? You've studied yourself into foolishness; you can't even figure out the simplest common sense. This Mrs. Qian of yours, can she measure up to the Communist Party? Did she participate in the Long March? Did she liberate China? What is she, after all, but a middle school teacher! Things are just getting a little better these few years, and only now can she come out and teach. I knew all along you wouldn't amount to anything. You don't read the important books; who knows what you're studying all night? Don't they teach you Party history in school?"

"No."

"They don't? Have you read from Mao's works? Have you studied Marxism?"

"No." I felt quite embarrassed, but it was true.

"You haven't, you haven't. Whatever counts, you haven't studied. Someday, this family is going to collapse, and it's going to be your fault."

Dad continued to rant and rave, and it was terrifying to see him so upset after I had tried so hard to please him in the past. My academic success and honor student awards had brought so much praise and honor to the family, but now, somehow, my refusal to apply to the Youth League would bring ruin?

My mother, who hadn't said anything up till then, spoke up in a tone much warmer than my dad's. "Old Chai, don't be too angry. Ling Ling has always been a bright and obedient child, and with such good grades. A lot of people wish they had such a child. If she makes a mistake, all she has to do is to make up for it . . ."

When she saw my dad was a little less angry, she turned to me and said, "Ling Ling, your dad has a temper, but he only wants what's good for you and the family. You don't know how many families were broken up during the Cultural Revolution just because they complained and reported their thoughts to the Party. Now things are better, but who knows whether in a few years things won't change back to the way they were then? Your mom and dad have put a lot into this family; we both came out of villages to go to school. When your dad went to school, his family set aside the best grain for him to eat; he had to eat dried sweet potatoes secretly so the landlord's kids wouldn't laugh at him. Your grandma didn't want me to go to school because I was a girl. Every day I came back from school carrying a plow and harrow and a stack of grass to do as many chores as possible so my mother would let me continue going to school. With school, your mother became a doctor and joined the army to follow your father. We have a beautiful family today. . . . Oh, Ling Ling, it wasn't easy for your mom and dad to get to where we are today. You're the eldest, and a national merit student. There are so many people looking up to you. Stop thinking of being like Mrs. Qian; you'll get us all sent back to the countryside, where there was no way to call that a life . . ."

Mom went on and on, until my dad interrupted.

"Enough, enough! Haven't we told her all this before and she didn't listen? It doesn't matter if this kid does well on her tests; in matters of right and wrong, she is a fool. I'm not going to talk all night about this, either. You tell us, Ling Ling, what's the next step?"

Drying my tears with my hands and biting my lip, I said nothing. After a long time, Dad realized I wasn't going to respond, and he became angry again.

"Tell us, what are we going to do? Get an application for the Communist Youth League and fill it out tomorrow. From now on, you are not to write or talk any nonsense about not joining the Party—or ask any questions about the Party. You will begin to study Party history, and until the issue has been cleared up, you are not allowed to speak any more rubbish on the topic. Can you manage these things or not?"

I said nothing.

"If you can't do it, then you won't be going to school anymore. You're suspended! It would have been better not to bring you up at all than to bring up an idiot to bring grief on this family!"

"Ling Ling, don't be stubborn," Mom broke in. "Just nod your head to your father, say you'll do it, and that will be the end of it. Your dad lost his temper, but it's for your own good. You don't understand, but you will when you grow up."

Tears were running down my cheeks. Hearing I would not be allowed to go to school made me feel terribly wronged. I loved school. My best teachers and friends and the things I was interested in learning were there. And there was hope for a different world from the one my mom and dad were talking about. I didn't want to give that up.

"Ling Ling, give your dad a nod—that looked like a nod," Mom said as she caressed my head. She turned to my dad and said, "Old Chai, simmer down. Ling Ling nodded already. She's just a kid after all, with such good grades. There's no one in the neighborhood who doesn't sing her praises, and she hasn't really brought any calamity on us. This time you got through to her, and that's enough . . ." Mom was a mother, after all.

"Enough, enough," my father said. "You just want to protect her. Sooner or later you're going to spoil her rotten." Though his words were no less harsh, his temper had obviously cooled down. "From now on, you're to stay away from that Mrs. Qian. Do your homework exercises at home. Your bike is confiscated."

As I continued to cry, he brought a big package of books and tossed them in front of me with a thud. An assortment of Party histories, Mao's *Selected Works*, and the writings of Engels scattered across the bed and floor.

"No more nonsense until you've read all these! Chairman Mao said, 'If you haven't investigated something, you have no right to talk about it.'"

By the time I emerged from my parents' room, it was almost midnight. Grandma was in the room outside, craning her neck. When she saw my eyes were all puffed up and my chest was convulsing with sobs, she looked at my dad and said, "Son, why pick on my eldest granddaughter? Shouldn't a family just get along, no matter what?"

My dad turned around and shouted at Grandma, "Don't you start, or I'll lock you up too!"

Grandma immediately shut her mouth and turned her eyes away, like a rabbit forced into hiding. As I prepared to go to bed, Grandma said quietly, "Eldest granddaughter, don't go to sleep crying; the soaking will wreck your eyes." I didn't listen and covered my head with the quilt, letting the tears come down in torrents. My self-respect had been deeply injured. The next day I walked an hour to school on foot.

I was deeply shocked by my father's brutal judgment of my secret, inner world. The self-respect and diligence I had developed since I was little, together with my consistent academic success, had brought me considerable honor. As the number one student in our county, year in and year out, I had found even the most fastidious teachers were respectful to me. Also, my national honor student status continued to draw attention. I was asked to give speeches on the army base about how best to educate one's children, and my parents were asked their advice for raising good children. Those requests had brought so much joy and pride to my mom and dad, far exceeding my own feelings. In my heart, I had my doubts about being honored as a Three Merits Student. I had never sought that kind of recognition and would not have envied students who had. But all the reporters coming to interview me and the speeches I was asked to give made my parents incredibly happy. Each time they became unusually enthusiastic—interrupting my study, calling me out of my room to speak to reporters or pose for pictures—and then they would talk about it for a long time after the reporters left, seeming to savor the feeling and wanting to prolong it.

Every time I saw Mom and Dad like this, I felt a greater loneliness in my heart. It seemed they were happy they had brought up a giant panda they could show off to others, yet I didn't know for sure they really loved me. But at least I had earned the respect of my father, who initially did not believe in me. So for him to treat me like a criminal or a third-class person was more than I could bear. What hurt even more was that he was partly right. I really hadn't read those political books, and I really did not understand the Communist Party.

———————

The next evening I came home as usual for my study time, but I stubbornly refused to speak to my father, and the atmosphere in the house was tense. Later that night I was suddenly awakened by the sound of moaning. Under the light, I saw that Grandma had gone into the bathroom and now could not get up. In my shock, I immediately awakened my little sister, hoping the two of us could carry Grandma back to her bed. But her frail little body was heavier than it looked, and we could not move her. When Mom and Dad heard the noise and commotion, they came running from their room and took Grandma to the hospital.

On the third day after Grandma went to the hospital, I visited her before going to class. My dad was there too, and I shut my mouth tightly, refusing to speak to him. The morning light shone through the white gauze curtains and illumined Grandma's pallid and anemic face. I wondered whether something I had done had caused her to suddenly become ill. Terror at the thought of losing her welled up in my heart and mixed with deep gratitude for all the years she had taken care of me.

When my father saw my sadness and fear, he reassured me with patience and tenderness. "It's not that bad, Ling Ling. It's not life-threatening. Grandma suffered dehydration, but we can treat her with an IV. In a few days, she will be home again."

I exhaled with great relief, and in that moment I almost felt a trace of forgiveness for my dad and deep regret for saying what I had said to get him all fired up. Wasn't I just being selfish, thinking only of my own feelings?

Despite my father's reassurances, I still felt somehow responsible for Grandma's illness—as if my words and actions had brought her to this state. If I continued to grow and develop according to my own nature, how could I avoid bringing disaster to the people I loved? But if I could not be true to myself, what could I be?

Caught between two powerful feelings, I had neither the strength nor the ability to assuage my deep sense of hurt. I felt as if I had been roughly thrown to the ground by fate, my body lying immobile, without the strength to escape or fight back because the powerful sense of pride and stubbornness that had always been the anchor for my personality had been brutally shattered. After all the respect I had earned through an immaculate academic record, I couldn't believe my father was treating me like a third-class person.

As I lay alone in my little room that night, I heard a cat meowing. It was the mate of our family cat, who had recently died after eating a poisoned rat. We had already buried her, but her suitor didn't know that. He was still patiently, sorrowfully crying outside the window. Night after night he came and cried; it sounded like a human being helplessly sobbing. As I listened in my room, tears welled up and fell from the corners of my eyes. Before I knew it, my pillow was all wet.

I don't know how long it was after that, but suddenly I felt as if an enormous mass were pressing down on my body, choking my throat, and suffocating me. I struggled with all my strength, but my arms and legs—my whole body—felt immobilized. All I could do was sink into the suffocating darkness. Startled awake, it seemed as if a black presence instantly disappeared out the window. When I rubbed my eyes and looked around, it was the same room I had seen before I went to sleep: table, chair, bed, and a beam of moonlight reflecting coolly on the wall opposite the window. When I tried to move my arms and legs, they felt numb. There was a clammy, cold sweat all over my face and neck.

The next night, I had a similar nightmare. After several nights of this, I began to experience severe pain in my lower belly and below my ribs on the right side. It was even worse after I ate. All I could do was take pain relievers until it gradually faded away. But later on, every time I felt sad or hurt or torn between my own feelings and my loyalty and love for my family, the pain would reappear.

Outwardly I changed as well. Once again I became a quiet, pensive child, sealing off the deepest part of my heart. A teacher who knew me well said, "Chai Ling, look what you've become. You used to be such an open, cheerful, and lively child!" I ground my teeth fiercely and didn't say a word.

This was a profound lesson for me. In order not to make the same disastrous mistakes again, I made two decisions: I would leave home, and I would never touch politics again. After months of hard work, I escaped the last grade in high school and tested into Peking University. With millions of students studying hard to get into the top universities each year, this was no small task. I had to block all my emotions and confusions, focusing my mind on two goals: to make up for the courses I would miss by skipping a grade and to prepare for the university test.

That year, 1983, our high school, which had not sent many students to college in the past, had three students test into Beida, and many more into other colleges. Our principal and the teachers were thrilled. They credited my parents as role models—meaning it was their influence that led to the positive changes in our small, sleepy country school. But I knew in my heart that if not for the influence of Mrs. Qian and the fight with my father, I would not have made the decision to escape from the family by skipping a grade or have made it into Beida. But the conflict with my father did take its toll when a boy in my class took the top score from me by a few points. It was the only time in high school I lost top academic honors to another person.

We arrived in Beijing after a long day's bus ride and a sleepless night's journey by train. I had not been to Beijing before, and it was only the second time my father had set eyes on the capital city and Tiananmen Square, the vast, sacred space that attracted millions of visitors every year and enchanted the imaginations of many more people who had never seen it. Our bus from the train station took us alongside Tiananmen, the Great Hall of the People, and the Forbidden City. On the north side of the Square, I saw for the first time the huge portrait of Chairman Mao above the entrance to the Forbidden City and the ramparts above the

Tiananmen Gate where Mao had first declared, in 1949, "On this day, the Chinese people have stood up."

In my childhood fantasies, I had been there, in that crowd of thousands, when Mao appeared on the vermillion rampart to celebrate his victorious revolution. My mind now raced with those memories as we rattled past the Monument to the People's Heroes and the newly built memorial that housed Chairman Mao's body.

Six years later, I would be commander in chief of a student movement on the Square, protesting for government reform, organizing thousands of students for a hunger strike, setting up Democracy University, and erecting the statue of the Goddess of Democracy. But as the bus transported my father and me from the train station to Beida, I found it hard to believe I had actually arrived in this ancient city of glamour and mystery that had filled my imagination ever since childhood.

At Beida, I was assigned to a standard room that could accommodate three bunk beds and two desks. The walls were bare and white, and the floor was concrete, but through the single window I could look out on lush green trees, which had an immediate soothing effect on my frazzled state. Dad helped me unpack and settle in.

A few days later, when the time for his return arrived, he took out the last two apples we had brought for the trip.

"Keep them, Dad," I told him. "You can eat them on the way home."

"I have lots of apples at home," he said. "You're all alone here. You might get hungry."

"No, Dad," I said. "You keep them."

I put the apples back in his bag. In our family, we never make an open display of affection. Instead, we offer each other food.

I walked with my father as far as the campus gate. We were both alone in our thoughts.

Finally my dad broke the silence. "There is an old saying— 'mountains beyond mountains, skies beyond skies.' This is a difficult place, and you are on your own. You are far from my protection now, Ling Ling. But just remember one thing: No matter what happens, you can always come home."

I nodded, and we waited in silence for the bus to arrive to take him on his homeward journey. I waved to him as he stepped aboard and disappeared into the crowd.

As a flock of migrating birds flew across the sky, I proudly thought to myself, *Dad, like those birds above, I've finally flown out of the sky you can cover.* Somehow I did not feel as joyful as I would have imagined. Instead, I felt alone again.

When the afternoon sun began to set over campus, a deep sense of homesickness settled in my heart as well—though I bravely and stubbornly refused to admit it. As I walked numbly back to my dorm and slowly climbed the stairs, I remembered a time when I was a little girl and my dad put me on his bike to go to the fishing port for fresh seafood. I could almost smell the aroma of freshly cooked fish. I thought of the time he had surprised me with a visit to my school and brought me steaming dumplings from home. I thought of how excited I had always been when the bright lights of army trucks returning to the base at night signaled the arrival of my precious parents from one of their rescue missions.

Trying to shake off these thoughts, I abruptly opened the door to my room. There, in the slanting rays of the late afternoon sun shining on the study table along the wall, I saw the two apples waiting for me.

5

PEKING UNIVERSITY

IF THERE'S ONE PLACE in China where a young person can be transformed by education, it's Beida. It's the country's most competitive school, especially for applicants from a rural background, which is why it became a gathering place for the best and brightest students. Words cannot adequately describe how much Beida shaped me and how much I loved the time I spent there.

Founded in 1898 by an American missionary, Peking University sits at the northwest corner of the city on a campus studded with buildings modeled on traditional Chinese architectural designs. The lake, the bell tower at the top of a little hill, and the gardens that flower year-round give Beida a feeling of secluded peace and privilege. In such an idyllic setting, it was hard for any young student not to feel the zest of enthusiasm. The Triangle was the heart of campus, the place where, all day long, students' paths crossed on the way to class, to the dining hall, or to exercise. And it was there at the Triangle we encountered a blizzard of postings for lectures by famous visitors, English contests, sporting events, weekend dances, musical performances, film showings, and flyers for the occasional demonstration or local election. The bewildering array of announcements gave a newcomer the sense of a campus bursting with fresh life. This intense atmosphere stimulated students' ambitions.

In my newfound freedom, I still had not completely escaped my father's sphere of control and protection. Somewhere in my subconscious lurked the fear that getting involved in politics would endanger my loved ones. Memories of my grandmother's pale face reminded me from time to time of the risk of wandering into dangerous territory. During my four years at Beida, I managed to steer clear of anything that resembled political activity, such as local elections in our district or the occasional salon where discussions centered on Western influence or liberal bourgeois thought. For me, life at Beida went on with continued vitality and youthful spirit.

Mrs. Qian, my beloved physics teacher, had taught me about Madame Curie. After I read a biography of the great French scientist, my dream had been to become a physicist like her. But the one boy who had outscored me by a few points on the final exam also took the physics spot. Instead, I was assigned to the department of geology. My second choice at Beida was psychology.

Psychology was a forbidden subject for many years under the Chinese Communist system. During the Cultural Revolution, Beida had responded to Chairman Mao's disdain for intellectuals and intellectual theories by eliminating the psychology department. Professors who had taught there were criticized, tormented, and eventually hounded out of the city to perform manual labor alongside peasants in remote rural areas. There, as Mao instructed, they could undergo reeducation and thought reform. In 1983, seven years after the Cultural Revolution officially ended, Beida's department of psychology offered one small class, open to twenty students. Only two or three other universities in the entire country were allowed to hold classes in psychology. So I couldn't take psychology courses during my freshman year, but I was able to attend lectures.

The lectures on Maslow's hierarchy of needs opened up a whole new dimension to me. During my growing-up years, my parents had exemplified devotion and discipline. They subordinated their personal needs and sacrificed their lives for a cause larger than life: the nation and its people. They were my role models, together with a cultural icon named Lei Feng, whose sacrificial service to the army and China was highly praised throughout the country, and they had instilled in me a belief in these ideals. But I could never truly relate to them. At Beida, I discovered a theory that addressed human psychological needs. I began to understand that we have a need for physical safety and well-being, but also for love and belonging, esteem, and what Maslow called self-actualization, or realizing one's full potential.

This was extraordinary. Never before had I questioned my fundamental beliefs. I'd grown up in a system that divided people into opposite categories: good or bad, red or black, hero or enemy. Things were either right or wrong; there was no middle ground. These new psychological theories fascinated me. As I began to question the assumptions that had formed who I was, I realized there might be more than just two sides to human behavior. I wanted to learn more by declaring a major in psychology.

In those days, students weren't supposed to switch majors and transfer between departments. But I stuck to my guns and continued to take courses the psychology department offered while I fought to convince the university to let me transfer. By the beginning of my third year at Beida, I was allowed to switch my major from geology to psychology, but I had to work extra hard to make up all the credits I'd missed in the first two years.

Socially, Beida never failed to live up to its reputation. It didn't take long for any young person to blossom within its protective walls. I, too, emerged from the shell I'd erected around myself in my last year of high school, when I had been a quiet and melancholy recluse, alone with my books. At Beida I became the real young woman I was created to be: radiant, active, curious, trusting, and full of zest.

I loved the way spring burst forth all of a sudden after the long, cold, gray winter months. The trees turned green. The flowers blossomed. The air was soft and fragrant. The night breeze felt like a soft caress on the cheek. After nightfall, students began to appear outside, returning to their dormitories beneath the starry sky along winding paths under the leafy trees. You'd see students walking in pairs, holding hands and confiding their secrets until the last bells rang and the girls had to run to get inside their dorms.

For my first two years at Beida, I lived in Building 35, a girl's dorm. The girls on the ground floor of my building were foreign language students, and they attracted many good-looking foreign male students to our building. Our dorm was locked up at 10:00 p.m. and guarded by an old lady who kept the girls tucked away and the boys at bay. This only enhanced the romance of those spring nights because the brave, young suitors sat under the trees around our building, played their guitars, and serenaded the girls, who lay inside on their bunk beds drifting off to sleep on clouds of love. Youth is such sweet wine.

On campus, I had many interests and activities. I quickly made friends with my fellow students—including one of Beida's child prodigies, a bright young girl from Hunan, Chairman Mao's home province, who had come to Beida when she was fifteen. Like me, she was taking geology and was crazy about Madame Curie. We bonded instantly. She was a brilliant student of many talents who possessed a wide-ranging curiosity about music, poetry, and art. She added a new richness to my life.

The 1980s were vibrant, dynamic times at Beida. China was just beginning to shake off the debris of the Cultural Revolution, and the university brought a stream of celebrities and experts to lecture on campus. My young friend and I attended all kinds of lectures and seminars together. One time a well-known opera singer came to give a lecture on the opera *Carmen*, by composer Georges Bizet. The title character is a Spanish girl working in a cigarette factory who falls passionately in love—body and soul—with a young soldier. When she demands the same total commitment from her lover, there are tragic consequences. Carmen's bold character made a powerful impression on me. She was liberated—a real contrast to us shy, reserved, and submissive Chinese women. Bizet's flamboyant score, with echoes of flamenco and bullfights, was still rampaging through my head days later.

We also went to lectures on makeup, skin care, and the proper use of shampoo and hair conditioner, all of which were just beginning to appear on the Chinese scene. You might think a lecture on makeup is a laughable subject at the country's most elite university, but it typified Beida's role as a pioneer on the forefront of Chinese society. Just seven years removed from the end of the Cultural Revolution, we were still emerging from a dark age when the Chinese authorities had condemned anything remotely related to beautification. The Mao suit was our national uniform—the last word in fashion during the Cultural Revolution. Until I attended the makeup lecture at Beida, I had never used lipstick. When I was a girl, nobody had ever heard of shampoo or hair conditioner. Back then, only the most elite families had private bathrooms. My family bathed once a week in a communal bathhouse on the army base, and even that was a luxury. The peasants had no place to bathe.

Another experiment was also underway at Beida: entrepreneurship. One of my friends opened a café on the south side of campus—arguably the first coffeehouse in Beijing. Coffee was an exotic item at that time, and you could find it only in a few international hotels in the city. Somehow my enterprising friend managed to convince a shop attendant at the Friendship Hotel to sell him a can of powdered coffee. He invited me to help him, and we cleared out a small room and set up a café of sorts. The minute we opened, business boomed. The small place was packed with good-looking men and women. This was long before Starbucks came to China. I have no idea how my friend concocted the fancy drinks that lured so many students to our little café. But every so often as I was taking orders and serving drinks, I glanced back and saw him crouched on the floor behind me, furiously mixing his potions. For a serious nerd like me, this venture was exciting and fun.

At that time, many students were interested in studying abroad. However, learning English, preparing for the Test of English as a Foreign Language (TOEFL), and applying to foreign universities was daunting and expensive. A friend of mine took a shortcut by marrying an overseas Chinese man to go to America, even though she didn't love him. That was inconceivable to me. Yes, I wanted to study overseas and advance my career, but I wouldn't trade the hope of true love simply for the convenience of going to America. Though I was wide eyed about all the new things I was learning at Beida, I still had my head on my shoulders.

I joined Beida's long-distance running team as a backup runner my first year and became a reporter on the school newspaper in my second year. I was always thrilled when my name appeared as a byline over a story. After that, I joined the student government as a volunteer in the academic division. When I was assigned to organize a workshop on campus, I worked on one called "Do You Want to Be a Journalist?" I was stunned when all the seats were taken and students lined up to get on the waiting list. Like a child just learning how to walk, I almost couldn't believe what I had accomplished.

During the registration for my workshop, in the noisy and crowded student government office, I met a young man—his family name was Wang—whose quiet presence stood out amid the clamor. A chemistry student who also excelled in the martial arts, Wang was several years older, of average height and build, and possessed an unusual aura of peace and calm, which I found very soothing. He soon opened a world to me I had never known before: faith in God. This was another taboo in China, where all forms of spiritual belief were condemned as capitalism's poison to the working-class soul.

Wang told me he had spent the previous summer traveling by bicycle along the Yellow River, the birthplace of our ancient civilization. He had wanted to see the lives and culture of the Chinese heartland with his own eyes. On his journey through six provinces, he came upon a mountain village so poor that no woman could marry into it. When the local girls reached the age of matrimony, they left the village to marry elsewhere. No one in the village knew how to read, and the villagers clothed themselves in rags. It shocked Wang to see such dire poverty.

When the people heard that a college student had wandered into their midst, a village elder gathered everyone, young and old, into a small, mud hut and invited Wang to join them. As everyone stood around a tiny oil lamp, the elder brought out a bundle wrapped in black cloth. Slowly, with trembling hands, he unfolded the cloth, one layer at a time, until it revealed an old Bible. The pages were wrinkled and yellow.

The old man told Wang that, many years before, an American missionary had left the Bible before he was driven out of China by Mao's liberation. Because none of the remaining villagers knew how to read, when they gathered to secretly worship, they simply passed the Bible around, hand to hand, and each person was allowed to touch it once. In this way, they received the presence of God. Still, they longed to know what was in that Bible, and they prayed for someone who could read it to them. When Wang showed up, they were overjoyed and said their prayers had been answered. Wang had no idea what they were talking about, but he was happy to oblige their request.

With all eyes on him, he read the Word of God as the people listened intently. He said it was as if they had all fallen into a trance. No one moved or left. Wang, too, felt the special bond these people shared. Without feeling tired, he kept reading late into the night. Each time he paused, the peasants begged him for more. Before he knew it, the rooster was crowing, and the peasants went out to work in the fields. Wang took a nap. After sunset, the peasants returned, and Wang continued reading to them.

After several days, Wang had to resume his trip in order to be back at school on time. The entire village turned out to see him off. They presented him with a large sack of sweet potatoes and would not let him leave without it. It was the best they could offer him from their village. Although Wang had many more miles to cover before he returned to Beijing, and he gave up many things along the way to lighten his load, he carried the sack of sweet potatoes on the back of his bicycle all the way home.

When Wang told me this story, I felt like one of those villagers who had longed to hear the Word of God. Though religion was outlawed in China when I was growing up, to me it was neither foreign nor intimidating. As I listened to Wang, I was strongly attracted to that powerful spiritual force. How much I wanted to be a part of those people who had such a strong devotion. I also realized I was strongly attracted to Wang and his peaceful demeanor. In my longing for love, I developed a huge, secret crush on him. But unlike Carmen, who could be so open with her emotions, I was shy and buried my feelings deep within. In my mind, Wang was like Apollo, shining and mysterious—someone I could admire but not get close to.

6

THE COST OF LOVE

On Saturday nights at Beida, the weekday seriousness was replaced by youthful exuberance. In the mid-1980s, a newly popular thing on campus was a weekly dance in the student cafeteria. After all the tables and chairs had been pushed against the walls, the students formed an electrifying crowd, swirling and swinging, or stepping on each other's toes, under the bright lights. I loved the movement of the dance. When the music played, I could close my eyes, let my body melt into the pulsing beat of the rhythm, and release all worry and control. For me, it was a new form of freedom.

One Saturday, when I went to the dance with my young friend from Hunan, I was surprised to see one of my colleagues from the student government there, a tall, handsome young man named Qing, who was a good student in physics and reminded me of a younger version of my father. Qing was not one for flowers and poetry, but he was a practical, solid, and steady young man. Like my father, he was strong and kind, a man of few words. Working together at the student government office provided a natural environment for us to get to know each other without the shyness and embarrassment I often felt around other boys.

One day Qing walked me back from class, and in his typical, straightforward way said, "You can see what kind of person I am. If you like what you see, would you be my girlfriend?"

In those days, agreeing to become someone's girlfriend was the equivalent of getting engaged in America. It was a commitment. We didn't date different people and then decide to go steady. Being boyfriend and girlfriend meant we could have lunch and dinner together between classes, and go to the library together in the evening to study. And it meant that sometime after we both graduated, we would get married. Qing's directness was refreshing, and his solid character made me feel protected and safe. I agreed to become his girlfriend.

Qing was not the first boy to express interest in me. For many, finding a girlfriend seemed to be part of their college curriculum. With all my campus activities, I got to know a lot of nice young men, but I politely and carefully managed to keep them at a safe distance without hurting their feelings or breaking up the friendships. Shy and reserved, I carefully guarded my heart for that special one, the one who would bring true and everlasting love, the kind of love I had read about in stories like *Romeo and Juliet, Gone with the Wind*, and *Doctor Zhivago*.

In my mind, I had a romantic image of my future love. He would be shining, handsome, strong, brave, kind, and tender—the kind of man who would devote himself to me no matter how difficult the circumstances. Together we would overcome every obstacle, and nothing would ever tear us apart.

Qing was not the perfect love of my imagination, but from the world's point of view, he was a good man—bright and stable, with a promising future. Part of me felt I should say no to the proposal and wait for my shining knight; part of me felt that maybe I didn't deserve perfect love and I should settle for the best the world had to offer.

One fall evening during my sophomore year, after a student government meeting, when everyone else had left, our hugs and kisses turned into something more. Neither of us knew exactly what was happening. When we parted ways, I ran back to my dormitory, feeling my face burning as I thought about what I had done. It was a feeling I had never experienced, and it was a bit frightening. I remembered one young couple who had been expelled for dating and being caught together.

Boys and girls still had separate dormitories, and the old ladies dutifully locked the doors to the girls' dorms at a certain specified hour. Later on, the dating rules were loosened at Beida, but any intimate encounter was like playing with fire. I was determined not to let it happen again.

One evening toward the end of the semester, Qing returned from a party where he'd had a few drinks. Whether it was actually the drink or just an excuse, I don't know, but he began pressuring me, which was unlike him. In retrospect, I wish I would have been stronger to resist him; but my traditional upbringing taught me to be accepting and not reject him or hurt him.

During the winter break, while I was home to visit, my mother observed my exceptional fatigue and took me for a blood test. When she came back with the news that I was pregnant, my father was furious. He was so mad, it was as if the sky had fallen. All I can remember is that he locked me in his bedroom again, like he had during the big fight we'd had when I was in high school. But this time I didn't fight him. I felt terrified and ashamed. This time I had become a disgrace to the Chai family, the family for whom I had worked so hard to bring respect, honor, and glory. I was ashamed that now, before I could finish school, I would have a child. A flurry of terrifying thoughts came to my mind. For the first time in my life, I had gotten into something I couldn't get out of by myself. I was really scared.

The next morning, my dad woke me up early and took me on a bus to a town two hours away—to a clinic where they would perform an abortion. Even though there was a hospital about twenty steps from our house, my dad was so ashamed he would only take me to a place where no one would know or recognize us.

After my father registered me, I was taken into an operating room, where a middle-aged woman was waiting. She wasn't mean, just matter-of-fact, as if accustomed to this kind of operation. The room was cold. With no anesthesia, she inserted a long tube into my body, and I felt the pain of cutting and heard the sucking sound of a vacuum. I was in agony, but I couldn't move or cry out. Next to me, an empty bottle began to fill with pinkish white foam. I felt the blood drain from my face, and my heart was in shock. As I felt I was about to faint, I heard the woman's harsh voice.

"Are you okay? If you can't do it, I will leave and come back later."

"Oh, please don't leave," I begged. "Just finish it." I could not imagine having to go through this procedure again. Clearly not pleased, she looked at my face carefully and then continued for what seemed like a century before the noise finally came to an end.

When she left the room, I looked at the bottle by my side. It was filled with redness.

Half an hour later the woman came back and told me I could go. I managed to walk out of the room and saw my father in the lobby. When the woman told him the procedure was finished, he nodded and started walking. I followed along behind. Pain and shame engulfed me. We went back to the bus and rode the two hours home without saying a word.

That evening, the pain became even more profound. I lay in bed, listening to my father's angry outbursts as the tears ran nonstop down my face. I was mad at myself for giving in. I was mad at Qing for making demands. Now I was paying the price. And it was my family who would bear the shame.

As smart as we Beida students looked to the rest of China, we had no knowledge of how to protect ourselves from the most basic risks in life. We spent all our waking hours learning and preparing for tests, and we had no sex education at home, in high school, or in college.

When we had studied the reproductive organs in a high school biology class, all the girls blushed and looked at the floor, while the boys stopped their silly acts and paid rapt attention. The classroom was so quiet you could hear a pin drop. I was simply too embarrassed to remember anything we were supposed to learn.

Even if I had known everything about how reproduction works, there was simply no place to acquire protection. In China, couples could not purchase contraception unless they were married. Sex was a subject nobody talked about; yet young men and women were thrown together on college campuses, hundreds of miles from home and away from their family network of support. Disaster was bound to happen, and it did.

Although Chinese society was puritanical in its expectations, it left a vacuum for how to prepare for and deal with our youthful emotions.

———

Qing did not learn about the pregnancy or the abortion until I was back on campus. He was sorry and treated me tenderly. We talked it over and hoped we could put the pain behind us.

I soon became busy with my transition from the geology department to the psychology department, and time flew by. A year later, after the memory of the pain and shock had faded, an innocent hug and kiss caught both of us by surprise and led to my becoming pregnant again. This time I was even more upset. I blamed Qing, but inside I was angrier with myself for allowing it to happen. I wrote a letter to Qing's family and told them. His father came to Beijing, and we were all embarrassed and upset. There was no discussion of any options—unlike America, there *were* no options. Under the one-child policy, unmarried couples were not allowed to have children. In addition, pregnant couples would be expelled from the university and sent home, where they would suffer social disgrace and be assigned to meager jobs. That would be their future. All the years of study, preparation, hope, and dreams would be gone. Qing's father was well aware of the consequences. He took me to a nearby hospital, and this time I was given anesthesia before the abortion. I never told my own father what happened.

The second time around left a deep emotional wound that Qing and I could not heal easily. He became more involved with the Communist Party, and I buried myself in the study of human psychology. As Qing became more rigid in his Party views, I started to have more doubts about our future. By the end of my junior year, our relationship was on the edge.

To any observer, we were the ideal couple—young, smart, well educated, and Party affiliated. China's best future belonged to young professionals like us. But my vision of the future was less optimistic. I imagined what life would be like with Qing—marrying and settling into a stable career path in China's upper class of scientists and educators. Once we had kids, the whole neatly dressed family would walk down the street together, the children proud as peacocks, with giant hair ribbons for the girls and toy guns for the boys. (As one of three siblings in my own family, I forgot we would be allowed to have only one child according to Chinese law.) This was the secure life everyone dreamed of, and as long as I dutifully did what I was supposed to do, I would have it. But imagining a traditional Chinese life made me feel claustrophobic. I simply couldn't breathe in it. I was longing for something more, something different from the life my parents had—something more fulfilling.

Beneath the surface of my day-to-day life, part of me yearned for a mysterious, unknown world that would excite and inspire me. I was still waiting for someone special to lead the way. My father continually urged me to join the Communist Party, but now that I was far removed from his protective influence, I ignored his requests. I knew genuinely good people at Beida who honestly believed joining the Party was the right thing to do as an early step in their life journey in China. Other students joined the Party because it was useful. Membership came with benefits, such as a good, secure job after graduation. But that was not enough for me. The Party was supposed to be the *servant* of the people, but I had my doubts. When I was a child, I always did whatever my parents told me to do, and they had always followed Party instructions. Nevertheless, even as a young girl, I cherished the notion I would live a life different from that of my parents. I sensed the existence of a dynamic force—perhaps even a spiritual force—that held life together. And though I wasn't a rebel or a revolutionary by nature, I wanted to find out for myself.

A new spring was flowering in China, and all my friends and fellow students were full of hope for the future, thanks to our beloved leader, Deng Xiaoping. After many years of grief and turbulence, famine and civil strife, he had brought joy back to our lives.

By 1984, eighty-year-old Deng was at the zenith of his popularity and power. He'd suffered many setbacks as a loyal servant of the Communist Party, yet he was still standing. Twice during the Cultural Revolution, Mao had humiliated Deng and banished him to the countryside. His son, Deng Pufang, had been permanently crippled when members of the Red Guards forced him to jump for his life from the third-story window of a building at Beida.

Eventually, however, Deng proved indispensable. Mao brought him back to Beijing—and then overthrew him a third time. But Deng triumphed in the end. After Mao's death, Hu Yaobang brought Deng out to help clean up the mess left by the Gang of Four. Deng launched education and economic reforms, which won him widespread support, especially from intellectuals. After decades of puritanical self-denial, prosperity once again became acceptable in China. Democratic reform seemed sure to come soon enough.

Meanwhile, Deng made an almost inconceivable decision when he volunteered to step aside to let relatively younger men run the country and Party affairs. This added to his popularity. Deng brought Zhao Ziyang to Beijing and installed him in the role of premier to oversee economic reform on a national scale. Zhao, the political leader of Szechuan, Deng's home province, had allowed fundamental reforms in the countryside. Deng then named Hu Yaobang to the position of secretary general of the Communist Party. As the head of the Communist Youth League, Hu had become popular throughout China among the younger generation as a liberal innovator always ready to entertain new ideas. Hu had also endeared himself to many older leaders when he helped the country recover from the trauma of the Cultural Revolution.

In the early 1980s, a genuine spirit of reform inspired the new leadership after Mao. Even Deng wanted to know how to build true democracy and freedom in China. He commissioned Hu's brain trust to recommend reforms for the country. True to his word, the only title Deng retained for himself was chairman of the Central Military Commission, which guaranteed him the supreme power to exercise military force. That spirit of reform and sense of hope was quickly embraced by the students at Beida and other elite universities.

On National Day, October 1, the thirty-fifth anniversary of the People's Republic of China, Deng stood on the rampart of Tiananmen Gate, just as Chairman Mao had done many times in the past, to review the military procession on the Square and wave to the immense multitude of people assembled below. I was there with a group of students from Beida.

When night came, the Square was filled with people dancing and singing. Fireworks burst overhead and spread out in brilliant array across the sky, lighting up the hearts of millions. For the first time in years, people were happy.

When another group of college students approached Tiananmen Gate, they broke formation. Shouting, running, and waving their arms, this horde of happy kids wanted to get a close-up glimpse of Deng Xiaoping. Out of the dancing throng, the students all of a sudden lofted a large banner emblazoned with four characters visible to the whole world: "*Xiao Ping Ni Hao*" ("Hello Xiaoping"). In China, elders are never addressed by their given name, and the thought of calling the paramount leader of the Chinese people by his given name was unimaginable. Yet this simple public greeting from the students said it all: We loved our leader and thanked him for all he had done for our country. The spontaneous banner caught Deng's eye. He smiled and waved to the students. It was the first time I had experienced the power of emotional force that such a massive gathering can arouse.

7

A DREAM AND A NIGHTMARE

AT THE END of my junior year, I stayed at Beida during the summer break to catch up on my psychology courses and prepare for the graduate exam, which I would take after fall term. One afternoon, I took a break from my studies to swim at the campus pool. As I came out of the water in the midst of a rainstorm, there was Wang. I was surprised he was still on campus. We went to our respective locker rooms to dress, and by the time we walked out, the summer storm had ended and a beautiful rainbow appeared in the sky.

Wang said, "Do you know the meaning of the rainbow?"

"Of course," I replied. "The humid air reflects the light and breaks it into its many parts."

Wang looked at me as if he were going to say something, but he decided to swallow his words. "Want to take a ride?" he said instead.

"Sure."

I was delighted. Wang represented a mysterious world I wanted to know. I felt intimidated, but my curiosity won out. We rode to Yuan Ming Yuan Park, the Garden of Perfect Splendor, just north of campus, and biked alongside the newly restored, man-made lake known as The Sea of Good Fortune.

It was a beautiful, warm summer evening. Wang pedaled, and I sat on the seat behind him as we meandered along the shady, tree-lined pathways. The fire-red sun had burst through the clouds and enflamed the western sky with blazing color. Wang stood on a boulder at the edge of the lake, arms at his side, gazing at the sunset. He looked like a bronze statue, floodlit by the last brilliance of the sun before it disappeared below the horizon.

I broke the spell. Seized by some inspiration, I leaped into the lake. The water crashed around me like sparkling diamonds. I swam out toward an island silhouetted in the middle of the lake, imagining I was a mermaid. Swimming was another thing that always made me feel free.

When I turned my head, I saw that Wang had stripped to his bathing suit and was swimming toward me. He swiftly reached my side. Fearing the darkness would be upon us before we reached the island, we turned back to be near the shore. The universe became still as we floated serenely on the surface of the water and gazed at the darkening sky. One moment it seemed close enough to touch with my fingers; the next moment it seemed unimaginably distant. Farther out, the water and sky seemed to merge. We lay on the surface of the lake like the children of earth and sky meeting at twilight. The moment was infinitesimal, yet eternal. I felt like a newborn child, innocent and peaceful.

Afterward we strolled along the deserted pathway in the half-light, and Wang told me stories of his youth. Before we knew it, we were back at my dormitory. Even though it was summer break, the dutiful old lady still guarded the door.

It was late, but the pathway outside the dorm was illumined by lights shining out from the windows. Under the harsh glare, everything seemed common and ordinary, no longer lyrical. The magic aura of the night vanished.

Wang stood next to the bicycle, gazing at me as if he could read my troubled thoughts and knew I had a big crush on him. Perhaps he could see how helpless I felt and how upset I was. I wished all this could have happened before I met Qing, before all that had transpired, so I could start fresh and whole again.

"You remind me of when I was young," he said. "Once, I was really attached to a girl, but when I got to know her, I was disappointed. The sadness I felt was close to despair. I'm afraid you, too, might be hurt by a rude awakening." Then, abruptly, he pulled out of his heavy mood and began to laugh. "Little Chai Ling, you're still in the monsoon season."

"Monsoon season?"

"That's right. From the story by San Mao. It's about a girl who gets turned upside down by love. She finally shakes the rain and teardrops from her hair and marches forward in great strides. And the monsoons never come back." He looked at me and said, "I am old, Chai Ling. I've experienced too much."

For a few moments, I didn't know what to do. My lips trembled as I tried to think of something to say. Fearing I might do something embarrassing and regretful, I blurted out, "Good-bye, then," and turned and ran into the brightly lit doorway. Back in my room, I poured out my feelings in my diary.

The next morning, I went for a ride on my bicycle. I wanted to know what attracted me so much to Wang—the source of his tranquility. I visited a church near campus, where I saw an older man in a black robe. I sat in one of pews and waited. I didn't feel anything.

Not quite ready to give up, I put on a straw hat and rode my bike outside the city limits. I was hoping to have an encounter like Wang had had in the countryside. Despite being harassed by some young men along the way, I managed to ride all the way to Miyun Reservoir, about fifty miles outside Beijing and the city's largest water source. It was as big as the ocean to me. In the afternoon sun, I sat on the shore, looking across the immense expanse of water, and quietly recited a poem in my heart.

Either it was the distant waves of the sea
Or a mother's call to her child in the twilight
When they asked me what this is all about
I could not give them your name

I could not give them your name
When they asked me what this is all about

Either it was a mother's call to her child in the twilight
Or the distant waves of the sea

I wasn't sure what I was looking for. Was it Wang or the spirit I sensed in him? In my imagination, I pictured a woman nursing her child, full of grace and peace, while surrounded by the chaos and clamor of a sinking ship. For some reason, that picture made me think of Wang and his calm demeanor. As I rode back to Beida in the early evening hours, I sensed I should leave campus before I could get into trouble with Wang. As soon as my classes were finished, I bought a train ticket and went home to see my family.

―――――――――

Soon the fall term arrived, my last year at Beida. Shortly after I arrived, Qing came over to help me with some laundry. Under my pillow, he found my diary and read the part about Wang. He later wrote me a note saying that after reflecting on our relationship during our time apart, he was ready for us to start over again, but when he read my diary, his heart became like a flowing stream that suddenly dried up. I felt bad about it, but I could no longer deny my attraction to the light Wang represented to me. I wanted to know what it was.

A friend told me that another classmate of ours, Shen Liang, who had also transferred to the psychology department, happened to be from Wang's hometown. With my typical, naive directness, I told Shen Liang I would like to know more about Wang and would appreciate anything he could share with me. He looked at me as if he could not believe I would be interested in Wang. In some ways, I almost hoped he would tell me something bad about Wang—something to knock him off his pedestal so I could move on with my life. But Shen Liang didn't offer anything useful.

One day I ran into Shen on campus and noticed he looked more pale than usual. When I asked him if everything was all right, he told me his grandmother had died and that he was feeling torn up. I asked if I could help in any way. At the time, we were both under extreme pressure to pass a difficult exam to determine whether we could continue our studies in a graduate program.

"Maybe you can help me," Shen said. "I'm so distracted I can't concentrate. Why don't you come to my dorm on Friday so we can study together. My roommate won't be there, and we can study all day to catch up."

This sounded like a good idea, so I agreed.

When I showed up first thing Friday morning at his dorm, Shen seemed restored to his old self. He was a thin, bookish student who wore glasses and wasn't at all in Wang's league, though they had grown up together in the same factory unit and learned martial arts in the same club.

He offered me some of his "power drink," a white, creamy beverage that had a funny taste. After a few sips, I stopped drinking it. Soon I began to feel sleepy and asked Shen if he had any tea. He said he did not, but he happened to have on hand a medicine that would give me energy like tea or coffee. "Why don't you try some of that?" he said. "These are what I take when I get sleepy. They are supposed to be for children, so you should take about six of them."

Shen opened a small bottle, shook out six little white pills and offered them to me on the palm of his extended hand. I took the pills without a second thought, just as I had when I was a little girl and my mother or father, both doctors, told me to take medicine when I wasn't feeling well.

Instead of perking up, though, I soon felt overwhelmed by drowsiness. I told Shen I had to leave, and I prepared to go back to my dorm. But he grabbed my bag before I could pack up my books, and said, "Just take a nap here. I'll wake you up in half an hour."

"Okay," I said. "But make sure it's just half an hour."

I dropped onto the bed with my coat on and fell into a deep sleep.

When I woke up, I couldn't breathe. A towel was stuffed in my mouth, some kind of blindfold was covering my eyes, and I was being held down on the side by a heavy weight. I thrashed my body against the weight, and this loosened the towel enough so I could shout. All at once, the weight lifted. I sat up and tore off the strip of cloth tied around my head. Shen was standing over me.

"I was just playing with you," he said. "That's all."

I heard laughter floating up from the campus. When I glanced outside, I saw students coming in and out of the dining hall. It was noon. I grabbed my bag and went straight to my dorm room, where I collapsed again on my bed and slept.

I gradually regained my equilibrium about forty-eight hours later, on Sunday afternoon. When I went out on the street, I felt disoriented, like an alien wandering among busy people who were shopping and chatting. I couldn't make any sense out of what was going on. By sunset my mind began to clear, and I tried to understand exactly what Shen had done to me.

Physically, I felt no pain. When I had awakened, my clothing was still intact and my coat was still on. There were no marks or other evidence to suggest Shen had done anything, but I began to think he had intended to rape me. Even if he hadn't succeeded, I knew he had done something evil to me just by drugging me and pinning me to the bed with a gag and a blindfold.

That evening, I went to the movies with some friends. One of them brought an acquaintance who turned out to be a police officer. He was at Beida for a special training course.

Without revealing I was the real victim, I told the officer what had happened. He listened and started telling me about the dark side of society. He told me he had once heard of a man who had drugged and raped a girl. The girl and her single mother were so ashamed, they never reported the incident. Instead, they drowned themselves in a river.

This was how I learned that women who are raped in China try to hide their pain because society assumes they must have invited the rape with seductive behavior.

I had heard about the dark side of society, but my world had been so sheltered that I'd never experienced it firsthand. I thought about Shen and what he had done, and I wondered whether I had the courage to report him or if I should just forget the incident and avoid the whole humiliating ordeal.

Shen wrote me a letter, which I found when I got back to my room. He told me he was sorry and explained that he'd been under psychological pressure. He hoped, since we were both psychology students, I would understand how this worked and just let it go.

The phrase "psychological pressure" got to me. How could that excuse his criminal behavior? I understood that human beings have certain basic needs, so I was not judgmental about that, but how did that justify what he had done? His letter wasn't a confession, actually. He just wanted me to keep the incident between us.

"Ling Ling," my mother used to tell me, "people in our family are too simple and naive. If you aren't careful, you'll be taken advantage of in the real world."

As I sat in my dorm room, Shen's letter in hand, I began to understand what she meant. It occurred to me Shen might be a serial rapist, given the evident planning that had gone into what he'd done, with the drugs, the gag, and the blindfold. I was aghast. I wanted to find the strength to report him, even at the cost of humiliating myself, so he would not do the same thing to someone else. At the same time, I was afraid to say anything.

The next day, I saw Shen in the library. I went right up to him.

"I am ashamed to know you," I said to his face. "I will never respect you again."

From there I went to his dorm room to look for the bottle of pills he'd given me. I wanted evidence. I searched the bookshelf and his desk, but he had removed the bottle.

I went to a nearby hospital and waited in line. The receptionist was a young woman with a nasty temper. She was bossing people around. When my turn came, I told her I wanted to have my urine checked.

"Check your urine for what?" she asked in a loud voice.

"For sperm," I whispered. "I think I've been raped."

"How many days has it been since it happened?"

"About three days," I mumbled.

"How can you check that?" she said loudly enough for everyone in the waiting room to hear. "Three days is too long."

My face was burning as I quickly walked away. I could imagine all the people in line asking the receptionist what had happened.

I had to do something. I felt so isolated. I went to Wang to ask him for help, but he was cold and indifferent.

"I thought you would understand," I said. "You are so strong, brave, and honorable. Besides, Shen comes from your hometown—"

"Strong? Oh, no, you have it all wrong," Wang said. "I can't protect anyone. I can't even protect myself in a system like this. You are too naive. You'll learn. You'd better go. Maybe one of your friends can tell you what to do."

I looked at Wang, not believing what I was hearing. This was the noble and mighty Wang, the one I had admired for so long, the one whose calm demeanor had always soothed me. I never pictured him this cold and afraid. With one last look, I walked out of his room without a word. The image of the woman sitting peacefully on the sinking ship broke into pieces.

8

FENG THE REVOLUTIONARY

On January 1, 1987, the Triangle was crowded with agitated students as I crossed through it on my way to lunch. It had just snowed, and everyone was wearing coats and hats. I asked a boy next to me what was going on.

"This morning the police arrested thirty-six students on the Square," he said. "We're all headed to the president's house to demand their release. Come with us. We need you. The more students the better."

Students in southern China had called for open elections, and the local Party leaders had complained when the students demonstrated publicly. "Haven't we given you enough democracy?" they said.

When news of this fledgling democracy movement was posted in the Triangle at Beida, the mayor of Beijing issued an edict banning demonstrations in the Square unless the Public Security Bureau—the police—gave its approval. When three Beida students applied for the right to demonstrate, the Party chiefs told them they would jeopardize their prospects for good jobs after graduation. Unfazed, the students had gone to Tiananmen Square to demonstrate without a permit.

The enthusiasm of the crowd impressed me. Not much time had passed since the incident with Shen and the disappointment with Wang, and my relationship with Qing was hanging by a thread. I had been living under a dark shadow of loneliness. I didn't know what the arrested students had done, but I was pulled along by the energy of the crowd to the president's house, called the Red Temple Building. It gave me a sense of warmth and belonging, which was a welcome change from the isolation I'd been feeling.

The Red Temple was flooded with lights, inside and out. Thousands of students were packed around it on all sides. I could hardly see the building over the sea of heads in front of me. Soon after I arrived, the voice of Ding Shishun, president of Beida, rang out over the broadcast system.

"Students," he announced, "after negotiations between our school and various departments of the central government, they have agreed to release our students. You may go now to welcome them back."

A cheer went up. "We've won! Long live President Ding!"

We made our way to the South Gate of campus to greet our returning student heroes. After waiting for more than four hours in the cold, we learned that the students had been dropped at the West Gate, far from the waiting crowd, and most had already gone back to their dorms.

A few days later, I went to the library to study. On the steps out front, I saw Feng Congde, one of the Beida students who had been arrested. He was one class above me, and I had seen him here and there. He was tall and slender, with a dark, tanned complexion, strong shoulders, and muscular arms and legs. His angular face, with a straight nose and flared nostrils, gave him a look of perpetual intensity. He was talking to some girls at the door, and it was impossible not to linger on the threshold to listen. I couldn't ignore his passionate, deep vibrato as he spoke about the incident. Here was someone who believed in something—to the point he was willing to go through a terrifying experience.

Before long, the other girls drifted away, and Feng was talking to me alone, telling me about the entire experience in a way that was both earnest and charismatic.

All sense of time vanished. My curiosity and admiration seemed to encourage him to talk more. Though I could never have imagined we would soon be lovers destined to marry and lead a student revolution, I was attracted to his spirit—sincere, pure, and brave.

He said he had gone to the Square only out of curiosity, which I later learned was an ingredient at the core of his being that seemed to pull him into crazy situations.

"Thousands of people had gathered there," he said. "There were students, curious citizens, tourists, and casually dressed secret police. It was odd how all these people had randomly assembled. Plainclothes policemen were filming us with camcorders, and as the insatiable, prying, greedy eye turned on one individual after another, they each would turn away, with their arms over their faces, because no one wanted to be identified and later punished.

"It was tense. People darted back and forth. No one knew what to do. Then an old man from the countryside, who was carrying his wares strapped to a basket on his shoulders, began shuffling around like someone who had wandered onto a movie set by mistake, oblivious to his surroundings, completely relaxed. As he meandered about, people unconsciously followed him, until a slowly moving tornado of bodies had formed behind him. By the time the poor man realized he was being filmed, he was scared like an animal caught in a net. Finding a small gap, he sneaked away from the crowd. A loud laugh burst out from the crowd.

"We were all embarrassed and wanted to do something," Feng said, gripping my arm, "but we couldn't. Those cameras were following us, whirring like insects. That's when someone began to hum the tune of 'The Internationale.' You know the song: 'Arise, you prisoners of cold and starvation!' It was bitter cold, you see, and we were all bundled in winter garments, and if you kept your head down, you could hide your face enough so they couldn't see if you were singing. So, in this muffled way, this strange crowd began to sing that somber anthem to revolution."

Feng grabbed both my arms and sang the entire song to me in his deep, low voice, intoning words that made the hair on the back of my neck stand up: "The blood in our bodies boils, we'll fight for the liberty of all people and destroy the old world we know."

That's when some students had unfurled a banner that said,

"Support Deng Xiaoping, Continue Reform." Feng had held one corner of the banner as the students marched together to the People's Congress—which, under the mayor's edict, was strictly off limits. Within fifteen minutes, he'd heard a strange whistling and was forced into a police car.

"They were police," Feng said, in almost a whisper, his face close to mine as he spoke, still urgently gripping my arms. "The people marching beside me, behind me—they were all plainclothes cops. I'm telling you because I want you to help me. I want you to tell everyone you know. Tell them what I've told you. I want them to see the true face of our national machine. Promise me you'll do that."

"Yes," I whispered. "I will." And I did.

Feng opened a whole new world to me, a world both refreshing and different, a world in which there was hope for a better and freer society, a world where I felt I could breathe. This glimmer of hope gave me the courage to formally end my relationship with Qing. He and I hadn't talked much since he discovered my diary, but I knew he disapproved of the recent student demonstration. I didn't know what lay ahead, and it was scary to break up with a man of such stability and a bright future, but I could no longer pretend to fit into his world. To all outward appearances we were a model Chinese couple with great promise, but I knew—and maybe we both knew—it wasn't going to work. No matter what the future held, I was ready to move into the unknown, to start over.

I had reported the Shen Liang incident to the campus security department, though as far as I knew, they never investigated it, and once I finished my graduate school exam, I was ready to enjoy my last few months at Beida. I felt the dark clouds were finally clearing and I could return to the happy and cheerful disposition I'd had during my early days at the university.

Several weeks later, I was astonished when Feng walked through the door of the dance club where I'd been selected to perform on the dance team. It turned out this passionate revolutionary also had an interest in dance—which, as he later confessed, provided him with an opportunity to meet girls.

Before our first dance rehearsal, Feng showed up uninvited at my dorm and asked if we could walk together to the dance club. While I was getting ready, he picked up my roommate's guitar and started strumming. Beautiful music flowed from his fingers as he played "Love's Romance." In the middle of the song, his fingers suddenly stopped strumming, and I looked at him. Our eyes met for an instant before we both looked away, embarrassed.

On the way to the dance club, we chatted casually and talked about philosophy.

"Ideals and theory are supplements for the flaws and imperfections in reality," I heard myself say, as if some invisible force had supplied the words.

"I had no idea girls could be so intelligent," Feng said.

After class he escorted me back to my dorm. From my third-floor window, I watched him hurry away into the night. Something about him was special.

The following Monday night, Feng came to visit again. I was boiling a few eggs and invited him to join me. He seemed troubled, and he struggled to talk about the difficulty as I listened intently.

The night we had met at the library, he'd returned to his dorm to find the area alive with the flashing red lights of police cars. He was certain they were there to arrest him, and his legs had frozen in fright. With great effort, he was able to climb the stairs to his room. Inside, he expected to find a plainclothes policeman waiting with handcuffs; instead, it was only his roommate, playing guitar in the mellow lamplight. He realized he was shaking—and how helpless it made him feel, how powerless against the specter of arrest. He later learned the police had come to his dorm because a boy had killed himself that night by jumping from the roof.

Feng sat forward on the edge of the bed as he told me the story, with his elbows on his knees and a blade of fine black hair hanging across his forehead. As he spoke, he occasionally glanced over at me with his serious, dark eyes to make sure I understood—and he'd crack his knuckles.

My heart ached for him. I knew that unspeakable sense of terror and loneliness. For marked men or women in Chinese society, the whole world as they knew it disappeared and all that was left was isolation and an endless fear of the unknown.

As I looked at this once brave, now troubled man beside me, a flood of compassion rose up in me. Almost like a mother wanting to comfort her frightened child, I wanted to brush back that stray lock of hair, soothe his disquieted spirit, and let him know I understood and that he was no longer alone.

In the past I had looked to Wang or Qing as my source of strength and protection. This time I was the strong and protective one. Feng's vulnerable confession made me want to hold him in my arms, comfort him, heal him, and make him whole again. As we sat in silence, my eyes told him everything.

Soon after that evening, Feng and I became a formal couple.

For two young people in love, Beida in springtime was a garden of enchantment. The singing of the birds, the blooming of the flowers, and the sunsets filtered through the trees around No Name Lake were all tinged with new meaning as we walked or rode our bikes together across campus. Together we raised two white rabbits as pets, and they would stand on their hind legs in the front baskets of our bikes as Feng and I explored the parks and rode alongside the lakes. In the evenings, as we rode back to the dorms together, our hearts were filled with joyful laughter and limitless dreams.

My fourth year at Beida would have had a picture-perfect ending if not for one unfortunate event. One Sunday afternoon, Feng and I stepped inside the university store to buy some snacks. I placed a twenty renminbi (RMB) bill on the counter and waited for the saleswoman to come and take our order. She was talking with someone and gave me a look that conveyed annoyance at my presence. This was not uncommon at Beida. The staff resented college students. We waited for a long time as the saleswoman continued her conversation and deliberately ignored us, even though she was only a few feet away.

Finally Feng grew impatient. When he caught the woman's eye, he indicated we would take the merchandise and leave our money on the counter. The saleswoman's eyes grew wide, and she began to shout, "Thief, thief!"

"What are you talking about?" I said, pointing to the twenty renminbi bill. "Our money is right here, and you still owe us change."

The saleswoman snatched up the bill and tore it to pieces. When Feng reached out to stop her, he accidentally grabbed her watch and ripped the timepiece off its band. As I picked up my books from the counter, the saleswoman tried to pull them out of my arms. In the ensuing chaos, she managed to rip off my watch as well. It was a violent explosion in the middle of a quiet Sunday afternoon. Finally officers from the Beida security department arrived, and they escorted all three of us to their office.

The officer who handled the matter seemed to resolve it in a judicious manner. He listened to each of us in turn and then rendered his judgment. He said the saleswoman had no proof we had tried to steal anything. He advised her not to accuse customers so casually and not to rip up money belonging to other people, because it was private property. He then admonished Feng for grabbing the woman's watch and breaking the strap, even in the heat of the moment. He insisted it would have to be repaired. Feng apologized to the saleswoman, who seemed reluctant to accept this resolution. The security officer decided to hang on to my watch until the saleswoman's watch had been repaired.

My watch was important to me. It was a gift from my father. I immediately went out and found someone who could repair the strap on the saleswoman's watch that afternoon. When I returned to exchange it for mine, the original security officer had left for the day, and a tall, skinny, unsmiling man had replaced him. He took the saleswoman's watch into another room to determine whether it had been repaired. When he returned, he refused to give my watch back. He told me I would have to return for it later, when the other officer was around. He spoke to me with such arrogance, as if the original resolution had been reached without his consent and he wasn't going to comply with it.

I immediately went and told Feng, and he went back with me to try to get my watch. This time the officer yelled at both of us as if we were criminals and again refused to return the watch. I later learned this man was a holdover from the Cultural Revolution, and this was his way of harassing people. The way he shouted at us stripped away all our pride and dignity. Feng refused to help me after that.

This was the same security department where I had come to report the attempted rape. Now I just wanted my watch back. My father was pressuring me to come home for a visit, and I knew he would notice if I wasn't wearing my watch. Remembering how upset he'd been when I had made him waste the valuable bag of grain with the foster family, I did not want to disappoint him again. I had to have my watch back before I could go home.

Despite all the shouting and insults, I went back again and again for my watch. Each time I got a new story, a new runaround, along with more humiliation. The saleswoman must have had some influence over this vicious man because all her wrath was poured out through him.

The security officer also used his authority to investigate Feng and me. He quickly ferreted out Feng's arrest on January 1 and my report of the attempted rape. Unpleasant rumors began to circulate about both of us. So, instead of getting my watch back, we were being slandered by rumor and innuendo.

I continued to return to the department, until one day I demanded to see the top official, a man in his sixties with a kind face and a patient demeanor. He reminded me of the early members of the Chinese Communist Party, who used to evoke trust and respect from people who went to them for help. The man listened as once again I explained what had happened at the store. Then he asked me the name of the officer who had handled the matter. It was a risk on my part, but I had no choice. When I told him the man's name, he said nothing more. He asked me to wait while he went next door. A few minutes later, he came back with my watch.

Later that day I bought my train ticket home.

These experiences deeply wounded me. They broke my spirit and undercut my pride. When the saleswoman attacked my reputation, it went straight to my heart. And when the rumors began to fly, I felt surrounded by a cloud of condemnation with no way to vindicate myself. My only choice was to suck it up and endure.

On the way to the train station, Feng told me the head of his department had asked him whether he knew what kind of woman I was. When Feng assured him he did, the director urged him to think twice about his involvement with me, as if he were offering advice to his son. I felt powerless to defend myself. And I felt injured and betrayed— because, as Feng told me all this, I could hear a certain doubt in his voice, a hesitation, as if he could not quite summon up the conviction that all the rumors were false.

9

RESOLUTIONS

Aboard the train, the seats and aisles were packed with sweaty passengers. The dusty air reeked of body odor and cigarettes. I squeezed into a corner, with my hands on the frame of the overhead luggage rack, and rested my head on my shoulder for the long ride home.

Crush, crush, crush. The voice of the train spoke to me as we hurtled along the track. Four years earlier my father had brought me to Beida on this very train. Then he was beaming with joy, confident in the vision he entertained of my great future. Now, after all my studying and training, I was bringing back nothing but broken dreams and a bleeding heart.

At Beida, when I transferred to the psychology department, I believed people could be healed through the help of others, and I was ready to charge out into society to use what I had learned to help and to heal—just as my parents had once been sent to the countryside to rescue the poor and the sick. Now that I was the one in need of rescue, the people I encountered seemed hateful and cruel. I felt confused and weak. If I could not even save myself, how could I save anyone else?

Crush, crush, crush. In my misery, as I thought about all that had happened, I blamed myself. It was only a watch, after all. I could have let it go. It did not have to become the agent of my destruction. Instead, my future graduate studies were now in question, and so was my relationship with Feng. A simple, well-intentioned visit to help a depressed classmate had become an ordeal of deceit, violence, and slander. As a result, a hostile department could easily decide to send me to some remote province to complete my graduate studies. It was my dream, and Feng's, to study overseas together. Now I could lose the man I loved and the opportunity to travel abroad.

I understood as never before that in China virtue and merit are not rewarded like a stable currency with a fair exchange rate. Instead, you have to purchase opportunity on the black market, through the medium of *guanxi*, a system that depends on the power of connections and favoritism. That's not how I was raised, trained, or educated. The real Chinese system was not for me.

Crush, crush, crush. At the ripe old age of twenty-one, I had tasted the bitter cup of defeat and despair—the feeling that, no matter how hard I tried, I could not overcome the inner hurt and outward assault of the world. These were not physical beatings or the severe kind of punishments that people considered enemies of the state suffered. Yet the whispers and insinuations swirling around me seemed no less terrifying.

Tears dripped down my cheeks. For the first time in my life, when I was supposed to know everything—or at least more than I had known before Beida—I simply did not know what to do. I was in such pain that the other passengers' curious looks were the least of my concerns.

Hush, hush, hush. As the train barreled on through the dark night, each stop reminded me I was one step closer to home, my rock and my refuge—the home my father had promised I could always come back to, no matter what happened. Today I needed to be there more than ever. I felt like a five-year-old girl again. I could no longer afford to be proud or stubborn. Like Scarlett O'Hara, I felt that once I got home, I would be strong again.

I arrived unannounced, to surprise everyone, as I always liked to do when returning home on break. I loved how everyone crowded into the living room, screaming and hugging me with tears of joy to welcome me home.

This time no one seemed surprised or particularly delighted when I arrived. As I stepped through the door, my dad was busy washing the dinner dishes in the kitchen, and my sister was in her room preparing for an exam. Dad looked older than I remembered, his usual ramrod-straight posture now hunched over like that of a man who had spent his life bearing loads of firewood on his back. I had always thought of my father as strong. Now he looked frail. And I detected unease behind his smile.

"Where's Mom?" I asked him.

"She's out running some errands." As he spoke, he rapidly blinked his eyes. He did that whenever he had something on his mind.

"Why don't you get some dinner, Ling Ling," he said. "You must be hungry from the long trip. Sit down and eat."

When I had finished my dinner, my father took my sister and me to show us the new apartment they would soon occupy. It was on a long street flanked by single-story apartment buildings. Chickens pecked at the ground in the late evening light. An older woman, a soldier who worked in the hospital with my father, called out to us as we walked along.

"Ling Ling, welcome back!" she shouted. "Did you come to visit your mom?"

"I'm just back for a short break," I told her. "What about my mom?"

The woman started to say something, but my father intervened.

"We're on our way to visit our new apartment," he said. "Ling Ling hasn't seen it."

"What's this about Mom?" I asked him as we hurried along.

"Oh, it's nothing. She's been a little under the weather, but everything's fine."

"What's wrong with her?"

"Well . . . it isn't exactly life threatening. She's had a nervous breakdown."

"What! Where is she?" A familiar sensation clenched at my throat. "I want to see her. Where is she?"

"Calm down," Dad said. "We'll go see her. It's no big deal."

We skipped the apartment and headed instead to the business district. Before long we were marching down a long hospital corridor with green doors on either side. Outside an open doorway to a darkened room, Dad motioned for my sister and me to stop so he could go in first. I heard him talking in a low voice, the way one speaks to a child who might be sleeping.

"Ling Ling just got back," he said. "She's come to see you."

Slowly, my mother pushed herself up to a sitting position. Her face was puffy, and she was definitely a mess. She had been sedated, so when she tried to smile, it was hard for her to move her mouth.

"Oh, Ling Ling," she said in a tiny voice. "You've come back."

This was not the delightful mother I knew, the playful and bright woman who always came home from work smiling.

"Mom," I said, hugging her. "What happened?"

Instead of hugging me, she pushed me away and said, "Ling Ling, you have to go. Right now. Go back to school. They're after us. They want to get us. They want to chop our heads off. They say I stole the microscopes. They want us to pay for them, but we don't have any money, Ling Ling. We spent it, we spent all of it, don't you see? We spent it on school. Where will we find the money?" Her eyes were filled with terror. "Where? The security people are coming to get us."

I turned to my father. "What's this all about?"

Dad forced a dry, tight smile.

"This is how she talks when she gets sick," he said. To my mother he said, "Don't talk like that. Ling Ling just got back."

"They had a meeting," Mom persisted. "They're coming to the house in a few days to shake us down."

Dad's face was somber. "When did you hear about this meeting?" he asked.

"This afternoon," Mom said. "The head of the Party was here. I heard them talking in the hallway. Old Chai," she said, addressing my father by his familiar patronymic, "take all of our money out of the bank and give it to Ling Ling and her sister before they come to take us away."

"There isn't much money in the bank," Dad said, in a voice of resigned patience. Then, tenderly, he added, "You need to rest. Ling Ling wanted to see you right away, but she's tired too. We'll come back later."

On the way home, my father told me my mother had not invented the story about the microscopes. Two valuable microscopes had vanished from her department at a time when my father happened to be absent on a long trip. Mom was the department director, an object of people's envy, and a rumor had begun to circulate that she had stolen the microscopes to pay for my college education. Evidently people were saying the offense called for the death penalty. Because my mom was alone at the time, with no one to talk to, all the rumors and sideways glances began to gnaw at her. She'd finally broken down.

"When I came back and found her babbling like this," my dad said, "I was just as shocked as you are."

"Why hasn't the security department made an investigation to find out who took those things?" I asked when we were in the safety of our home.

My father didn't immediately reply. In his grief, he stared at the floor, trying to compose his response.

"You have to understand, Ling Ling. Your mother and I lived through the Cultural Revolution. It was a time that turned good, well-intentioned people into evil human beings, who—to save themselves, perhaps, or merely out of spite—accused others, who were utterly innocent, of being enemies of the people."

He paused to rub his eyes with his forefingers, and sighed. "In those days, you were guilty until proven innocent. Any accusation automatically implied guilt. All they said about your mother was that she had keys to the storage room. Naturally, that meant she must have sold the microscopes on the black market. It's the Cultural Revolution all over again."

Dad paused again before concluding, "I think the people who stole the microscopes are the ones who have accused your mother."

"Maybe we could investigate it ourselves and find out who stole the instruments," I said in a burst of optimism. "Maybe that would help Mom recover."

"That's an excellent idea, Ling Ling," Dad replied, "but I'm afraid it's not that easy. This ordeal has been going on for months, and it has a life of its own now. Your mom held the keys to the storage room, but she would lend those keys to anyone who wanted them, and she never kept track. At one time it would have been hard to sell those things, and whoever tried would stick out in a crowd. Not anymore. Not now. We live in a free-market system. You could unload those things in any hospital, no questions asked. It's just not that easy to find out who did it."

That summer, in my mother's absence, I reassumed the role I'd held when I was younger—planning the family meals, preparing the food, and caring for my siblings. I knitted a sweater for my little brother and repaired my sister's skirts.

One Saturday we brought my mother home from the hospital so we could make dumplings together. A young nurse we knew came over to help. Sounds of laughter and joy filled our house for the first time that summer. I was taking a break from making the dumplings when Mom came out of the bedroom.

"Ling Ling," she whispered. "I just put my finger in the light socket. How come it didn't kill me?"

"What are you talking about?" I said.

Mom took me into the room, unscrewed the lightbulb, and before I quite understood what she was doing, she stuck her finger into the socket.

"It's such a little shock," she said. "It's supposed to kill me."

I grabbed her and held her in my arms.

"Oh, Mom," I said. "How could you do that? How could you? If you die, what will we do? What will the children do? Father can't take care of them."

"I'm useless," she said. "If I could die, I wouldn't be a burden on the family anymore." She said this without emotion, as if stating a simple fact.

I was weeping. She looked at me as if she didn't know me.

"Okay," she said flatly, "I won't do it again." She looked at the light socket with curiosity, as if she still couldn't figure out why it hadn't killed her.

I removed the lamp from the room, and when I left, Mom was still sitting on the edge of the bed, staring at the wall.

When my dad returned from visiting patients, the dumplings were ready. The nurse insisted she had to leave, even though Dad wanted her to stay for dinner. She was a good family friend who always came to see if we needed help. When she was gone, I told my father what had happened.

He was horrified.

"Why didn't you say something?" he shouted. "The nurse was right here. She could have done something. I don't care anymore if outsiders hear about our family shame. Let the whole world know! Let everyone come and see what they have done to your poor mother!"

I watched him in silence as he fumbled for a cigarette. He had always been the source of our family's strength and pride. Now he seemed so broken and defeated. When he finished smoking, he seemed calmer. We sat down to dumplings, with Mom and my brother and sister, and ate without talking.

Over a span of one hundred days, my life and the life of my family had turned upside down. We had been one of the most promising families in the army compound. My parents had become directors of their respective departments, and even now my father was in line for chief executive of the hospital. I was on the verge of graduating from the nation's most elite university. Yet three small incidents had upended these stellar accomplishments—my visit to a disconsolate classmate, a dispute over a wristwatch, and the disappearance of two microscopes. That's all it took to shatter the dreams of three generations of a Chinese family.

There was something terribly wrong with this situation. As a family, we were far too naive. We were not well equipped to survive in a system like this. It defied our family's bedrock belief in the goodness of life and the value of love and hard work.

As I sat chewing my dumplings, I made a resolution: I would marry, and I would apply to graduate school in the United States. There I would acquire a home for myself and my family, where someday my father and mother and brother and sister could join me in a new land, no longer subject to the tyranny of fear. We would rebuild our lives and be happy. As I sat in silence, surrounded by my most precious loved ones, I promised myself I would be the rock for my family; I would rescue them and take them out of this scary society, no matter what obstacles awaited me.

TIANANMEN
SQUARE, 1989

10

NIGHT AT XINHUA GATE

FENG AND I got married in the spring of 1988, shortly after I graduated from Beida and started graduate school. What prompted our decision was another pregnancy. Feng and I now attended separate universities, but one night we went to visit his brother and sister-in-law. When it got too late for us to return to our own places, I made the mistake of agreeing to spend the night there.

Feng casually remarked that I should keep the baby. He wanted me to quit graduate school and go to his parents' home to hide and give birth. I think he thought of me as some sort of tragic heroine, like Tess of the d'Urbervilles, who would drop all responsibilities and family obligations and risk being marginalized in society to prove my love for him by having the baby. Then he would love me back. Feng said he felt a great sense of pride walking around campus thinking he would be a father.

I said nothing. I could only imagine what my own father would say and do, and the potential shame and devastation were unthinkable. Despite Feng's bravado, we both knew it was legally mandatory for a woman to have an abortion if she did not have a birth permit—and in those days, birth permits were not issued to unmarried women, or even to married women under the age of twenty-five.

On the way to the hospital, Feng was regretful and tender with me, but on the way home, seeing my brief moment of relief, his face darkened. He quickened his pace, leaving me to trail slowly behind in the bitter wind. When we got back to my dorm, he said, "I'm ashamed of you for not wanting to be a mother."

I felt deeply hurt, both emotionally and physically. On top of that, I felt I had let Feng down. Anger rose in my heart. If only I could tell him how shameful and irresponsible he had been to pressure me. But I was too ashamed myself. I never felt it was safe to tell him about my past experiences, and I didn't tell my family about any of this.

How we moved on from there, I don't exactly remember. One turning point came a few weeks or months later, when it occurred to us that we didn't have to wait until we were done with school to get married. The hope of being together and having a place of our own—a place where we could prepare for a future family and for studying overseas— lifted us out of our feelings of hurt and despair.

In hindsight, this might seem like an obvious decision, but it wasn't at the time. And we soon discovered there was a legal barrier as well. When we went to acquire a marriage certificate, we learned that a couple's combined age must be at least forty-eight; ours was forty-four. Feng managed to charm and distract the female clerk when she examined our identification, which he had altered to make us both twenty-four. Within a week, we were legally married.

* * *

After our wedding, Feng and I were able to find off-campus housing together. I had been accepted as a graduate student at the Child Psychology Institute of Beijing Normal University, and he continued his graduate studies at Beida. After sharing a dorm room with as many as five other girls and eating at the college cafeteria for four years, I was happy to have my own space and to cook my own meals over a simple coal stove. As a graduate student, I received a stipend allowance of seventy-four renminbi a month, the equivalent of ten dollars. This small salary established my financial independence, which made me happy and proud.

On the outskirts of Beijing, just south of the Beida campus, I found an available room in a *siheyuan*, a traditional Chinese family house with walls all around it and an open courtyard in the middle. Traditionally, several generations of a family might live inside a *siheyuan*. However, over the years, as the urban population increased, many of these courtyards were shared by different families, and rooms were added to expand the living space, leaving the original structure and charm of the courtyard completely unrecognizable. The room I found was attached to the left side of the main house. A side path led to the main entrance, and a smaller yard formed an inner quarter within the large courtyard. Cooking and washing were done beneath a huge, leafy tree in the center of the inner yard. There was no hot water or sewer system. The wastewater was absorbed by the dirt.

Feng and I furnished our little room with two twin-size beds joined together, two writing desks, and some old chairs purchased at a second-hand furniture shop. I covered the worn-out surfaces with handmade tablecloths and cushions. A wobbly bookcase stood between the two desks. We had an armoire for storage and a charcoal brazier to provide us with heat in the winter. With a pink mosquito net draped over our bed and some colorful curtains, our little home was cozy, warm, and romantic. During the day, the place was quiet and peaceful. The only sound was the clacking of my typewriter. At sunset, when the neighbors returned from work, the courtyard came back to life. I loved that time of the day, with the smell of dinner cooking, the chatter of conversation, and the anticipation of Feng's imminent return.

April 15, 1989, my twenty-third birthday, is a day that history will remember for the tragic death of Chinese leader Hu Yaobang, which ultimately triggered the student movement that shook the core of the Communist regime. I spent most of the day filling out an application for an American graduate school. Feng had already started the process for studying in America.

When I heard the familiar ring of Feng's bicycle, I rushed to open the fence door. With his arrival, the lonely little room was instantly transformed into a warm home.

"Look what I brought you," Feng said as he offered a fancy-looking box. "A birthday cake. You almost forgot, didn't you? Today is your birthday."

As I set the table for dinner, my lovely cat, Blackie, rubbed my ankle, begging for his food. Growing up with Grandma, we always had little animals in the house—cats, chickens, or rabbits, but never dogs, which were seen as playthings for the bourgeoisie.

Feng was in an unusually good mood as he began to cook noodles in a little electric pot. He added some meat sauce and vegetables left over from the day before, and the two of us sat on folding stools under the tree, while the steam gradually rose from the electric pot.

At the dinner table, Feng mentioned he had received a reply from Li Shuxian, the wife of noted professor Fang Lizhi. Feng had written seeking advice about whether studying abroad would be seen as abandoning our country. Li told him not to worry, that once he learned more skills, he could return and be of greater service to China. That explained why Feng was in such a good mood. During that quiet evening, we talked about our life together and our dreams to study overseas.

A chilly breeze sent us back into our little room, and gradually a fine rain began to fall. Feng put twenty-three candles on the cake, and I solemnly made three wishes: "Please bring my sick mother back to health, let Feng and me be together in love forever, and make our plans and dreams come true soon!" I blew the candles with all my strength, but there were three that stubbornly kept burning. I guessed that some of my wishes would not be granted that year. I sighed, cut the cake, and casually turned on the television. A funeral dirge instantly dampened our mood, and the familiar solemn face of the anchorman on the Central Television Network appeared:

The Central Committee of the Chinese Communist Party announces with deep sorrow the passing of the long-tested, loyal Communist fighter Hu Yaobang, a great proletarian revolutionary, politician, and outstanding political worker in our military, and an excellent leader

who had long shouldered important Party leadership responsibilities.
On April 8, as he participated in a meeting of the Politburo, Hu had
a sudden, massive myocardial infarction. The utmost efforts were
made to rescue him, but were in the end unsuccessful. At 7:53 a.m.,
April 15, 1989, he died at the age of seventy-three.

We froze. Feng was the first to react in the darkness, cutting through
the heavy atmosphere by saying, "I feel bad. Our demonstration at the
Square contributed to Hu's downfall. We will have to do something to
pay our respects."

On April 19, Feng came home in the evening and told me that Beida
students who had gone to Tiananmen Square to mourn the death of
Hu Yaobang needed food and water. I agreed we should go to help our
school friends.

Supplied with canisters of water, Feng and I bicycled through the
warm, early spring dusk. The breeze was soft, and the sky was apricot
tinged with lavender, which gradually became a deep purple blue as
night fell. On the road, sailing along ahead of me, Feng was rhapsodiz-
ing about our future together as I pedaled faster to catch his flow of
words.

"We'll get into one of the American universities," he sang out,
"and we'll get our degrees. Then I want to find a place where I can do
research. I want to create the world's best invention, and maybe we'll
have a house full of rug rats. I'd like that."

Feng's words filled me with hope. He sounded so confident. I loved
hearing my young husband's big dreams, his plans. His commitment
to our future together filled me with a sense of relief after what we had
gone through only a month earlier.

The most recent episode had left me feeling deeply bruised. It was
unexpected and made me doubt the future of our marriage. It began
with a disagreement that quickly turned ugly. After Feng and I had
watched the English-language version of *Doctor Zhivago*, based on the
novel by Boris Pasternak, we compared our impressions of the movie. I

was moved by Lara, who inspires poetry; and Feng, in my view, seemed to resemble Lara's absent husband, Pasha, whose devotion to revolution displaces family life. As I look back on that moment, I realize I was communicating my fear that Feng's passion for political affairs would shatter our life together. My comments angered Feng because they sounded critical, as if I disapproved of him. We had walked the rest of the way home in uncomfortable silence.

At home, Feng told me how much he had once been infatuated with a tall, beautiful girl he had seen at Beida. Every time he caught even a glimpse of her, his whole body would start to tremble. This was not exactly what I wanted to hear. I felt hurt. Our conversation moved on to things like open marriage, love and care, truth and honesty, life and family. It made me sad to realize how profoundly I disagreed with my new husband about so many important matters. When he told me about his plans to go abroad, he made it clear I was free to join him or to go my own way. He sounded like a different man, remote, foreign.

The morning after this unsettling conversation, Feng simply took off and went to his lab, leaving me alone in our empty room. When Feng stayed away for several days, all sorts of dire consequences raced through my mind. Then one day, he came home as if nothing at all had happened. We both avoided the subject, and I made a serious effort to steer clear of another fight.

That's why, as Feng and I bicycled through the warm evening air on our way to Tiananmen Square, his words brought delight to my heart. As we prepared to deliver food and water to the students on the Square and pay our tribute to Hu Yaobang, life seemed beautiful, bright, and full of promise.

I adored Feng for all the same reasons that had made me want to marry him. I admired his brilliant mind—his ability to hit the books the night before an exam and walk away with the top grade. He was hot and peppery, a hardworking boy from Szechuan Province, like our leader, Deng Xiaoping. Feng was someone who put moral values ahead of self-interest, as his parents had taught him. And I was still under the spell cast by his handsome good looks. He was a beautifully built creature, lean and masculine, yet sensuous: I adored his dark skin, strong chin, and sudden, brilliant smile. Above all, I loved his large, soft, brown eyes. He was a serious, passionate man who wanted to change the world. Yet he could be so warm and gentle.

What I did not know was the plan B he was hiding from me. As we breezed down Xidan Street into the heart of the city, I was unaware Feng was entertaining ideas that completely contradicted what he was saying. At the same moment he was telling me about studying abroad, a conviction was rising in his heart that he could make a bigger difference for China right where we were. As we rode toward Tiananmen, he felt an enormous pull, a magnetic attraction. He kept it to himself, but he already knew the road we were on would change our lives forever.

When word of Hu's death had rippled across the Beida campus the day before, it had cut into the hearts of the students like the cold blade of a steel knife.

We were all so young and full of hope. We revered Hu Yaobang, the secretary general of the Chinese Communist Party, whom Deng Xiaoping had demoted two years earlier. We were told that Hu loved us, and we had ached for the day when he might return to power and pave the way for freedom in China. Hu Yaobang stood for reform and justice. He had rescued many outspoken opponents of the regime from certain imprisonment or worse. He was the foremost champion of change and democracy in China. He was our friend, and now, all at once, he was dead of a heart attack. He had died suddenly, after an emotional meeting with the same Party leaders who had brought him down.

When the rumor that Hu had died reached campus, students began to gather outside on the Triangle, the grassy space at the center of campus where so much activity took place. By nightfall, the Triangle was boiling with angry, grieving students, some of whom carried posters with provocative slogans:

"Forever Yaobang."
"Those who should die did not, and those who should live have gone."
"Some who already have died live on, others who live have died."
"The warm one died, the cold one buried him."

Feng and I turned left on Chang'an Avenue at the corner where it meets Xidan Street and rode toward Tiananmen Square. Up ahead we could see people sitting in front of Xinhua Gate, the southern entrance to the compound known as Zhongnanhai, where the Chinese Communist Party headquarters and other government offices are located. Zhongnanhai is where day-to-day administrative activities take place. It is home also to top government officials, such as Hu Yaobang's successor, Zhao Ziyang. Until his death in 1976, Chairman Mao had made his residence there in a comfortable courtyard apartment.

As we passed Xinhua Gate, we heard sounds of quiet laughter and conversation from the cluster of young people who had settled in for the evening on the sidewalk under the dim glow of the street lamps. All seemed at peace.

At the edge of the Square, on Chang'an Avenue, Feng and I dismounted and carefully leaned our bikes against a tree. Across the Square, a crowd of people surrounded the People's Monument. Together we headed in that direction and worked our way into the crowd.

A young man was giving a speech when we arrived. Every time he posed a question, he aroused the crowd to a fervent response.

"Is there a single person in this crowd who has never been bullied by a Party boss?"

"Why can't we choose our own jobs?"

"Why must we let the Party assign us to a workplace?"

"Why does the Party keep a personal file on each of us, and why don't we have the right to see it?"

That last one got to me. I thought of how the security man at Beida had used my personal file to almost ruin my life. The speaker called it a "black file."

He talked about the meaning of democracy and called out, "Are we not entitled to some basic rights of freedom?"

The crowd cheered. The words he spoke went straight to my heart.

Then a voice cried out that police were attacking students in front of Xinhua Gate, and someone said we should all go over there.

A row of armed soldiers stood in front of Xinhua Gate, guarding the entrance to Zhongnanhai beneath a royal blue escutcheon.

The students sat on the ground facing the soldiers, separated from

them by a few feet. Onlookers formed a human wall behind the students. When we arrived with people from the Square, we immediately
enlarged the throng of student protesters. Some of the new arrivals
started throwing things like hats and gloves, and someone even threw a
shoe that struck a soldier in the face. (Later we wondered if the person
who did that had been planted by the government.)

From time to time the crowd took up a chant: "Come out, Li Peng.
Li Peng, come out."

Li Peng was the premier and had gotten the job at the expense of
Hu Yaobang. In January 1987, when Hu was forced to resign, his position of Party secretary general went to Zhao Ziyang, Deng Xiaoping's
handpicked premier. That left the premier's seat vacant. Li Peng was an
engineer with no political expertise, but he had conservative views and
close ties to the Party elders. Nobody knew if Li Peng was in Zhongnanhai. The student representatives who had disappeared inside the compound earlier in the day to deliver a petition had not emerged. Outside
the black gate, the crowd had grown to several thousand strong. Some
people impatiently pushed against the cordon that kept protesters at
arm's length from the soldiers, who stood motionless, their backs to the
gate, their eyes blank, facing straight ahead.

Suddenly someone shouted, "The police are coming!"

I looked down Chang'an Avenue toward the west, away from
the Square. People were stampeding toward us up the wide avenue,
like a herd of frightened impalas on the Serengeti Plain, pursued by
truncheon-wielding police. At once the night air was filled with screams
and the thunder of running feet. When the police reached Xinhua Gate,
they started beating people with nightsticks to clear the way. I ran with
the crowd in sheer panic as fast as my feet would carry me.

When I finally slowed down to catch my breath, I was burning
with shame and rage. I had never felt so humiliated in my life, chased
down the street like a dog. Feng was by my side, and I could feel the
heat of his body. Our eyes met and we were instantly united in the fury
of insult. We were at the rear of the crowd, and together we turned to
see a battalion of police running directly toward us about thirty feet
away. They looked like ghost runners in the night, spread out across the
eight-lane avenue. The vanguard was followed by more police. We stood

stock-still, in the middle of Chang'an, and faced them. Others in the crowd came up from behind to join us.

I had come to the Square that night with a simple thought: to deliver food and water to some school friends and to pay tribute to a fallen leader. But within a few hours, I was transformed. Being chased by the police and seeing others unjustly beaten triggered the pain of the unresolved wound left by the Beida security officer and the angry saleswoman. In my heart, I determined I would no longer be the young woman from two years before who had cried all the way home on the train. My wounded pride and a newfound rage dried up my sorrow. From now on, I would not run away, and neither would Feng.

On my way to the Square, I had worried about the crumbling edges of my life with Feng. Now all that was no longer important. When we stopped running and looked into each other's eyes, a bond deeper than ever was born between us. I knew then that we shared something larger than life, something more profound than any future plan. We must live like human beings and protect our dignity.

That night, when the government sent the police to Tiananmen Square and compelled the younger generation of China to stand up, a new chapter in our country's modern history began.

11

SEARCHING FOR FENG

THE MORNING AFTER our confrontation with the police on Chang'an Avenue, Feng and I awoke to hear the government radio denouncing the spontaneous student gathering at Tiananmen Square. A government spokesman described the grief-stricken crowd as a handful of ill-meaning troublemakers who had seized on the death of Hu Yaobang to conduct illegal activities—which would not be tolerated. With this outright lie, the government threw down the gauntlet to the students of Beijing.

Feng and I went to the Triangle that evening to see how students had responded to the government broadcast. Feng was on fire. He had an astonishing ability to devour and digest volumes of complex material in one sitting, which had made him a star at Beida, and he'd spent the day in the university library poring over *The Constitution of the Chinese Republic*, *The Constitution of the Chinese Communist Party*, *The American Government and Its Politics*, and a biography of Mahatma Gandhi, among other tomes. He wanted to be prepared for what was about to happen. He could feel the breath of destiny on the back of his neck.

Two or three thousand students had already gathered at the Triangle.

Various students gave speeches, and soon they were focused on forming an organization to lead a movement. Feng made his way to the forefront to propose his ideas for student leadership, including the creation of an independent newspaper that would advocate for free assembly and free speech. I stood and watched from afar as Feng became a founding member of the Preparatory Committee, one of seven people designated to establish an independent student leadership organization. I was there as Feng's supportive wife. I was not going to stand in his way. I was determined to show solidarity.

I truly loved Feng. He was at once vulnerable, passionate, and brilliant. And I yearned for his respect. I was never so proud of him as I was the night I watched him take command of the student movement with his six colleagues. At last, I thought, all that frustration will be released as a positive force.

The next morning, I mailed my application to a graduate program in child psychology at Columbia University's Teachers College. I was not going to waste a nanosecond before following up on Feng's enthusiastic declaration about studying abroad together. Then I went over to the Triangle again because Feng had not returned home the night before. There I found a big poster announcing that students had returned to the Square. A bloodstained shirt hanging next to the poster bore silent witness to the risks of joining the protests. I began to worry. Feng could have been at the Square. It was easy to imagine him being singled out for a beating, to teach him a lesson, so to speak. I began a frenzied search.

Four hours later I had looked for him everywhere on campus. Twice I had gone back to our little room, hoping to find Feng asleep and out of harm's way. He hated it when I worried about him. He hated any demonstration of concern or affection he hadn't initiated. I couldn't help myself. Finally I wrote him a note and left it on the bed before going back out to look for him.

I took a bus to Tiananmen. A huge crowd had gathered there, bigger than any I had yet seen. It would be impossible to find someone in such a teeming mass, but like a crazed woman at a rummage sale, I pulled people aside by the shoulder in search of Feng's face. Nobody seemed to notice—maybe because it was raining so hard. I found my bike next to Feng's, where we'd left them two nights earlier. By the time I got home, pedaling through the dark streets in the rain, it was almost midnight. I couldn't stand the idea of waiting at home again for Feng to come back, so I bicycled over to Beida through the dark alleyways.

Back at the Triangle, I once again questioned the students there. One of the stalwarts holding an all-night vigil in the rain immediately took me to Dormitory 28, one of the boys dorms on campus. I followed him upstairs to the second floor and to a room down the hall. He knocked on the door; when no one answered, he barked out Feng's name. A man opened the door and immediately closed it again. Moments later, Feng appeared.

When he saw me, he held me so tightly I could feel his heartbeat. We kissed in the darkness. In that instant, we rediscovered how much we missed each other.

"Oh, baby," he said. "I can't tell you how much I want to go home and curl up in bed with you right now."

The man who had opened the door reappeared.

"You can't take Feng away," he said. "We need him."

I could see the man wanted me to go, and that Feng was going to tell me to wait for him at home. I wasn't about to let that happen. Now that I'd found him, I didn't want to give him up.

I followed Feng and the other man into the dorm room, where five or six students were huddled by candlelight, talking in low voices. It reminded me of stories I'd read about the early days of the Chinese Communist underground movement.

This was the beginning of the democracy movement, when few people even knew how to conduct a productive meeting. These boys were debating proposals and taking votes. Whoever lost to the majority would protest by citing Lenin's claim: "The truth is often in the hands of the minority." As the only girl present, I was the true minority in the room. I sat on the fringe of their debates and listened. Soon enough I could see why they were having trouble resolving their disagreements. I offered to mediate. I just wanted them to get the job done so Feng and

I could go home. That was my sole objective. They all listened to what I had to say, probably because I spoke in a soft, feminine voice amid this conclave of males.

I told them we all came from different backgrounds and experiences, so of course we would have disagreements. That was normal and should be accepted. Though each student had important ideas, it was vital they work together as leaders and compromise, if necessary, to agree on one action plan they could execute. Then they could lead the other students in constructive action.

This may seem like common sense in a free world. But in a Communist dictatorship, we did not have much leadership experience. That's why we tended to act like little dictators, fighting hard for our own ideas. But democracy requires listening and working together.

The meeting broke up at dawn with one decision: They would call for a student strike, a boycott of all classes.

1 2

THE FUNERAL
FOR HU YAOBANG

THE FUNERAL FOR HU YAOBANG was scheduled to take place at the Great Hall of the People on the west side of Tiananmen Square on April 22. On the twenty-first, the government announced that the entire Square would be closed to the public on the day of the funeral, starting at eight o'clock in the morning. To the students of Beida, this was unacceptable. We wanted to pay our final respects to this man who, more than anyone, had stood up for democracy in China. The Preparatory Committee decided to move students onto the Square during the night, before the police could close it off and shut us out.

When I returned to Dormitory 28, the scene of our candlelight gathering had morphed into a hive of energy, buzzing with activity and excitement. I went to work on preparations for our march to the Square. We had to work fast. Within hours, the march grew to include students from all the major universities in Beijing, including Beijing Normal University, Tsinghua, People's University, and others. It was a massive job to coordinate so many people in such a little time, and when we were all finally on the Square, it was thrilling to see thousands upon thousands of students all standing in formation. We almost entirely filled the vast space.

I devoted my efforts that first day to creating slogans and preparing banners. Students assembled in columns beneath the banner for their particular school. Student marshals with red armbands formed picket lines around the perimeter. We took the government by surprise, and not a single policeman appeared on the scene to disperse this well-ordered open defiance of a government decree. We settled down for a long, cold, early spring night on the Square. While Feng went off to another meeting of the student leaders, I stayed with my group from Beida. Together we would greet the dawn on Tiananmen Square and take part in a memorial service from which the government had intended to exclude us.

After a cold night on the hard concrete, I woke up with a terrible sore throat. The day began when a troop of honor guards marched out of Tiananmen Gate and stopped at the foot of the national flagpole on the north edge of the Square opposite the Forbidden City. Tens of thousands of students stood at attention as the flag slowly rose against the brilliant golden rays of the early morning sun. We all raised our hands in salute and then thundered the Chinese national anthem in unison. We filled the vast Square with roaring, heartfelt song. When we'd sung the national anthem, the flag began a slow descent from the top of the pole to the middle, to honor the passing of Hu Yaobang. We all began to sing "The Internationale," a somber dirge that reinforced the death of a lost leader. Many wept.

After the honor guard marched back to Tiananmen Gate, loudspeakers on the Square broadcast the voice of a government spokesman.

"Students on the Square," the voice screamed, "there has been misconduct in the city of Beijing these past days. You should all be aware that a small handful of people are using the death of Hu Yaobang to attack the government. If these people continue their actions, they will have to take full responsibility for the consequences."

Unease spread quickly through the students gathered on the Square. Feng met with the other student leaders to discuss what to do. A few minutes later, a group of students from the University of Law and Politics raised a big wooden banner on which were emblazoned the words

"According to the Chinese Constitution, Article 35, the citizens have the right to free speech and assembly."

The crowd broke into applause.

The funeral began at ten o'clock, as scheduled, inside the Great Hall of the People. All the major political figures of China were present.

A later report revealed that Deng Xiaoping stood before Hu Yaobang's casket in the company of all those who had conspired to remove Hu from power, while Zhao Ziyang read a eulogy, calling Hu "a great Marxist and Leninist." One can only imagine what Deng must have been thinking.

Then, apparently, Deng heard the great noise outside the hall. He asked someone standing at his side what the noise was all about. When the man whispered something in reply, Deng walked over to the window. There, on the Square below, he saw a roiling sea of people. In full view, on the steps leading up to the entrance to the Great Hall, three students knelt, holding an unfurled roll of paper above their heads. Deng stared through the glass window, trying to make sense of what he saw. It must have seemed to him as if the black hands of the Cultural Revolution had returned to haunt him.

Another old Party cadre who had fought with Deng alongside Mao Zedong in the early days of the revolution walked over to Deng and stood next to him, pounding the floor with his cane.

"They call us dictators," he declared in a loud voice broken with age. "They call you the Emperor."

That moment determined the fate of the student movement and all that followed. Deng would not tolerate anyone who called him a dictator. He had sent Wei Jingsheng to prison for fifteen years for calling him a dictator on Democracy Wall. He hated Fang Lizhi, the astrophysicist who had openly called for Wei's release. More recently, the United States had invited Deng's bitter resentment when it stood by Fang Lizhi, inviting him to a US embassy banquet.

Deng Xiaoping gazed out the window for a while longer and then walked away without a word.

Chen Mingyuan, a much-honored professor of Chinese language, emerged from the Great Hall and ran down the steps. He stopped in front of the three kneeling students and embraced them. "This is China's conscience," he cried, "embracing you all." He burst into tears.

Seated on the ground, the students covered the Square like a human carpet, waiting for our turn to pay our respects to Hu Yaobang. Hunger and thirst had begun to take their toll, and some in the throng had gone off to buy food. Most of us, however, remained where we were as funeral music from the loudspeakers floated over the Square. Our opportunity to say farewell to Hu was going to come as soon as the service inside the Great Hall ended. The casket containing his body would be placed in a hearse, which, according to tradition, would drive slowly around the Square before it headed out to a crematorium on the western outskirts of Beijing.

We waited for what seemed an inordinately long time, even for a state funeral. And then came shocking news: The hearse had surreptitiously departed from the Great Hall, bypassing Tiananmen Square. It was now heading west down Chang'an Avenue, followed by a long trail of people on bicycles ringing their bells while residents of Beijing stood on either side of the avenue as the procession went past.

Students on the Square exploded in outrage. They pushed forward toward the gate of the Great Hall.

"Come out, Li Peng!" they thundered. "Come out, Li Peng!"

I could see catastrophe looming. If the students began to stampede, causing people to be trampled underfoot, the student leaders would be blamed for the chaos and imprisoned—including Feng. The fear I might lose my husband gave me the courage to climb onto a wall before the raging crowd.

"Let me go to the front!" I called out. Those immediately below where I stood stopped shouting to listen. "I'll go see what's happening and what's being negotiated. I'll come back as soon as I find out. Please don't do anything crazy. We don't want a bloody conflict."

I seemed to have captured the allegiance of the crowd. They made room for me to fight my way toward the Great Hall, where students had clashed with the soldiers guarding the steps. When I reached the front, I saw a rope running between the soldiers and students. The crowd was packed tight, body to body. An empty space existed between where the soldiers stood and the steps leading up to the Great Hall. Scattered around the empty space were some army officers and a few students.

I felt a sense of kinship with the officers as I approached them. I was at home with men in uniform. At the army base, I used to call them "uncles."

"Please let me cross the defense line," I said to one of the soldiers standing at the edge of the crowd. "I have to find our student representative so I can report back to the crowd."

I begged the soldier, telling him the crowd had been waiting without food or water for twenty hours, they had become emotional, and we had to keep them from getting violent.

The soldier was clearly moved. He directed me toward an older officer.

"He's our lieutenant," the soldier told me. "Ask him."

The lieutenant categorically refused to let me through. Twenty minutes had passed since I'd left the students in my group.

"Then maybe you could go in there and find our representative," I said, almost pleading with him.

He shook his head.

Just then I saw a student in a green military jacket walking toward the crowd. I shouted at him, but he did not appear to have heard me. One hundred meters from where I stood shouting, he turned back. Someone in the crowd handed me a megaphone. I aimed the megaphone at the Great Hall and addressed the leaders inside.

"Please come out," I shouted. "Please hear us. We've waited for a whole day and night. We're exhausted and upset. We don't want a bloody conflict. We just want to talk."

I went on and on. My throat was burning with pain.

A PLA soldier standing nearby said to me, "You don't need to shout anymore. You should protect your voice." Then he added in a gentle voice, "That megaphone doesn't work. They can't hear you."

A second soldier passed a water bottle to me. "Your voice is cracking," he said. "You need water."

At that point, I had not had food or water for more than twenty hours. The water soothed my burning throat and cooled my head. I thanked the soldier with a deep, grateful look as I handed the bottle back.

Thirty minutes had passed. I felt I was under a death sentence if I couldn't get information.

Three students appeared on the steps leading up to the Great Hall. Like the earlier petitioners, these students went down to their knees and raised a large paper roll over their heads. The entrance to the Great Hall remained shut.

Around me I could hear students weeping as tears ran down my own face. Even the soldiers wept. We felt betrayed. Our government officials had turned a deaf ear to us. The image of students weeping while our petitioners sat on their knees on the steps of the Great Hall before a silent bastion of stone became the symbol to me of our humiliation.

I was back with our Beida contingent when Feng reappeared. He had been gone for ten hours and looked distraught. He handed me a handkerchief on which he had written, "Premier Li Peng, people" with his own blood. He had intended to write, "Premier Li Peng, people were calling you," but he could not force any more blood to flow from his fingers.

Suddenly there was another massive push from the crowd toward the Great Hall.

A cry went up. "Let's break into the Great Hall!"

A tsunami of people pushed forward to crush the thin line of resistance formed by the soldiers. This could mean only one thing: bloodshed.

Feng and I exchanged glances. We both knew we could not allow this to happen.

"If we hold hands in a line, we can stop the momentum," Feng said.

We moved among the Beida students, quickly urging them to join hands to stop the rush to violence.

Students at first were reluctant. I had to force them to join hands.

"This is a tragedy in the making," I told them. "We have to stop it."

Gradually, students began to link arms, standing protectively around the Beida students who were sitting on the ground. When I looked around, I saw other student marshals doing the same thing.

Feng and I exchanged smiles of relief and solidarity. It was a moment of supreme understanding and unconditional unity that gave me a surge of joy. Our action had created a sense of purpose and clarity that transcended the angry chaos of the crowd. In the seething ocean of people, Beida students formed an island of calm.

At 1:30 p.m., a new wave of anger caused the crowd to surge forward again. Feng saw soldiers rushing down the steps of the Great Hall and became alarmed.

"Beida students," he called out. "We have to leave. Form a line. We'll follow each other. Let's get out of here." Ten students fought to make a path through the crowd so our students could make a break from the Square, like water flowing through a dike. I was thrust forward against my will until I saw a break, an open space. Feng called to me and I ran toward him, tripping over myself to catch up with him. When I looked back, I could see the crowd was following my lead, pouring after me and Feng. We knew that without any other form of communication, a body of movement could direct an entire crowd. That's the lesson Feng had learned from observing the old man in the Square in 1987.

As Beida students took the lead, thousands of students from other universities began to follow us out of the Square. We had avoided a huge tragedy.

"You did an amazing thing," I later told Feng. "You saved lives today."

He blushed and was too moved to reply. Instead, he gazed at me silently, tears rising in his large, deep, brown eyes.

It took us three hours to make the trip on foot back to Beida. "Boycott classes, boycott classes," the students chanted along the way. Citizens of Beijing lined the streets, cheering us on.

"Students, we support you," they cried out.

I felt someone pull on my arm. I looked to see a short man in gray, shabby clothes, a local worker with a pale face and big eyes full of fear, shyness, and embarrassment. He pushed a piece of paper at me. I took it, and he stepped away. When I looked at my hand, it held a rumpled five renminbi bill, old and soft, like a little rag.

I left the march and found an ice cream stand. An old couple at the stand gave me a box of ice cream for my five renminbi. Then they added another half box on top of that. I distributed the ice cream to my fellow marchers, all of them parched and hungry. As I moved back and forth among them, I saw other residents who had come out to line the streets bringing water to the students. It made me profoundly grateful to the good people of Beijing.

I believe the way the government treated the students on the day of Hu Yaobang's funeral incited their anger and led directly to the demonstrations on Tiananmen Square and the aftermath that shocked the world. As a beloved leader was laid to rest, a movement was born. I have often wondered whether events might have turned out differently if the government had invited a few students to attend the funeral.

13

DAWN OF NEW BEGINNINGS

LATER MEMOIRS AND REPORTS recorded that the next day, April 23, Zhao Ziyang, the general secretary of the Chinese Communist Party and Hu Yaobang's successor, boarded a train in Beijing and departed on a scheduled state visit to North Korea. Zhao, who was the second most powerful leader in China after Deng Xiaoping, later professed to be sympathetic to the students on Tiananmen Square and their peaceful agenda, but it seems odd in retrospect that he would leave Beijing at such a pivotal moment. That decision cost him the power to influence events and ultimately his political career. In leaving, he turned the situation over to Li Peng, his rival for the ear of Deng Xiaoping.

Zhao's instructions to Li Peng were as follows: Make sure the students return to classes immediately, avoid bloodshed at all cost, and open a dialogue with the students. Zhao Ziyang secured Deng Xiaoping's approval before he handed the instructions over to Li Peng, who then could be counted upon to turn them to his own advantage.

That evening, Chen Xitong, the mayor of Beijing, convened a meeting between Party secretaries and the presidents of seventy Beijing colleges and universities. Students from eighteen schools had announced plans to boycott classes, and some were setting up new organizations to replace their official student associations. The mayor scolded the university officials and told them to go back to their schools, gather information through the Youth League and the official student organizations, and come back with a solution.

At about the same time, students from twenty-one universities gathered to establish the Beijing Students' Autonomous Federation, which was charged with the mission of leading a citywide student movement. Based on someone's suggestion, democratically electing a true student leadership group had become a new focus for the movement.

Feng remained busy with the Preparatory Committee, which was setting up an election for a new organization to replace the official student association at Beida. It would be the first time any such election was held on our campus.

The room in Dormitory 28 became the Preparatory Committee's command central. Feng and his committee members met continuously, and I took on the job of running secretariat, fielding questions and registering the innumerable ideas that a stream of visitors brought to the Committee. I was the liaison with the general student population at Beida, and I created a press center at my desk out in the hallway. On the first day alone, I met hundreds of people and gathered many suggestions that helped to shape the direction of the movement. An older man who stopped by told me he saw in us the same passion and enthusiasm he recalled from the early days of the Communist Party. That made me proud.

It was midnight before the last people lingering in the headquarters room began to leave. I was exhausted. A student who had helped me at the desk began to play his guitar. The music filled me with tranquility. It sounded like soft raindrops in the fragrant spring night. I jumped up from the bunk bed where I had been resting to look for Feng so we could share this moment. He was out in the hallway, engaged in a heated discussion. I dragged him into the room.

The magic of the music began to work on Feng. His whole day had been filled with political debates and strategy sessions; but as he began to relax, the romantic Feng, the young man with whom I had fallen in love, returned.

A girl named Tang Ye, who had also helped me at the desk, sat curled up on one of the beds, quietly listening to the song.

"Isn't this the life we've been struggling for?" she murmured, to no one in particular. "A peaceful life, without fear?"

Her words touched my heart, but Feng shot into a sitting position.

"Yes," he announced in a loud voice. "That's why we're here. To fight. That's why we have to boycott classes." He was back in debate mode.

"Oh, Feng," I said. "Please don't ruin it."

He flopped back on the bed and flashed me a boyish grin. I forgave him anything when I saw that grin. Still, he'd broken the spell. The student went on playing a little longer, but when he finished the song, he put down the guitar and stood up.

"Feng is a politician now," he said. "Whenever he opens his mouth, out pops a speech."

But Feng was fast asleep, the faint trace of a smile still on his face. I pulled up a blanket to cover him.

The next day, sixty thousand students from forty-eight colleges and universities in Beijing refused to go to class. The boycott was official. It was also a reprieve. At Beida, students streamed over the campus in a holiday mood. Our first independent election was scheduled for two o'clock in the afternoon on a large sports field known as the May Fourth field on the eastern side of campus.

On May 4, 1919, almost exactly seventy years earlier, Beida students had led a demonstration on Tiananmen Square, which in those days was a bucolic, grassy field. They were protesting the Treaty of Versailles at the end of World War I. One provision of the treaty, which established new boundaries and rearranged entire countries, permitted Germany to transfer its rights to Shandong, my home province, to Japan. The warlord government ruling China at the time was allied with Japan, and the Peace Conference justified its decision on the basis of that somewhat covert relationship. But in handing this rich, delicious coastal province to the Japanese, the Great Powers ignored the sovereignty of China.

It would be hard to compare the students of 1919 with those of 1989. The students who opposed the Treaty of Versailles took the future of China into their own hands. Their boycott throughout China inspired a national resistance movement, called the May Fourth Movement, and workers went out on strike. The Chinese government never signed the Versailles treaty and soon crumbled in the face of opposition.

The May Fourth Movement had started a revolution. That was real power. Seventy years later, nearly eight thousand students gathered in the May Fourth field to exercise our vote because we wanted to advance democracy in China. We wanted to make a discovery, not a revolution. Yet we were always aware of those brave students from an earlier day. Political reality had forced them to grow up fast. To save China, they'd had to confront a weak, corrupt government. We were only trying to capture the attention of the monolithic, all-powerful leadership that had grown out of that earlier movement. We were children fighting to grow to maturity within a system ruled by a generation demanding total submission.

As I was leaving for the May Fourth field to cast my vote, a student appeared at the Preparatory Committee headquarters and announced that Li Peng had called a politburo meeting to address the students' concerns. This, I thought, was promising news. At last the central government was beginning to pay attention to us. I asked another student to post this news at the Triangle. One boy created a poster with beautiful calligraphy. Another student reminded him not to leave any trace of handwriting the government might later use to incriminate him. The calligrapher, without skipping a beat, switched his brush from right hand to left and finished the poster.

Terror was present in ways the May Fourth students could never have known. Feng's department head had warned him not to get too deeply involved in the student movement because the government had been recording all its activities with infrared cameras. After I heard that, I was always nervous for Feng, who was never afraid to stand up in front of a crowd. In the words of a Chinese proverb, "The wind always destroys the tallest tree in the forest." Only recently we had found a listening device in our makeshift office. The government was everywhere, an unseen presence.

At the election on the May Fourth field, Wang Dan gave a speech, followed by other candidates, who introduced themselves and explained where they thought the movement should go next. Everything seemed to go smoothly. Tang stood with me in the crowd and we watched from a distance.

Then two students who were not scheduled as candidates wanted to get up on the podium to speak. Students sitting in the field shouted, "Let them up! They have a right to speak too." Another student climbed onto the podium and grabbed the microphone. "He's a spy!" he shouted, pointing at one of the two students. "Don't listen to him."

The outcry sent a wave of commotion through the field of students. Somehow Feng ended up with the microphone. He'd been preparing for this moment all morning in the library. He was so intent on his speech, he somehow failed to notice the agitation in the crowd.

"I have a dream," Feng declared. Martin Luther King's speech was not well known to Chinese students at that time, but Feng loved it. He'd won a prize for reciting it a few years earlier in an English language contest. It was not, however, what the crowd wanted to hear at that moment. They didn't care about somebody's dream. They wanted to know why one of the unscheduled speakers was being accused of spying for the government. The crowd began to jeer at Feng and laugh so raucously that he had to stop. By the time Wang Dan took over and urged the crowd to be patient, students were already drifting away. They had come to exercise their right to vote, and they voted with their feet.

Feng and the other candidates and organizers were left marooned on the podium in embarrassment. We were all crushed. Tang Ye looked as if she'd witnessed a public hanging. I patted her on the back, but I couldn't find anything encouraging to say. We walked back to the Preparatory Committee headquarters in silence.

The student who had interrupted the speaker and called him a spy was Xiong Yan, a law student from a peasant family in Mao's home province of Hunan. He had been involved with the Committee from the outset. His passion, his direct temperament and fearless personality, and his resounding Hunan accent endeared him to us all. We had heard his open critiques of the government as early as 1987, when he gave speeches at the Triangle. Once, referring to government officials who fattened their pockets at the expense of reform, Xiong had called them "well-fed ghosts." This time, however, Xiong's hot temper had undermined the election. He was mortified.

Back at headquarters, Xiong's face was red hot and his breathing was heavy. We were all too upset and embarrassed to speak. No one came to our office anymore, while life on campus continued to bustle with noise and energy. Morale was at an all-time low. Already some students had criticized members of the Committee for kneeling on the steps of the Great Hall when they tried to present their petition after Hu Yaobang's funeral. They said we should never kneel before the Communist Party, never "beg for democracy." Today, however, Beida students had gone beyond criticism. They had walked out on the Committee. In our discouragement, we said to ourselves, *It's over.*

Chen Mingyuan, the professor who had embraced the Committee members on the steps, came to our improvised command center shortly after the failed election. He was a poet in his forties, who had twice been imprisoned during the Cultural Revolution. When Chen was released after the death of Mao and the arrest of the Gang of Four, he was hailed as a hero.

"Don't be discouraged," he told us. "You are excellent kids. I've been through the April Fifth Incident and many other things, and I know how hard it is to organize an event like this. It's perfectly okay to fail the first time. Don't worry," he said. "This is just a small setback on your long journey. Next time you'll do much better."

"But I don't think the students will trust us anymore," one member of the Committee said.

"Let's do this," Chen said. "I'll give a speech to the students, and then I'll come back to talk about what to do next."

Minutes later we heard his voice booming out over the campus, telling everyone how significant it was that Beida students had decided to hold the first democratic election in China in forty years and what changes would come about if our model was adopted throughout the country. His speech was interrupted many times by thunderous applause. Immediately student attitudes began to shift. By nightfall, all kinds of people had begun to show up at the office, many of them students from master's and doctoral programs, older students who came in response to the criticism that student leaders were too young and inexperienced to run an election. They came to help and offered all kinds of suggestions to improve the movement.

The next day, we held another election—this time in a classroom. Approximately one hundred students, representatives from each department, cast their votes. Candidates once again had the opportunity to address the assembled voters before they cast their ballots. When Feng presented his qualifications, he talked about his involvement in the demonstrations of 1987 and 1988 and his more recent organizational activities. He also noted that the Preparatory Committee had conducted its meetings behind closed doors up to that point and expressed his fear it would become disconnected from the student body. Eventually, he said, with his characteristic dry wit, the student leaders could become the "small handful of people" the government liked to say was manipulating the demonstrations.

The six candidates who received the most votes were elected. Feng was among the winners.

What unexpected surprises awaited me when my victorious husband returned to headquarters at sunset. He looked relaxed and in a good mood. He borrowed some food coupons, telling the boys in the office he wanted to take his wife out to dinner.

"Chai Ling isn't *just* your wife," one of the boys replied, teasingly. "She's also our secretary general. If you want to take her out to dinner, you have to ask our permission."

"It's okay," said another student, who had appeared in the doorway. "Feng can take her to dinner. She's just been fired."

I thought he was joking.

"It's true," Feng assured me, smiling. "We're replacing you with Tang Ye. In fact, I insisted on it."

I was stunned. "What did I do to deserve that?"

"You haven't done anything," Feng said. "But you are my wife, and I'm a newly elected member. I can't have a family member working in the organization. It might be viewed as nepotism. You can be my personal secretary general if you want."

The boys in the office burst out laughing. They were intrigued to see a husband acting like a big shot and bossing his wife around.

I was not amused. We had weathered this storm together, and after all the hard work I'd done to prepare for his victory, this is how Feng had decided to thank me. I threw my food coupon on the floor and stormed out of the room before bursting into tears.

The last few days now felt like a century. I had worked hard to build an organization that could facilitate meetings, handle public communications, and set up student guards and working schedules. I had skipped meals. I had lost hours of sleep. I never knew where to find Feng, and because I was afraid to go home on dark nights, I slept wherever I could find a spare bed.

I had done all this out of a faithful wife's devotion to her husband, working quietly behind the scenes to do everything he and his colleagues could not do themselves. I never wanted credit. When students complained about the leaders, I took the heat and asked them if they wanted to help us. I was the one who saw how students walked away after waiting for the leaders to emerge from behind closed doors. I was the one who set up a channel of communication between students and leaders. I did all this to help Feng, so he could come home safe one day and we could get on with our life's plans.

It seemed Feng took all my contributions for granted, though. He constantly undermined my suggestions, which he called "the little lady's views." He was so eager to win the respect and trust of the boys he worked with that he was willing to do so at the expense of the one person who genuinely cared for and loved him.

Outside the dining hall young couples wandered around holding hands after another full day with no classes to attend. The girls looked so relaxed and carefree, and there I was, hungry, lonely, and exhausted. Why couldn't I have just one day like those girls? Feng was so busy with the movement that in order to be near him, I had to help out and put up with all sorts of insults. Now Feng himself had taken away the one opportunity I had to be near him.

I sat on the steps of the new education building with my head resting against the wall, watching the fading shades of pink and orange in the sky, wondering what color my love had become.

A student I vaguely recognized stopped in front of me. "Aren't you on the Preparatory Committee?" he said. "You are all so courageous. We really admire you. Keep going. We'll stand behind you."

I watched him walk away. If only he could have known how profoundly uplifting his words were. He made me think of all the wonderful people I had met in the past few days—the man who had pressed the sweaty five renminbi note in my hands, the old couple who had given me extra ice cream, and Tang Ye, who had sworn to visit me in prison if Feng and I were arrested. I recalled the night when the police had chased us down Chang'an Avenue and the oath I'd made never to run away again, and I realized I could no longer be a part of the movement merely as Feng's wife; I had to do it for me. I had to stand up for my own dignity and the dignity of my countrymen. From now on, I would help the movement, not as Feng's wife, to love him and support him, but as a citizen of China. With renewed determination, I resolved to face all the setbacks and insults and do whatever I could to help the movement.

On the same day that democratic elections gave birth to a new, independent student organization in China, a new, independent woman was born as well.

14

THE DONG LUAN VERDICT

WHILE BEIDA STUDENTS gathered at the May Fourth field on campus for our first trial election, Li Peng convened a politburo meeting to discuss the student movement. After Li Ximing (the Communist Party boss of Beijing) and Chen Xitong (the mayor of Beijing) reported on the situation—calling it *dong luan* (turmoil), unprecedented, and "evil winning over good"—the head of the State Education Committee reported to Li Peng what students had said and written in slogans and on protest posters in Beijing, as well as at top universities across the country.

In Li Peng's eyes, the student protests were "a naked and overt challenge to the Party." The meeting concluded with Li characterizing the student movement as "a planned and organized turmoil against the Communist Party and socialism." And he was determined to get Deng Xiaoping to agree.[1]

To make his case, Li Peng knew how to present "planned and organized turmoil" to Deng. He selected slogans and grouped them together in a way that made them appear to be anti-Party and antisocialist. Li Peng was like a tattletale with a teacher. "The spear is pointed at you," he told Deng.

Deng Xiaoping reacted just as Li Peng hoped he would. The old man couldn't swallow any criticism without a fight. Years of class struggle and the horrible times he had known during the Cultural Revolution had turned Deng into a man who believed he had to get tough with the student demonstrators. In the words of an old Chinese adage, he would "use a sharp knife to cut through knotted hemp." Though Deng had initially endorsed Zhao Ziyang's assessment that the students should be handled with persuasion, when he heard Li Peng's report, he summed it up by saying the Party was facing *turmoil*, and they had the ability to put a stop to it.

Deng was extremely sensitive just then about the situation in Poland, where, in his opinion, the ruling Communist Party was too soft on the Solidarity movement. At Beida, we used the same name, *Solidarity*, for our own organization, which in Deng's mind was clear evidence of Western bourgeois liberal influence that could not be tolerated. China could not become a second Poland.

Deng concluded, "This is a well-planned plot whose real aim is to reject the Chinese Communist Party and the socialist system at the most fundamental level. . . . We are facing a most serious political struggle. . . . We've got to be explicit and clear in opposing this turmoil."[2] His words became the official verdict on the student movement.

After a meeting lasting nearly two hours, Deng Xiaoping gave Li Peng the green light. Li Peng immediately ordered Deng's words to be printed as a speech and distributed as a central government document to Party officials at all levels across the country. He then called the *People's Daily*, the Party's official newspaper, to publish an editorial, which was lifted in large part directly from Deng's speech.

Over the next two days, as students boycotted classes and set up organizations, the government moved at top speed. On April 25, government radio announced the verdict nationwide on the seven o'clock evening news. The speech also appeared the next day as an editorial in the *People's Daily* and headlined all major newspapers in the country.

I remember as if it were yesterday the night we listened to the broadcast of the government's announcement. As Feng and I were walking back from the dining hall to our command center in Dormitory 28, the campus broadcasting system suddenly crackled. The voice of a familiar anchor from the Central TV station began his reading:

Following the memorial meeting commemorating the death of Hu Yaobang, an extremely small number of people with a hidden agenda continued to take advantage of the young students' feeling of grief for Comrade Hu Yaobang to spread all kinds of rumors to poison and confuse the people's minds. . . .

We stood and listened as the announcer continued to mischaracterize and vilify the student protests, saying our purpose was to "sow dissension among the people, to plunge the whole country into chaos, and sabotage the political situation of stability and unity." But it was what he said next that sent a chill wind down my spine.

This is a planned conspiracy and a dong luan *[chaos, turmoil, or upheaval]. Its essence is to, once and for all, negate the leadership of the CPC and the socialist system. This is a serious political struggle confronting the whole party and the people of all nationalities throughout the country. . . .*

If we are tolerant of this dong luan *and let it go unchecked, . . . a China with very good prospects and a bright future will become a chaotic and unstable China without any future.*

The whole party and the people nationwide should fully understand the seriousness of this struggle [and] unite to take a clear-cut stand to oppose the dong luan. *. . . Under no circumstances should the establishment of any illegal organizations be allowed.*[3]

I looked at the young students standing around me. Their faces were serious and tense. The government had called our movement a *dong luan*, a chaos or turmoil—the same verdict the Party had used against the crimes of the Cultural Revolution. No other movement had been labeled *dong luan*; that was a name for disaster. The government also called our student organizations "illegal" and accused us of attempting to overthrow the government and the Party. To any Chinese, no crime deserved a punishment more severe than the crime of "overthrowing the government and the Party."

As the broadcast continued, the entire campus fell into deathly silence. It was as if all creatures had ceased to breathe and the earth had stopped turning. Shocked disbelief, fear, and anger were the emotions coursing through my system.

A moment later, the sound of smashing glass exploded around me as small glass bottles were thrown from dorm windows and hit the ground. Deng's given name, Xiaoping, has the same phonetic sound as "small bottle." In 1976, when Deng returned to power for the third time, people showed support and good wishes by hanging small bottles on trees. This night, however, the students smashed bottles to show their defiance. After they had smashed all their bottles, students banged on tables and crashed pans and buckets together, shouting, screaming, and cursing. Anger roared into the night sky as the campus exploded with the cries of voices laced with the jingling and tinkling of millions of pieces of broken glass.

Then from our student broadcasting center, which had loudspeakers several floors above the campus speakers, came a strong voice:

In this China, the power, the law, the government, the army, the economic system, the country, the media, and the people are all controlled by one Party. The Party system and the legal system are one and the same. The Constitution can't reflect the people's will but it is simply a chapter of the Party. And the National People's Congress formed under this Constitution does not reflect the people's will either. Why in the past thirteen years, since the ending of the Cultural Revolution, did people not voice their opinions through the People's Congress or the Party organization or the government? The answer is very clear: The ruling Party, the government, and the People's Congress do not reflect the people's will. This is the result of corrupt politics, corrupt politicians, and a corrupt legal system. Can lies go on forever? To make the National People's Congress truly represent the people, the one Party monopoly must end![4]

The speaker was a longtime political dissident named Ren Wanding, who had recently been released from prison. I found his speech brilliantly insightful, but he was quickly interrupted by student leaders. "The one Party monopoly must end" sounded too radical for a lot of students at that time. The student leaders did not want the government to find more excuses to harm the student movement. They wanted to help push reform and clean up corruption and carry out some basic practices of democracy, first on campus. To overthrow the ruling Communist Party was definitely not on students' minds.

Calling us "an organized antirevolutionary conspiracy, aiming to overthrow the Party and socialism" was too much for us to accept. We felt we were being wronged. When you were wronged by your parents, you could run away from home; when you were wronged by your local Party boss, you could take it to a higher level, to the city, provincial, or central government. But when you were wronged by the highest authority in the country, the dictator of the land, where did you go? We took to the streets again.

Before the government verdict appeared in the *People's Daily*, the Beijing Students' Autonomous Federation, a new student organization that intended to lead a citywide student movement, had proposed a march to Tiananmen on April 27. Many students hadn't yet recovered from the fatigue of recent demonstrations, and some student leaders preferred to run activities on campus. But the *People's Daily* editorial changed the tenor of the movement.

The mood on campus was tense after the *People's Daily* editorial appeared. Some law students rushed to prepare a response to the editorial, which they broadcast over our loudspeaker system.

This broadcast eased the tension a little because it provided a great deal of clarity. It also supplied a legal basis for the ongoing student movement. Our immediate concern was whether the students should march to Tiananmen Square the next day. Throughout the morning, the Triangle was filled with new protest posters as the students' anger burst out in black ink.

Meanwhile, the newly elected student committee members and organizers gathered in a classroom. After an intense debate, five of the committee members voted 3–2 against the next day's march to Tiananmen. Wang Dan and Feng voted to go. The other three members insisted the government's tone had been too harsh, that it was better to focus our energy on the campus democracy. Wang Dan and Feng believed that before the government verdict, it was possible to make compromises by scaling down the activities on campus; but with a verdict of *dong luan*, we would be accepting the government's accusation if we didn't take strong action. They argued we must put more pressure on the government to reverse the verdict. Otherwise any further activities on campus would be labeled *dong luan*.

"If the Preparatory Committee decides not to go out tomorrow because we're one vote short," said Feng, "it would hurt this leadership's reputation. After our first failed election, this organization already suffered. If we decide not to support the demonstration, but the majority of students go out tomorrow anyway, we will lose the support of the students and be left in the dust. And if the students go out without any organization or leadership, the chance of bloodshed will be higher when they encounter the police."

Feng made a good argument. He then went back to the podium and suggested another vote—this time to include the head of each department under the Preparatory Committee. This time the majority voted to march the next day.

At sunrise the next morning, two thousand Beida students were out on the street, along with students from neighboring schools, many of whom had come out on their own. After a few confrontations between students and police, who staged blockades at all major intersections, more students joined the march.

I was still at the office, working with some students to make another banner stating our commitment to peace and support of the Four Basic Principles—upholding the socialist path; upholding the people's democratic dictatorship; upholding the leadership of the Chinese Communist

Party; and upholding Marxism, Leninism, and Mao Zedong thought. I wanted to make sure we could de-escalate the tension but focus on continuing reform and ending corruption. I later read in a government report that the leaders were confused by this "change in message." We never meant for war.

Before I could join the march, a man who claimed to have some kind of relationship with Deng Xiaoping and his family came to see me. He told me, "Deng and the other older leaders like young people very much. . . . But right now they are having a difficult time and hope the students will give them some time before pushing the movement further and bringing harm to everyone."

I was surprised by this information because it was entirely different from what the *People's Daily* editorial had implied. If Deng had been misinformed about the student movement, which was possible, then it would be helpful to let him know the peaceful intentions of the students. I asked the man to take back the message that we had nothing against Deng; in fact, we liked him and were grateful for the reforms he had launched and wanted him to stand behind the reforms and push them forward.

After saying good-bye to the man, I rushed to join my fellow students. As soon as we walked out of the Peking University campus, we met up with students coming from Tsinghua University. As we walked south to People's University, we encountered the first police blockade. The policemen formed a line in the middle of the street with their arms locked together. We had already decided to remain disciplined to avoid chaos and any clash that might give the government an excuse to call our movement a form of turmoil. We stopped and waited for the student leaders to talk to the police, but a great number of onlookers then moved into the street, chanting, "Move away! Move away!" and forced the police to the sidewalk.

As we marched on, many students from other schools were simply waiting at intersections to join us as we advanced toward the center of the city. When we reached Second Ring Road, a main boulevard circling the city, our march became more organized. Each formation proceeded under its school's flags and banners, and student picket lines protected the main body of the march, preventing nonstudents from mixing into the march. In front of each square formation, student leaders with whistles and bullhorns shouted slogans as they led their troops. Usually shy in public, I, too, held a bullhorn and led the shouting. The police blockades at all major intersections did not put up much resistance. Instead, many of the police cheered us on.

On Chang'an Avenue, we encountered armed soldiers, who formed a human barrier on the northern edge of the Square, determined to keep us from entering. But we were in such a happy, cheerful mood that the fear of bloodshed had evaporated. The march turned into something more like a festival as millions of Beijing residents filled the sidewalks and overpasses, giving us bread, water bottles, and ice cream bars. When we approached Tiananmen Square, we knew we were not there to pick a fight. Instead, we left the empty Square to the nervous soldiers and marched on to the far end of Chang'an Avenue, traveling from west to east, in the opposite direction of traditional, government-sponsored parades. The march became the single largest protest against the government since the Communist Party had seized power in China. For the first time since the *People's Daily* editorial had made such dire threats, the students and citizens of Beijing won a total victory.

At one moment, after we had reached Chang'an Avenue, I stepped to the side to take it all in. Before me, a sea of people—young and old, men and women—poured onto the eight-lane boulevard from all directions and all parts of the city. They joined together and became an unstoppable wave, pulsing and moving forward, full of vigor and vitality. That experience left a profound and lasting impression on me. For the first time in my life, I had experienced the massive power of the people's will for freedom. Despite all the intellectual analysis that came later, I knew in the core of my being that this was a force no individual, no organization, and no party could stop, control, suffocate, or manipulate. With joy and delight, I knew I was part of and deeply connected to this force.

15

SECRET MEETING

MY FATHER PAID me a surprise visit on May 1, which is Labor Day in China, a national holiday. He had not been to Beijing since 1986, when he and Mom came to visit me. It was not exactly the most opportune moment, from my standpoint, because Feng and I were deeply immersed in the gathering storm. We no longer even lived in our little one-room home, although as chance would have it, I happened to be there when my father unexpectedly appeared.

He seemed uncharacteristically relaxed. My mother, he said, had almost recovered from her nervous breakdown. The family crisis that had almost been too much for him to bear had passed, and that's why he felt he could pay Feng and me a visit.

I rushed out to buy a Peking duck and some ice cream so he and I could enjoy an afternoon lunch outside on our little patio. By the time I returned, Feng had joined us as well.

As we sat beneath the huge, leafy tree that shaded the courtyard, I delicately inquired of my father whether he had any inkling of the political situation in Beijing. He was blissfully unaware that anything was underway. Carefully, and with some circumspection, I filled him in on what was happening. I assured him none of the apparent brouhaha would interfere with his sightseeing opportunities. The Summer Palace, for example, was a short bus ride away.

I told him to make our little room his own for however long he wished. Feng and I would sleep at school. (Feng and I lived on campus all the time now, but I did not include that information.) I really wanted my father to enjoy his richly deserved vacation, but I could not bring myself to tell him I was too busy to take him out and show him a good time. I avoided direct eye contact and encouraged him to eat more duck.

He soon realized things were more serious than any other political movement he had experienced because this time his daughter was in the forefront. I saw fear flit across his face as he lit up a cigarette. He didn't say another word for the rest of the lunch. His ice cream turned into a bowl of pink soup while he burned through one cigarette after another.

At a traditional Peking duck banquet, the tongue of the duck is set aside and presented to the guest of honor at the end of the meal. The woman who packed the duck for me at the restaurant expressly reminded me not to discard it. Now, as I looked at my father's worried expression and saw the lines around his eyes, I couldn't find the heart to present him with the precious duck tongue, which now looked like a piece of dried rubber, worthy only of the garbage pail.

Dad spent the entire next day at my little home, consuming cigarettes, moving from the bed to the chair to a little stool out in the courtyard. He never touched the leftover duck. A growing turmoil, a real *dong luan*, was brewing inside him.

As much as I wanted to spend time with my dad, I had an urgent mission to accomplish. I had told the committee about the man who had approached me before the April 27 march claiming to have connections to Deng Xiaoping, and they had agreed to send me and another student representative to see if we could contact Deng directly through this man. My instincts told me that if we could speak to Deng in person on behalf of the student leadership, as the man had suggested, we could explain what was really going on with the students so he could see our true motives and our desire for democratic reform. Deng might not agree with us, but at least he would know that the students were not hostile toward him and the other leaders. I wholeheartedly believed that love and peace could bridge the gap of distrust, soften the hearts of the leaders, and end the escalation toward violence.

After traveling most of the day through the hot and sweaty city, by some miracle we were able to find the man who had come to see me. But by then his attitude had changed. No longer optimistic, he denied he had any real connections with Deng's family.

"They left the city," he said.

As we were about to leave in defeat, the man seemed to reconsider what he had said. Instead of sending us away, he invited us in to warn us of the dangers ahead. He told us the government could crack down at any time, and he did not want to see any more lives destroyed. "You youngsters do not know how dark and cruel the Communist system can be. You all should quit now." His wife, too, kept urging us to stop the protests, with sincere concern and worry written all over her face.

Later we learned that Deng's family had become alarmed by the mass reaction from the people on April 27. They felt Deng had been misled by Li Peng's exaggeration of the situation. Deng's family had all suffered from his banishments during the Cultural Revolution, but in many situations they had been helped, protected, and loved by the goodness of the common people. They had a tender spot in their hearts for the Chinese people and the Beijing citizens who had led them back to power. Two of Deng's children went to Beida to try to build a bridge of communication with the students, but when they came to the South Gate of campus, they were met with talk of revenge and retribution by some students and other bystanders, none of whom were part of the official student leadership. Deng's son and daughter had cut short their diplomatic mission, and Deng Xiaoping soon left Beijing for his summer residence in Beidaihe, an ocean resort a few hours north of the capital.

When our meeting with the man and his wife was over, he arranged for a car and driver to take us back to Beida. We were accompanied by two sharply dressed men, who were brisk in manner and conducted themselves with impressive efficiency. They told us they had watched tapes of the demonstrations and had easily identified the student who was with me in the car as one of the protesters. My heart froze, and my mind replayed stories of people who had disappeared to unknown places. These men were part of the national security force, which was different from the local police. Rumor had it their boss, who was one of the seven politburo members who made all the decisions for the country, was secretly pro-reform, but he did not like anarchy. "If you really want to do something," one of the men said as we sped along toward Beida, "get serious."

"What do you mean?" I asked.

The two men looked at each other and the one spoke again. "On the evening of April 19, on Chang'an Avenue, we saw a student sitting on a piece of white cloth that said 'Hunger Strike.' But when the police moved in, that student jumped up and ran like a rabbit. You can't be taken seriously if your protests are that laughable."

I looked at my fellow student, and neither of us could believe what we were hearing. Advice from the enemy? Who was with us and who was against us?

Before they dropped us off at the South Gate of Beida, the men handed us a business card. "Call us if you're in trouble," they said. "Don't sell us out." As soon as we stepped clear, the car sped away. I knew an important opportunity for peace and reconciliation had come and gone.

We walked back quickly to Dormitory 28 and told the other leaders about our encounter. Just as we finished our report, I was told someone was waiting for me outside.

It was my dad. He had changed out of his army uniform into civilian clothes and was standing in the shade of a tree with a piece of paper in his hand.

It was the note I had written to Feng the day after police had chased us down Chang'an Avenue. I had written the note in a state of rising panic when I couldn't find Feng anywhere and thought he'd been arrested—or worse. My father had found the note, which provided a much clearer picture of the situation.

"Ling Ling," he said in a heavy voice, "I should leave now. I understand how you feel and why you have to do this. I can only hope nothing bad will happen to you. You and I went through these debates in the past. What needed to be said has been said. There is no use for me to stay here; whatever will happen is beyond my ability to stop. Our family needs me; it will collapse without me. So I'll leave now."

My heart ached because I knew what was going through his mind. Years earlier, Dad had lost his younger sister to the Revolution. She had babysat for a village leader who was involved in land reform, and they had all perished in a fire set by an angry landlord seeking revenge after his properties were seized by the Communist Party. My father had never stopped blaming himself for not being there to protect his younger sister. Now his daughter was placing herself in harm's way, and there was nothing he could do to prevent another tragedy.

I felt terrible he had taken time from work and our family to come all the way to Beijing to see me, only to cut his visit short. He had come to celebrate my mom's recovery and the return to happiness at home and also to tell me—I found out years later—about his promotion to CEO of the hospital, the job he had worked his entire life to achieve. Now he had come to the realization that he might never see his eldest daughter again. To comfort him, I said I would send him a telegram every three days.

"What if three days go by and I don't get one?" he asked. "Then what?"

"I don't know, Dad," I replied. "If that happens, maybe you should stop waiting for me."

I couldn't believe I had uttered those words. We looked at each other, and my tears began to flow. Never in my wildest imaginings had I ever expected to say farewell this way to my father.

"Don't cry, Ling Ling," he said. "Crying is not a good thing to do for farewell. Bye now!"

He walked away, and then suddenly stopped. His voice trembled a bit as he said, "You built such a nice home. It is hard to watch it being destroyed."

How I longed for him to forgive me for all the pain I'd caused him in my growing-up years. How I wished I could ask him to forgive me for all the grief the impending storm was going to bring. All I could say was, "I am so sorry, Dad."

The gap that had opened between us during my headstrong teenage years, the gap across which I had never been able to build a bridge, suddenly closed in the presence of our unspoken words. I felt closer to my father than ever before. Through my blurry eyes, I saw the kindest and strongest man in my life fighting back his own tears to give his daughter the strength she needed.

It was the last time I saw my father in China. He received no telegrams, no phone calls, no letters, but he went on waiting for me. Like everyone else, he learned I was still alive after the massacre in Beijing when he read my name on the government's most-wanted list. God only knows how many nights he holed up in his room with his ear pressed against his shortwave radio, hoping to hear my voice or any news of me from Voice of America.

———————

Looking back twenty years later, it's clear the students wanted more than Deng was willing to give. After suffering greatly during the Cultural Revolution, Deng wanted people to have food on the table, but he had no stomach for democracy, freedom, human rights—all that Western, liberal nonsense, which he believed would only lead to turmoil, chaos, and tragedies similar to those of the Cultural Revolution. Deng envisioned an economically prosperous China and an obedient Chinese people, and he believed preserving a democratic dictatorship was the way to achieve it.

Other advisers, including Ruan Ming, felt that Deng had wanted reform and democracy in the late 1970s but that he had changed his mind after Wei Jingsheng posted his famous critique on Democracy Wall: "Do we want democracy or new dictatorship?" Deng had suffered plenty of name-calling during the Mao era. Enough was enough.

When Zhao Ziyang came back from North Korea, his power struggle with Li Peng intensified. Deng had made it clear before he departed for Beidaihe that he wanted the situation in Beijing cleaned up in time for Mikhail Gorbachev's state visit in mid-May. Zhao and Li differed on how to accomplish that objective. While they battled it out, Deng rested at his summer home—though he closely monitored the situation in Beijing. In the words of an old Chinese adage, he was sitting on a mountaintop, watching the tigers fight. If Zhao and Li failed to clean up the mess, Deng knew he had yet another option at his disposal: He could call in the army.

We students knew very little about the power struggle at the top. We were caught up in trying to read the tea leaves to determine what we should do next. After the April 27 march, some students were intoxicated by the apparent victory. Others insisted that nothing had really changed. A staged dialogue on national television between the government and some handpicked student leaders made the students appear unorganized, ungrateful, and spoiled. The phony dialogue punctured the illusion of victory and drove the students back into the streets. The Beijing Students' Autonomous Federation coordinated a march to celebrate the seventieth anniversary of the May Fourth Movement, commemorating the youth movement that led to the birth of Chinese Communism. On the morning of the march, we left the Beida campus at eight in the morning and arrived at Tiananmen Square around three that afternoon. The police were out in force, but they mostly acted with restraint.

Students from fifty cities all over China staged demonstrations, and hundreds of journalists joined our march on the Square, protesting the closing down of the *World Economic Herald*, a Shanghai newspaper that had run a long article commemorating Hu Yaobang on the day of his funeral. When Jiang Zemin, the local Party boss in Shanghai, fired the *Herald*'s editor in chief and then closed down the newspaper, the journalists fought back. They appeared on the Square with banners and slogans, such as one that declared, "Don't Force Us to Lie Anymore." This was unprecedented. Under Communist rule, newspapers in China operated under tight censorship.

After the May Fourth demonstration, the student movement began to lose steam. One demonstration after another, and what did it prove?

On campus, we seriously debated whether to end the boycott. When we distributed a questionnaire on the matter, two-thirds of the students voted to continue. Feng, meanwhile, discouraged by the endless debates between student leaders, returned to the lab to continue his research. On Beida's campus frustration was building even as the energy ebbed.

Still, we kept up the pressure. On the Triangle, we selected and formed a dialogue delegation, led brilliantly by Xiong Yan. Anyone who wanted to join the dialogue team had a chance to mount the podium and present his or her speech skills. Yet as the government continued to ignore our demands for dialogue, we held brainstorming sessions to discuss ways to pressure them into meeting our demands.

Marching yet again to Tiananmen Square was out of the question. We'd been there, done that. Someone proposed a hand-holding rally encircling the entire city. Another person proposed a bicycle parade around the city. Yet another student proposed holding an event in a giant wasteland, a sort of Chinese Woodstock.

The idea of a hunger strike had been floating around for some time. It was nothing new. Boycotts and hunger strikes seemed to go hand in hand. I first heard the idea from Zhang Boli, one of a group of talented writers who came to Beida for a one-year residency. Boli raised the subject in a writing class I attended. He was inspired by Gandhi's autobiography, *The Story of My Experiments with Truth*. He told me with great excitement how Gandhi had used hunger strikes to achieve political goals, notably against British colonial rule in India. Boli could quote Gandhi's words: "When I despair, I remember that, all through history, the way of truth and love has always won. There have been tyrants and murderers, and for a time they seem invincible, but in the end, they always fall—think of it, always." These words struck a responsive chord in my heart.

But most of the student leaders at Beida and the Beijing Students' Autonomous Federation argued against a hunger strike. They opposed it because they thought it was too drastic. There wasn't enough of a rationale to justify a hunger strike, they insisted, even as they wavered indecisively and waited for permission to enter into a dialogue with our government leaders.

Days went by. Students at other universities went back to class. More than a week passed, and Beida students began to run out of patience.

Finally, we held a debate at the Triangle to discuss whether or not to stage a hunger strike. Thousands of students showed up.

It seemed like the right time to do it. Mikhail Gorbachev, the Soviet leader and a political reformer, was scheduled to arrive in Beijing on May 15. If we launched a hunger strike to coincide with Gorbachev's visit, we would give the Chinese leaders a reason to engage us in discussion.

16

HUNGER STRIKE

ON MAY 12, WANG DAN came to tell me he had decided to join a hunger strike. Only forty Beida students had signed up by then. He told me with some frustration that because the student organizations had voted against it, he could not join the hunger strike as a student leader. He'd sign on as an individual. Without hesitation, I told Wang Dan I'd be on board too.

The Beijing Students' Autonomous Federation did not support the hunger strike because they didn't want to take responsibility for people's lives. Their leaders stayed behind closed doors, talking and arguing, seemingly out of touch with the sentiment of the students. They said if we'd mellow out, the government wouldn't settle scores too harshly with us later.

At nightfall, I went to the Triangle with Wang Dan. As usual, he was simple, clear, and direct when he spoke. "My name is Wang Dan. I am going to join the hunger strike." With his calm demeanor, his young face shone with inner strength.

Then I went to the podium.

This was the only time I stood on the Triangle and addressed my fellow students. The microphone felt heavy in my hands, but my heart was heavier. I scanned the people in the crowd surrounding me. Their heads were like black ocean waves under the glittering night stars. I saw many young faces in the first rows, unwashed, unshaven, and earnest. They reminded me of myself, five years earlier, when I'd first come to Beida from an army base near a fishing village. I knew where they came from and what they had brought with them. I could feel the crowd's heartbeat and energy. We'd shared the same kind of love, the same kind of dream, and now we shared the same frustration and hope for our country. I knew the truth was on our side. I knew our hearts were filled with love. What more could I ask for at that moment? To speak truth to power, to sacrifice our health to win freedom, to face the unknown with calmness—these were the great notions with which I and my generation had been raised.

As I stood before the crowd, I was overwhelmed with emotion. All at once, the agitation was gone. The rippling ocean waves gave way to a smoother, silky sheen. The crowd became quiet. Even the cries of cicadas behind the tree leaves were subdued. Longing seemed to fill the evening air. They were waiting for me to speak.

"My name is Chai Ling," I said, "and I would like to share with you my reasons for joining the hunger strike. I understand we are all frustrated with where we are with the movement and confused regarding what to do next. We are infighting about whether to continue boycotting our classes and whether to continue waiting for a dialogue to take place before we take further action on a hunger strike. I understand both sides. If we didn't like to go to school, we wouldn't be at Beida; and if we didn't love our country, we wouldn't be worrying about demonstrations, dialogues, and hunger strikes. So we are all great students and great patriots. But what is the truth about our country, and what is the truth about our government and people? Why, when we asked for freedom and democracy, were we called *dong luan*? Why do the police beat us up when we shout slogans like, 'Long Live the People! People's Police Love the People!,' and why are the people always the ones to run?

"Some say if we just wait for the dialogue to take place, we can continue our campus democracy movement; but at the same time, we also learned the government is using its Party system to reinforce the verdict of *dong luan*. And we all know that's a marching order for crackdowns and arrests. As the old saying goes, 'When a bird's nest is smashed, it's hard to expect a whole egg to survive.'

"From the sidelines I have watched carefully how several movements came and disappeared in the past. Each time sacrifices were made, but no progress was achieved and recorded. So each new movement started from square one and met with the same fate. Will this movement in 1989 be different? Will this movement expose the truth and leave a record for history to continue?

"This is why I feel we have only one option left: a hunger strike. Our last freedom is the freedom to starve ourselves. Because the time is short, we should make the goals achievable by narrowing them down to two requests: reverse the verdict of *dong luan* and give us an equal dialogue. If the government won't reverse the *dong luan* verdict, we will at least have communicated the truth about our movement so history will be clear.

"Dear fellow students, when we sacrifice our health, we want to see the true face of our government. When we were growing up, we were raised to say, 'We love our country, we love our people.' Now we want to see if our country loves us and if our people will stand up for us. We want to know if this country is still worth our struggle, our sacrifice, our devotion. I want to use the courage to face death to fight for the right to live life."

Loud applause interrupted my speech many times. As I was speaking, I observed the change of expression on their faces—from agitation to agreement, from agreement to endorsement, and from endorsement to hearty support. I knew my words had reached their hearts and their hearts were connected to mine. In unison, our feelings rose and fell and rose again to new heights.

I ended my talk with certain specifics about the actual planning of the strike, such as what clothes to wear, how to form support teams, what medical assistance we would require, how to organize communications, and what work the period following the hunger strike might entail. As I closed my address, a new surge of confidence and renewed hope erupted with thunderous applause.

After I finished, another student climbed onto the podium and grabbed the microphone. "I will join the hunger strike!" he declared. "I—I—"

He was so overcome with emotion that he began to stutter. The crowd laughed until I returned to the podium by his side and waved at them without saying a word. My eyes spoke for me. They said, *Be kind, be patient.* The crowd calmed down and then began to applaud. The applause gave the young man courage, and he continued his speech.

"I am a Beida sophomore, and I've never cared about politics. My only goal in life is to become a great person, like Chairman Mao. I never joined a movement before this. But today, while I was walking back from the library, I heard the speech. I was truly moved. Now I want to join the hunger strike because I'm a Chinese citizen and I want to do something for our country. I love you, Mom, but I love my country even more."

His brief speech ended to even greater cheers and applause. One by one, students went up to the podium and declared their decision to join the hunger strike.

That night the number of students who enlisted in the hunger strike rose from 40 to 220. Many of them were like the stuttering student— brilliant and hardworking. They did not care about politics in general, but they signed up for the hunger strike to demonstrate the love and passion they felt for their country.

I awakened the next morning to confront the realities of the night before. Until that moment, the implications of the hunger strike had not entirely sunk in. I was asked to write a speech that would speak from the heart to the common man on the street to explain what motivated us to take on this crusade and to leave a record for later generations. As I sat in a quiet place to write my speech, the gravity of facing the unknown began to pull on me—saying farewell to the beautiful things of life and all the people I loved. Grandma, Mom and Dad, and my younger sister and brother all came to mind.

Bai Meng, a poet from the Beida writers' class, found me overcome with emotion and offered to take a look at my draft. An hour later, when he returned the speech to me, something on his face showed how deeply my words had touched his emotions. I hurried back to Dormitory 28, where the broadcast center was stationed.

As I looked out the window from the second floor, the hunger strikers were organizing to march out to the unknown, uniformed with white T-shirts and headbands. Flags were waving, and bicycles were gearing up. I started reading the speech into the microphone. Feng was speaking loudly in the background. Somehow, as I was reading, the crowd became silent. Feng saw the expression on their faces, realized what was going on, and pressed the record button on the tape recorder.

> On this glorious, sunny day in May, we are on our way to a hunger strike. In the most beautiful moment of our young lives, we have no other choice. We must put behind us all the beauty and wonder of life. But how we don't want to; how we are not willing.
>
> However, the country has reached this moment: Inflation is rampant, corruption is raging, the authorities are powerful, the bureaucracy is rotten. Many people with high learning and integrity have drifted overseas. Our social order and security are deteriorating day by day. At this life-and-death moment, fellow countrymen—all fellow countrymen with a conscience—listen to our cry!
>
> The country is our country.
> The people are our people.
> The government is our government.
> If we don't shout, who will?
> If we don't act, who will?
> Our shoulders are still tender. Death still seems too heavy for us. But we go on. We must go on. History has called upon us.
>
> Our passion and loyalty for our country have been labeled dong luan, a "chaotic disturbance" with "hidden motivations manipulated by a small gang."
>
> We ask every honest Chinese citizen—every worker, peasant, soldier, intellectual, government official, policeman, and those who have fabricated our crimes—to place your hand over your heart and ask your conscience: What crimes have we committed? Have

we caused turmoil? We boycott classes. We march and protest. We go on a hunger strike. We give our lives. But our emotions have been repeatedly played. We suffer through hunger to pursue the truth, but in return we get beatings from soldiers and the police. When we kneel down to beg for democracy, we are ignored. When we ask for dialogue on equal terms, we are met with delay after delay. Our student leaders face grave danger.

What are we to do?

Democracy is the noblest human aspiration. Freedom is a sacred human right, granted at birth. Today, both must be bought with our lives. Is this fact something about which the Chinese people can be proud?

This hunger strike has been forced upon us. It is our last resort. We will use the spirit of facing death to fight for the right to live. But we are children, still children! Mother China, look at your sons and daughters. Hunger is destroying our youth. Will you not be moved when you see death approach us?

We don't want to die. We want to live, and live fully, because we are in the prime of our lives. We don't want to die; we want to learn all we can. Our nation is wretchedly poor. We do not have the heart to abandon our motherland through death. That is not what we seek. But if the death of one or a few can make the lives of many better, if these deaths can make our homeland stronger and more prosperous, then we have no right to live on in disgrace.

Fathers and mothers, don't feel sad that we are hungry. Uncles and aunts, don't be heartbroken when we die. We have only one wish, that the lives of everyone will be better. We have only one request, that you not forget that death is absolutely not our desire! Democracy is not a private matter, and the enterprise of democracy will not be accomplished in a single generation.

Good-bye, my fellow students, take care! The departed hold the same loyalty as those who stay alive.

Good-bye, my love, take care! I can't bear to leave you, yet I have to bid farewell.

Good-bye, my parents! Please forgive me; your child could not fulfill her duties to both you and our country.

Good-bye, my people! Please allow us to show our loyalty in such an unnatural manner.

Our pledge, written with our lives, will eventually brighten the skies of the Republic!

This speech became the manifesto of the hunger strike. It was copied onto thousands of cassette tapes and sent to many universities in Beijing and other cities across the country. It inspired thousands of students to join our hunger strike.

If my stomach hadn't hurt so much, I might have enjoyed spending the night on Tiananmen Square. The hunger strike officially began at six o'clock on the evening of May 13. Earlier that day, I'd been so busy with last-minute preparations that I had missed the lunch some teachers had hosted at a restaurant near campus for students who had signed up for the hunger strike. I bade farewell to Feng, who promised to join me later at the Square, though he didn't know when. He was on his way to the Soviet embassy to deliver a petition for Gorbachev, inviting him to visit Peking University. He'd managed to get some three thousand names on the petition.

On the Square, it was well past the dinner hour, and I'd been too busy all day to notice hunger creeping up on me. It hit me once I sat down on the concrete. My stomach felt so empty that the cool evening breeze seemed to go right through me.

Students from several other universities in Beijing had also joined the hunger strike, including students from Beijing Normal University, led by the charming and extremely popular Wu'er Kaixi, who joined forces with Wang Dan to work with the press and deal with the government on issues related to the dialogue we wanted to arrange. I undertook the tasks of helping the hunger strikers settle in and organizing picket lines to protect the strikers. By nightfall, eight hundred hunger strikers and two thousand supporting students were spread out in front of the Monument to the People's Heroes.

The cool evening breeze and the swath of brilliant stars in the heavens above bestowed on the scene a calm and quiet joy. Students clustered in small groups, chatted quietly, or sang, or read, while others told stories. It was like being at summer camp.

The beautiful monument was bathed in the light of the early summer night. It seemed to radiate bluish rays under the starlight. I had never taken a close look at this national monument, which was built to commemorate martyrs who had laid down their lives for the motherland.

I gazed upward at the structure for a long time until it seemed to come to life, swaying slightly in the night breeze. Sealed within, beneath its smooth alabaster surface, the monument enshrined the souls of hundreds upon thousands of heroes who had fought and given their lives for the better place where we now lived. I felt small yet inspired. The monument, in all its potent grandeur, reminded us that tonight a new chapter of history would be written.

Someone nudged me and pointed to the sky. A comet was falling through the heavens into the Forbidden City. Was this a bad omen? Some said it meant the beginning of disaster. Others said it signaled the end of an era. Whatever the fates may have decided, our young lives had arrived at the crossroads of history and the future.

It was past midnight. The temperature had dropped, and hunger and cold kept everyone awake. The strikers had long since walked off that earlier meal. We wore our white T-shirts over our springtime outerwear. On the back of my shirt, I had written from top to bottom on the left side, "A Heart Is Set to Save the Country." On the right side I had written, "Powerless to Turn Back the Ruler," and in the middle, "Grief." Some strikers wore white cloth headbands bearing the legend, "Give Me Liberty or Give Me Death."

From time to time I got up and walked around the picket lines to check on the students. Many were lying on the cold concrete. Some had insulated themselves with newspapers. They used books for pillows and lay closely packed together to stay warm. I felt like a mother passing over her slumbering children, and I bore the weight of obligation to protect them from harm if I could. I thought of Joan of Arc, with her troops on the battlefield, and wondered if she had felt the same burden of responsibility I carried in my heart that night.

"Mom, I Am Hungry," one banner read. These young students had grown up in relatively better times than their parents. They'd never gone hungry the way their elders had. They'd also been spared the worst chaos of the Cultural Revolution, which had broken up so many families and scattered them throughout the countryside. All they'd ever done was study, study, study, and that's how they'd earned admission to fabled Peking University. They were the "good kids," who had never done anything remotely like this: starving, shivering, lying all night in the open. Their parents would never have allowed it.

As I surveyed these brave, innocent child crusaders, my heart went out to them. I was profoundly moved by their willpower and devotion. No one had forced them to come, and no one was forcing them to stay. And yet they stayed for one shared reason: They loved our country.

I kept a vigilant eye on the eastern sky, hoping to see the first rays of dawn. Along with a new day came new hopes. Chief among them was the hope the government would accept our two requests so we could return to school and celebrate with a hearty meal. I expected that we would have to go hungry no longer than forty-eight hours. I believed the government would respond to our hunger strike before May 15, when Mikhail Gorbachev was due to arrive.

The cold and hunger had sapped everyone's energy. I could see the signs of fatigue. I talked to the students through a bullhorn and told them how encouraged I was by their unity and strength of purpose. Today, I told them, we expected to begin a dialogue with the government; and once we had arranged to do that, we'd all leave the Square and welcome the arrival of Gorbachev.

Feng was among the first to show up at the Square in the morning, and the sight of his smile and dark eyes filled me with a warm thrill. He was exhausted too. He'd bought a broad band of black cloth nearly sixty feet long on his way back from the Soviet embassy. Using a teacher's sewing machine at Beida, he'd turned it into a giant banner on which he'd painted two words in bright yellow paint: Hunger Strike. The rectangular black banner measured thirteen by ten feet. It was hoisted high above the crowd, near the monument. From a distance, its blackness added a somber, funereal note, conveying something tragic and heavy, as if it, too, were an omen. Black cloth is used in Chinese funerals to express mourning. There was a run on black cloth in Beijing after the massacre. People bought out the supply and tore the cloth into strips, which they fastened on their shirts as armbands. The sound the huge banner made as it flapped in the wind seemed to echo the words on the cloths of white we all wore around our heads: "Give Me Liberty or Give Me Death."

17

SOLIDARITY

ON THE MORNING of May 13, while we were preparing for our hunger strike, Zhao Ziyang went to see Deng Xiaoping. It was the first time he had visited the paramount leader since returning from North Korea. Deng, meanwhile, had come back from his summer retreat in time for Mikhail Gorbachev's impending state visit. President Yang Shangkun was also present at the meeting.

The three men talked at great length about the situation in Beijing. A hunger strike during the Soviet leader's visit would portend a massive loss of face for Deng, who had orchestrated the Sino-Soviet Summit to demonstrate his power to the world. Imagine the paramount Chinese leader playing host to the architect of *glasnost* at a state dinner while thousands of fasting students lay on the Square outside the banquet hall, demanding democracy.

Glasnost, which called for transparency of government and freedom of speech and information for the Soviet people, was the last thing Deng would permit the Chinese people. Indeed, when Gorbachev had first proposed a Sino-Soviet Summit to reinstate diplomatic relations and trade between the two countries, Deng had brushed him off. He was in no hurry to break the ice between the two countries. He had set the timing and the agenda for this summit, and it could only take place on his terms. Just as Richard Nixon had been the first American leader to visit Communist China, Gorbachev would be the first Soviet leader since the 1960s to come to Beijing.

Zhao Ziyang, not knowing the hunger strike would begin that evening, focused his discussion with Deng on ending corruption. He even offered to allow his own children to be investigated. Yang Shangkun, meanwhile, assured Deng that he could count on the army to line up behind the central government whatever it decided to do.

Though the hunger strike officially began at 6:00 p.m., when Wang Dan made an announcement in the presence of a few journalists, the 8:00 p.m. news broadcasts completely ignored it.

Support in the capital city, however, was unprecedented. The morning after our first cold and hungry night on the Square, when we stood to sing the national anthem as the honor guard in its daily ritual raised the national flag, students all over Beijing once again walked out of classes and streamed into Tiananmen Square, from all directions, to show their support. Teachers, professors, and intellectuals expressed solidarity, and a big poster signed by famous intellectuals, headlined "We Can No Longer Remain Silent" appeared simultaneously at Peking University and a number of colleges. The banner exhorted intellectuals to join a march of solidarity on May 15, the day of Gorbachev's arrival: "We must show the world our conscience, our courage, and our social responsibility! Let us write history!"

Three hundred teachers and professors at Peking University signed a letter addressed to the Central Party Committee, urging the top leaders to take the hunger strike seriously, to treat the striking students with genuine concern, caution, and kindness, and to use every available measure to safeguard their health. On the Square, we cheered—and wept—when a young teacher read this letter out loud.

All through the day, more students arrived on the Square with banners and pennants. Whenever a new contingent arrived, they first circled the Square and then merged with the vast sea of people already there. From their upraised flags, I could see more than forty colleges from Beijing, Tianjin, and Shanghai had come to support us.

I had told my fellow students this new day would bring us hope that our hunger strike would soon be over. Now it was happening before my very eyes as thousands upon thousands of students, teachers, and Beijing residents poured into the Square to support our demand for a dialogue with the government.

At 4:00 p.m. on May 14, I was called to join a student dialogue with the government, led by Yan Mingfu, head of the United Front Department of the Communist Party, whose offices were situated in a small alley across from the Zhongnanhai compound, a half hour by foot from Tiananmen Square. The United Front had been created in 1937 so the Communist Party could form a front line with Chiang Kai-shek's ruling Nationalist party to fight the Japanese. After Mao's victory and ascension in 1949, the department had evolved into a symbolic facade organization that worked with so-called allies of the Communist Party, such as ethnic minorities, Tibetan Buddhists, non-Communist intellectuals, and compatriots from Hong Kong and Taiwan, all of whom survived at the mercy of the Communist Party.

It was puzzling, to say the least, that the government would hold this hard-earned dialogue at the United Front Department. Did the ruling party view us as a potential ally, or was this the most idle government office, an empty shell that had time to linger with students? On the Square, some students were happy to hear we were about to have this dialogue. Others, however, were skeptical. They contended the government could not possibly be taking us seriously if they were assigning such low-ranking representatives to meet with us.

I could not give much thought to all this because I was preoccupied with other matters. The hunger strike had lasted more than twenty-four hours, and our second night was fast approaching. If we couldn't reach a satisfactory agreement during this dialogue session, how would I be able to help the striking students endure another hungry and chilly night on the Square? I gathered some banners, notably the one that read "Mom, I Am Hungry," along with the cassette tapes on which I'd recorded my hunger strike manifesto. We intended to ask the government to broadcast the dialogue live on Central TV so the whole nation could witness it, and I was hoping to play my tape on national TV so people would understand and support our action.

The setting for the dialogue was a conference room on the second floor of the United Front building. When I arrived, people were already seated at a large oval table covered with a white tablecloth. It was formally arranged like a diplomatic negotiation. On one side sat Yan Mingfu, flanked by ten government officers, such as the minister of education. The student dialogue delegation sat on the opposite side of the table. Each member had a topic to discuss, and they all seemed to have rehearsed their lines. This was their first opportunity to put their collegiate debating skills to use.

Two weeks earlier, State Council spokesman Yuan Mu had announced that the government would not, under any circumstances, hold a dialogue with an illegal student organization. So it was a big concession for them to engage in talks with our student dialogue commission.

Yan Mingfu had already warned us the welcome ceremony for Mikhail Gorbachev might not be held at Tiananmen, regardless of whether the hunger strikers evacuated the Square. So we knew we would have to settle for talking to minister-level officials, not to Zhao Ziyang or Li Peng. Yan Mingfu knew the decision had already been made to hold the welcome ceremony at the Beijing airport, but he thought he still had time to persuade the students to end the hunger strike. No one wanted to embarrass our country and disrupt an international event that the top journalists in the world had arrived in Beijing to cover.

The representatives from the hunger strike sat behind the student dialogue representatives, facing the government ministers. Our dirty clothes, drawn faces, and white headbands emblazoned with "Give Me

Liberty or Give Me Death" made a sharp contrast to the neat, well-dressed officials. We were serious, even solemn, and stood with composure, even though we had not eaten for twenty-four hours and had hardly slept. We wanted the nation to see us on TV and realize we were not playing a childish game; we were doing this in the best interest of the country and the people.

The dialogue began as a careful, cordial, sincere, and respectful discussion and then grew heated. At one point, student leader Xiong Yan asked Yan Mingfu, "What do you really think of the student movement?" This was the first time any of us had seen a government official confronted with an unscripted question. All eyes were on Yan Mingfu for his reaction.

Yan appeared taken aback by this blunt question, but he was in no position to speak freely. With evident discomfort, he looked at us and said, "Personally I'd like very much to say you are patriotic, but I can't say that."

"Why not?" Xiong Yan replied with great disappointment. He wasn't prepared to let the issue drop. A positive and affirming statement about the movement and assurances of no later repercussions might go a long way toward convincing students to return to class.

Yan Mingfu again looked pained as he searched for the proper words, and we waited in hope and silence. Just then, the door to the conference room burst open, and a loud shout came from the hallway: "Stop, stop the dialogue!"

With stunned faces, we all turned to look at the door. Outside, a few students shouted, "We cannot hear the direct broadcast as promised. The dialogue must come to an end."

Yan Mingfu seemed just as surprised by the news as we were. "Why was it not directly broadcast?" he asked one of his deputies. "I thought it was."

While the deputy went to the side door to see what was going on, the room lapsed into silence and a precious moment of a deeper connection with Yan Mingfu was gone.

Back on the Square, the hunger strikers had grown impatient and increasingly suspicious about the dialogue. They had not seen any sign of it on TV, as they had been promised, because the broadcast had been delayed for an hour. They felt they had made a sacrifice for this dialogue and were entitled to be kept informed. When no news was immediately forthcoming, they sent students to break in on the session and stop the dialogue. I was surprised that in one short hour the hunger strikers had become so impatient.

The dialogue ended badly soon after, and Yan Mingfu walked slowly out of the conference room. Soon after the Tiananmen crackdown, when the students looked up to him as an endearing father figure, Yan was accused of sympathizing with the students and stripped of his title.

When the dialogue ended with nothing to show for it, I had to hurry back to the Square. Outside the gate of the United Front Department, I met twelve leading scholars who had volunteered to visit the students at Tiananmen. By then, Chang'an Avenue had become a parking lot jammed with people. To move even a foot became almost impossible, and the mile-long journey to the Square was like going to the moon. We hoped somehow these scholars would bring the magic needed to bridge the gap between the government leaders and the students; but by the time we reached the Square and the scholars got a chance to speak, we realized how big the gap had grown. No one had the power to penetrate the bubble surrounding the Central Party Committee or to influence the Party leaders. Just like that, a critical deadline to change the minds of the government leaders and end the hunger strike before Gorbachev's formal visit came and went.

18

THE GREAT WAVE

AFTER THE SCHOLARS failed to persuade the hunger strikers to leave the Square before Gorbachev's arrival, most of us lay down on the concrete and drifted off to sleep. Support teams had brought us blankets and coats donated by people who had rallied to our cause, and students from Beijing Medical University circulated among the sleeping students to keep an eye on us in case we needed medical attention.

At four o'clock in the morning, an urgent voice began screaming over the loudspeaker, jarring the sleeping students out of their slumber. It was Wu'er Kaixi, the student leader from Beijing Normal University. He directed the students to move immediately en masse to the eastern side of the Square to leave the central area clear for the arrival of Gorbachev. He said we had to show the government we were true patriots and that we would not contaminate our national image. We were not withdrawing, he declared. We were just moving a little bit to one side.

There was no unified leadership on the Square at that time, and most students weren't happy to hear this sudden command shouted at them over the loudspeaker without any previous discussions between student representatives. But no one wanted to argue about it at four in the morning on an empty stomach. The students got up, gathered their few belongings, and trudged over to the east side of the Square. My heart sank at the sight. One-third of the hunger strikers were girls, and they looked so small and frail. Like fallen leaves drifting and floating in the darkness, some simply followed along with their eyes closed. Once they reached the new location for the hunger strike, they fell to the ground, and sleep once again consumed them.

During the migration, the student marshals lost their picket lines, and protection for the weak and hungry strikers vanished into quicksand. In our wake, the center of the Square looked awful—newspapers and magazines, empty water bottles and soda cans, food wrappers, hats and scarves, cigarette butts and boxes, and shreds of cloth littered the vast expanse of concrete.

Kaixi's spontaneous action took a serious toll on his reputation and credibility. He was soon voted out of the leadership. Undeterred, he continued to come in and out of the Square and subsequently made his mark at the forefront of the movement.

When dawn finally arrived on May 15, we awoke to the news that the welcoming ceremony for Gorbachev would take place at the airport. This information hit us like a cannon blast, and many students began to weep. The truth was evident for all to see: The government simply did not care about us. To many, the thought that we might actually die on the Square became a possibility for the first time. I was overwhelmed by the sadness I saw on those young faces.

Now what? I asked myself repeatedly. *How many more days will we have to continue our hunger strike?*

We had been fasting for forty hours. The hoped-for deadline to reach agreement came and went. More than three thousand hunger strikers lay on the Square like defeated and wounded soldiers. Most of the supporting students and residents from the day before had departed. Even Feng had returned to Beida. Now that we had moved to the east side of the Square, the morning commuters on Chang'an Avenue could barely see us. We were overwhelmed by the feeling we had been abandoned and left to die.

If I had a moment of despair, it was only fleeting. The words of the

Hunger Strike Manifesto once again rose within me. By then I had committed every word to memory. I knew I had to do something. I felt responsible for these students. The Square was in dire need of a strong leader.

It was at this critical time that Li Lu entered the battlefield and rose up as one of the core leaders at Tiananmen Square. I had first met him two weeks earlier on the Beida campus when he'd come to offer ideas and suggestions. Though he was from Nanjing, he seemed to have important contacts in Beijing. On the day we marched to the Square to launch the hunger strike, Li Lu had found me and offered me a ride on the backseat of his bicycle. He told me how moved he had been by my speech the night before at the Triangle.

Now Li Lu sought me out on the Square. After spending the night collecting salt water for the striking students, he was stunned when he returned to the Square and saw the condition we were in.

"How could this happen?" he shouted. "I was gone for only a few hours." After quickly assessing the situation, he declared that the hunger strike would die on the vine if we did not create a better organization to protect the lives of the students. "If the government is willing to stand by and watch the lives of these students waste away one by one, then we should take more extreme measures. To gain the support of the people, put pressure on the government, and prevent striking students from dying," he said, quite matter-of-factly, "we need leaders who will rise up and be willing to burn themselves alive, like that student in the Prague Spring."

Li Lu talked further about how we should organize the hunger strikers, but when he said "burn himself alive," I couldn't hear anything else. I began to weep uncontrollably. In my heightened emotional state—famished, exhausted, exhilarated—anything could set me off. I immediately thought of my aunt's tragic death by fire and the unending anguish it had caused my father. How would he be able to bear the news that I had set myself on fire? I could not begin to imagine the excruciating pain I would have to endure to burn myself alive, like Joan of Arc at the stake.

"Don't cry," Li Lu said. "This is not the time to cry. What other choice do we have?"

I knew he was right. If by dying I could prevent the death of others, then so be it.

I decided Li Lu should take command of the hunger strike. He possessed the strength, determination, presence of mind, and efficiency we needed just then.

"No, no," he said, when I told him, in no uncertain terms, what he should do. "People don't know me, but they do know you. Your speech inspired us all. You should be the commander."

My parents' lifelong devotion to service reminded me to submit my will to the calling, ready or not. Within half an hour, we had reconnected the broadcasting system, and I spoke to the students on the Square.

"The situation is very bleak," I said. "A prolonged fight lies ahead. In order to save the lives of our hunger strike students, we must organize." I volunteered to be the commander of the Hunger Strike Committee and declared that anyone who served on the Committee with me would have to be prepared to die. "If my death can save the lives of everyone else on the Square," I said, "then I will be the first to walk to death."

Many students began to cry. Many more applauded. "Fight to the end!" someone shouted, and others took up the cry. More than ten students came forward to volunteer as members of the committee.

As Li Lu and I stood together, surrounded by the newly formed Hunger Strike Committee, the hunger strikers, from more than forty colleges, swore a sacred oath. I was calm, and my voice was clear and strong. My spirits were lifted, and my determination returned. I read the oath slowly and distinctly over the loudspeaker as one thousand voices joined my recitation.

I solemnly swear that in order to promote democracy in the motherland and to bring prosperity to the country, I will go on a hunger strike. I resolve to obey the rules of the hunger strike committee, and will not break my fast until we have achieved our goals.

Through tears and cheers, we set to work. There was much to be done. We had to reestablish a line of protection for the strikers. No one could enter the protected area without a student identification card. We formed a pathway from the center to the edge of the Square so strikers who fainted could be carried out to waiting ambulances. By then, more than eighty students had already fainted.

Li Lu, as my deputy commander, invited two representatives from each college to attend a preliminary meeting. He was sharp, collected, decisive, and totally in charge. He earned immediate respect by leading a productive and efficient meeting while still giving everyone an opportunity to speak. At the end of the meeting, he delivered a quick, precise recap of what everyone had said and assigned each individual a clear task. I could see the students were happy and had found renewed meaning in the hunger strike.

On the third day of our protest, people from all walks of life stood up for us. When a few intellectuals called for a march that day in our support, 30,000 scholars from 230 educational and research institutions in Beijing responded. Students in fourteen provinces protested simultaneously on our behalf. While Gorbachev's motorcade was stuck in a Beijing traffic jam, trying to duck through the backstreets and alleyways, demonstrators marched on Chang'an Avenue, holding aloft banners of greeting for the Soviet leader—"Welcome Gorbachev, the True Reformer"—and reproof for our Chinese leaders: "Where is China's Gorbachev?"

On May 16, more than sixty-five hours into the hunger strike, the Square was alive with the piercing sounds of ambulance sirens, like a knife cutting to the hearts of millions of people. Two hundred students had fainted. But whenever one person went down, ten more stepped up. The number of hunger strikers soon increased to 3,100. More people arrived on the Square to support the hunger strike out of anger at the government's silence. Throughout the day, demonstrators marched along Chang'an Avenue: workers, farmers, government employees, middle school students—even military cadets, police cadets, secret Christians, and Buddhist monks in their bright orange robes.

In the ensuing two or three days, the number of demonstrators in Beijing swelled into the millions. In the words of Chairman Mao, "Where there is oppression there is opposition."

Medical students and hospital workers from Beijing helped establish and maintain our "lifeline," the pathway that ran from the center of the Square out to the edge and was essential for saving students' lives. Student guards on either side maintained a passage just wide enough to allow an ambulance through. These students stood with their arms locked to form a human chain. Day or night, under the scorching sun or in the chill night air, these human chains never broke down. The student marshals who formed picket lines around the hunger strikers also stood shoulder to shoulder without budging. No one without a student ID ever crashed their line of defense. The unity and determination of the supporting students was the source of my strength.

Despite our good intentions, it seemed Deng Xiaoping's worst nightmare had come to pass. As he met with Gorbachev inside the Great Hall of the People, the great people of China gathered outside, fasting and protesting. The guest of honor, the real socialist reformer in the eyes of the Chinese people, had to enter the Great Hall through a back door that opened onto a side street because the main entrance facing the Square was blocked by a bubbling pool of red-hot human lava.

When Yan Mingfu came out to the Square for a desperate final plea to the hunger strikers, he had to be escorted by Wang Dan and Wu'er Kaixi, who held him by his arms on either side as they pushed and squeezed their way through the crowd to our broadcast center at the Hunger Strike Committee headquarters. Yan was visibly overwhelmed by the masses of people he saw everywhere he looked. After giving an impassioned speech, imploring us to end the hunger strike and return to our classes, he offered to give himself up as a hostage to prove the good intentions of the Party leadership.

While Yan Mingfu was making his last attempt to end the hunger strike, Zhao Ziyang met his Waterloo. During a televised discussion with Mikhail Gorbachev, Zhao revealed to the world that Deng Xiaoping was truly the one in charge of China—which was the truth and a seemingly innocuous statement. But somehow it was interpreted, both by Deng's side and the intellectuals' side, as a signal to wage war against Deng. That night, before Zhao realized what was happening, Deng called an urgent meeting with Yang Shangkun. By the morning of May 17, when Zhao went to Deng's home to present a plan to end the student hunger strikes, Deng, Yang, Li Peng, and other leaders were ready for him. They announced a swift decision to impose martial law—which Zhao voted against. Zhao then cited health issues to avoid executing the decision. He was later charged with the crime of splitting the Party and placed under house arrest, where he remained for the last sixteen years of his life.

Though I was unaware at the time of the conflict among the top leaders of China, the competition for leadership on the Square had made an impression on me. By the fourth day of the hunger strike, many organizations had raised their banners and established headquarters on the Square. The Beijing Students' Autonomous Federation, which had originally voted against the hunger strike, now set up shop right next to us on the Square. The hunger strike students held an election, and I was elected commander in chief, with Li Lu and two other students as my deputy commanders.

Some volunteers who were not elected were unhappy about this turn of events. One student, Wang Wen, complained he should have been elected because he was one of the original hunger strikers. I assured him he'd be elected in the next round of voting, but I had no way of knowing his unhappiness would turn into a fierce resentment leading to revenge.

Finally, after seventy-two hours of no food, little sleep, and minute-by-minute tension, my body gave out. I was carried out along the lifeline and sent to the hospital. When I came to, I was in a hospital ward with an intravenous drip attached to my arm. There I spent the night, although I'd left my heart on the Square. Throughout the night, my mind crisscrossed the blurry line between dream and reality. When morning came, I ran out of the ward. A bus carried me and many other students from the hospital back to the Square.

After Yan Mingfu's visit to the Square, the hunger strike representatives held a vote: to leave or stay. The majority voted to stay. In the evening, a doctor from Beida came to the Square and coached the hunger strikers to drink fluids, including water, sugar water, soda, or even milk. He said Gandhi drank milk to sustain himself through long stretches of fasting. Many of the striking students brazenly rejected his advice and announced the start of a water strike. A school bus from Beida ran nonstop between the campus and the Square, bringing all kinds of supplies, including the only telephone on the Square and a TV set, which we set up in the communication center.

Just when we thought we'd done everything necessary to prepare for another night, a new challenge presented itself. The weather forecasters announced that a severe thunderstorm was headed our way and would hit Beijing the next day. How would we survive a downpour under these conditions? The garbage was piling up, and most student strikers were too weak to move.

After we had gotten just a few hours sleep at night, we were awakened by an urgent report of some strange activities on the Square. Someone said that government agents in white doctor's coats were taking students into buses. Fearing it might be part of a government plan to clear the Square, we had to awaken all the students and tell them to be alert. By the time we were able to clarify the confusion, morning had arrived and my body gave out again.

This time I was taken to a hospital and given a dose of drugs that prevented me from returning right away to the Square. Later, one of the leaders of the Beijing Students' Autonomous Federation told me she had suggested to the government that they put me under control so she could try to get the students out of the Square. I was frightened by her confession. What if the dose had not been a sedative but something stronger? We often heard stories of people who had vanished.

When I finally returned to the Square, I was astonished to see row after row of big buses parked on the north side of the Square, adjacent to Chang'an Avenue. Members of the Hunger Strike Committee had worked through the night to secure seventy buses from the city transportation company to provide temporary shelter for striking students when the thunderstorm arrived.

By the afternoon, when the first streaks of lightning sliced open the gray skies, all the hunger strikers had moved into the buses. Soon the Square, which only moments earlier had pulsated and throbbed with the energy of thousands, resembled an enormous pond of splashing water. Each raindrop hurled down from the sky sent out a ripple when it landed, and the ripples merged into a wave. I thought, *Just look at the wave we've created.*

19

MARTIAL LAW

LI PENG FINALLY agreed to meet with student leaders, but no one from the Hunger Strike Committee attended the meeting. When we heard that a dialogue had been arranged between student leaders and possibly high-ranking government officials, we were busy herding students onto the buses before the thunderstorm. We were more concerned with their safety and no longer put much stock in high-level discussions with the government. When the meeting ended, Wang Dan raced back to the Square with news.

"It's bad," he said. "Li Peng is hostile."

On May 19, day seven of the hunger strike, we learned the army would soon enter Beijing. Around four o'clock in the morning, news came that Zhao Ziyang and Li Peng had come to the Square. We dashed over to see them, but by the time we got to the scene, both men had departed. Those who had heard them said that Zhao Ziyang had been kind and sincere, but Li Peng was cold and phony.

We decided to call an end to the hunger strike. We held a meeting and swiftly concluded we did not want to give the government an excuse to bring in the troops and impose martial law. By day seven, the hunger strike had grown to four thousand people, but many were extremely weak, and some had to be moved on stretchers. We could not allow the army to march in and trample on our faithful comrades. I announced the decision over the loudspeaker and asked the students to start eating again. I urged Beijing residents to bring us food. I then went straight to Tiananmen Gate, where journalists were waiting for me to make an appearance. I declared we had won a moral victory and had earned the support of the Chinese people nationwide. Just then, the sun cast a wide shaft of golden light over Chang'an Avenue, and I felt as if a mountain had been lifted from my shoulders.

Not everyone agreed with the decision to end the hunger strike. An angry group surrounded our new headquarters aboard one of the buses, yelling that we had betrayed the hunger strike. They pushed the bus back and forth until it started to rock. Someone threw a stone that shattered a window. Out of nowhere, Feng and Wang Wen appeared and accused us of selling out the movement. They said the decision was undemocratic. Feng demanded another vote and grabbed a microphone to address the hunger strikers.

I thought he'd lost his mind. I seriously wondered if the Square had taken its toll on his judgment. As I struggled to wrest the microphone from his grip, the angry people outside continued to rock the bus. It was like battling aboard a storm-tossed boat at sea.

Li Lu, who had been at the forefront of ending the hunger strike, now just sat and watched, though he must have been dumbstruck by Feng's madness. Zhang Boli, who had been trying to calm Feng during the fracas, finally proposed a motion to remove Feng as deputy commander.

"I resign!" Feng screamed as he threw the microphone onto the floor and stormed off the bus. I was shocked and disheartened.

One hour after Chinese Central Television announced the end of the hunger strike, the Party Central and State Council held a meeting of high-ranking Party officials, the government, and the military to prepare for martial law. Zhao Ziyang had decided he would not be the one to carry out Deng Xiaoping's order to use troops against the students and took a three-day sick leave. Li Peng, however, was more than ready. He wrote the speech ushering in martial law, which was formally declared at 11:00 p.m.

In support of the declaration, Chen Xitong, the mayor of Beijing, signed an order banning demonstrations, student strikes, work stoppages, and all other activities that would impede public order.

When the decision was announced, the city of Beijing exploded. Three hundred thousand people were on Tiananmen Square that night. While the government's loudspeakers continuously broadcast speeches by Li Peng, we called on people to resist the troops in nonviolent, peaceful ways. We immediately organized able-bodied students to go to the outskirts of Beijing to block the army's advance. We also sent students to mobilize the citizens of Beijing for the resistance. All night long, the Square boiled with anger and disbelief. A sense of impending doom prevailed.

One question circled my mind a thousand times: *Why is the government so coldhearted, so blind to the good intentions of the students?* We had reduced our demands to only two particulars: direct dialogue and a reversal of the *dong luan* verdict. Our student movement was by far the most peaceful and organized protest the city had ever known. Four thousand people had joined the hunger strike, and by the time of the martial law declaration, fifty-eight thousand students from outside Beijing had come to the Square to join the movement.

People on the Square waited all night for the troops to arrive. At daybreak, we learned that residents on the outskirts of the city had stopped the troops. With joy and relief, I went out on a truck to check the major streets in the surrounding city. I saw roadblocks at almost every intersection on Chang'an Avenue, and Beijing residents filled the streets.

"Go back to the borders to protect our country from foreign invasion!" someone shouted. "You are the people's army. We don't need you in Beijing."

Back at the Square, I heard an unfamiliar sound overhead. Looking to the sky, I saw military helicopters hovering overhead. People began to curse and move around, waving their arms and covering their heads.

We thought because the troops on the ground had been stalled, they would drop down on us from above. The helicopters discharged a storm of paper. Leaflets, on which were printed the martial law declarations, drifted downward and soon formed a new layer of refuse on the floor of the Square.

At noon, some sympathetic former military officers visited our command post to advise us on how to organize a resistance to block the army's advance and cut off their supplies. They suggested we fly kites over the Square to stop the helicopters.

When the government declared martial law, the entire landscape of the protest shifted. Before, the slogans generated by students addressed government corruption and called for freedom and democracy. Now the protest became a people's movement directed against the regime. Throughout the day, angry protestors denounced the leadership. "Down with the puppet Li Peng!" they shouted. "Down with dictatorship! Deng Xiaoping step down! Down with Deng Xiaoping! Deng Xiaoping is like the moon: He changes every fourteen days."

Feng returned to the Square. He'd managed to recover his sanity after storming off the bus the night before. He told me he'd seen people lining up in front of banks and stores, buying up supplies as if preparing for a siege. The subway trains had stopped running, and the city had cut off the water supply to the public bathrooms near the Square, which had been our only resource during the strike.

The Beijing Students' Autonomous Federation assumed leadership on the Square, and they announced a sit-in to protest martial law. Hundreds of thousands of people had already gathered, and more were arriving all the time from other cities. As the daytime clamor gradually died down with the coming of night, we were convinced the arrival of troops was imminent. But the first night of martial law passed without incident.

The Square was a vast rumor mill. When word reached us that the government had sent trained killers to the Square to assassinate the student leaders, some students skilled in the martial arts immediately assigned themselves as bodyguards for Feng, Li Lu, Zhang Boli, me, and the other leaders of the hunger strike, though now that the hunger strike had officially ended, we were all "off duty." Discussions swiftly followed on the matter of how we should carry on the fight by living, not dying—how we should save "the revolutionary seeds" and spread the democracy movement to all four corners of the country. We still had a small fund of donations, enough to provide committee members with "escape money" in the amount of 1,000 RMB each. Safe houses were in the process of being arranged, and the committee decided Feng and I should go our separate ways to avoid being recognized. My heart was ripped by sadness. This was May 22, our first wedding anniversary.

Somehow my sentiments on this occasion inspired Li Lu to announce that, regrettably, he had never experienced marriage and sex. His girlfriend had just arrived from Nanjing and found him on the Square. "Why not get married now, right here?" I said. Everyone thought that was a grand idea. We were all familiar with the movie *Marriage on the Execution Ground*, which tells the story of two young Communists captured after an uprising against the Nationalist forces of Chiang Kai-shek in the city of Guangzhou. The couple decides to get married before they are executed, and they die in a hail of bullets while singing "The Internationale."

Tension and fear gave way to cheers and laughter on the Square. We all needed something like this. Thousands sang the "Bridal Chorus," and Li Lu invited Feng and me to be best man and maid of honor. Zhang Boli managed to produce a marriage certificate embossed with the seal of the Hunger Strike Committee. Followed by a fanfare, we walked around the Square and up the steps to the People's Monument. As flashbulbs went off all around us, Zhang Boli pronounced the couple husband and wife. As a beautiful sunset cast its glow on the scene, Li Lu gave a rousing speech. "We have to fight—but we must marry, too," he declared in his strong voice.

The crowd responded with a thundering cheer. We could not provide the couple with a wedding cake, but someone produced a big watermelon. It was a sweet, fond, parting memory before we said farewell to one another and prepared to go underground.

I left the Square that night for a safe house. A Beijing family let me sleep in a little bedroom in their apartment. For the first time in many days, I took a shower and slept in a comfortable bed. Alone in the quiet, moonlit night, I wondered about Feng. Where was he? Now, more than ever, exactly one year to the day we had married, I yearned for him and our life together. I drifted to sleep, alone in my safe-house bed, with memories of our wedding day swirling in my mind.

When I awoke the next day to news that nothing had happened on the Square during the night, it didn't take me long to decide to return. What use could there possibly be in hiding? A life on the run was not the life for me. I took two hundred renminbi out of my "escape money" allotment and gave it to the family who had protected me. They brought me several new outfits and a backpack so I could shed my dirty clothes.

Li Lu had remained on the Square overnight, and that's where I found him upon my return. He gave me a quick update about the chaotic situation. Several organizations were present on the Square, he said, but none seemed equipped to assume a leadership role. One group had changed presidents 182 times in just a few days. Anyone could organize a meeting, gather a group, and direct the people toward one purpose or another. Little groups took over areas of the Square and posted their own guards to protect their turf. This went on, back and forth, throughout the evening, Li Lu told me.

Sanitation conditions had become worse, and the risk of an outbreak of illness had increased. Many students were irritable, irrational, and easily angered—on the verge of emotional breakdown. Rumors of an imminent crackdown circulated constantly.

In the middle of the night, Wu'er Kaixi had again tried to move people off the Square, but before anyone could act on his hoarse exhortations, another voice had announced that Kaixi only represented himself, not any leadership group. This caused great confusion on the Square in the early hours of the morning.

The Hunger Strike Committee called for a meeting with representatives from many different groups. Li Lu wanted the Beijing Students' Autonomous Federation to turn the Square back over to the Hunger

Strike Committee for twenty-four hours so we could restore order, but the BSAF vehemently opposed this proposal.

That's when I stood up to speak. I said that little had been accomplished under BSAF leadership. They had voted against the hunger strike, but then assumed leadership after it was a great success. Since the strike had ended, they had failed to maintain order on the Square. Meanwhile, the hunger strike leaders had remained strong and united. We had kept the Square in order even when our leaders were suffering from hunger and exhaustion. I promised we would return leadership to the BSAF once order was reestablished on the Square.

This was a moment when fatal disaster could have struck from two directions: the martial law troops or the chaos that ruled the Square. The sheer size of the protests, the anger, the pent-up anguish, the long-suppressed revolutionary fever—not to mention the undercover government agents who mingled among the people stirring rumors and panic—could have set a match to the fuse that was just begging to be lit.

During the afternoon, three men threw eggs dipped in black ink at the giant portrait of Chairman Mao above Tiananmen Gate. This unimaginable act of sacrilege sent shock waves through the Square. This was an act the government could have used to accuse the movement of anti-Communist, counterrevolutionary turmoil. The three men were immediately apprehended, and to my regret, a zealous student leader handed them over to the police. The men each spent more than a decade in prison and suffered inhuman torture.

Just as the egg-throwing incident began to die down, a sudden high wind blew into Beijing from the Gobi Desert, sweeping with it clouds of sand that turned the sky a hazy yellow. But before the dust could settle, windblown rain and hail began to pelt us, scattering people in all directions. The storm brought a ghostly feeling to the Square. Before darkness fell, Mao's portrait had been cleaned and restored to its eminence above Tiananmen Gate.

The movement at this point desperately needed strong leadership. Amid the developing crisis, a new organization, the Capital Joint Conference, made its appearance. It was led by well-known figures from the 1976 April Fifth Incident at Tiananmen Square and various prominent scholars and intellectuals, who proposed a way to strengthen leadership on the Square. In the spirit of this proposal, a new leadership group called Defend Tiananmen Square Headquarters was formed, and they endorsed me as commander in chief for the Square. Zhang Boli and Feng—both of whom had returned from their safe houses—became key members of the new headquarters on the Square, along with Li Lu.

At 10:00 a.m. on May 24, with at least one hundred thousand people gathered in the Square, Wang Dan announced the formation of the Defend Tiananmen Square Headquarters. I led the assembled crowd in the annunciation of the following oath: "I swear I will protect the republic and Tiananmen Square with my young life. Heads can roll, blood can flow, but the people's Square can never be lost! We are willing to fight to the last person."

In the span of one month, I had gone from graduate student to student leader; from student leader to "mayor" of a small city, worrying about how to supply food, shelter, water, sanitation, and medical care to a growing population on the Square; from mayor to semi-military general, preparing to defend against martial law; and from general to spiritual leader—trying to overcome my own sadness and despair while continuing to cheer up thousands of young people and encouraging them to face the unknown with peace, strength, and purpose. I felt a greater, mysterious force was leading me and the entire movement into the realm of the unknown. All I could do was follow my instincts, keep pushing forward, and adapt to whatever circumstances lay ahead.

20

DEFENDING
TIANANMEN SQUARE

ALONG WITH MY new role as commander of the Defend Tiananmen Square Headquarters came the responsibility of caring for the lives of the people on the Square. Though I hadn't been trained or prepared for this task, I had a sense of what needed to be done from a big-picture perspective. First and foremost, we had to set up a broadcasting system so we could quickly establish authority and issue instructions. Second, we had to direct the student marshals to build a defense line to control the flow of traffic around the Square. Third, we had to establish a secure, central location for our headquarters so people would know where to find us and we would be able to protect the leaders dependably. We also needed a system to manage the donations of money and goods and provide food and water to the people on the Square. Finally, we must open a channel of communication to reach the news media and other organizations inside Beijing and beyond. To make a prolonged movement sustainable, I felt we needed to set up tents on the Square as shelters. I remembered how quickly the army had set up tents on our military base in the aftermath of the Tangshan earthquake when I was ten years old.

One week into martial law, the troops had been kept at bay and the subways were running again. Tiananmen Square truly belonged to the people. It was free and open to all kinds of activity, from political debate to rock concerts. The initial tension and fear provoked by the threat of martial law had vanished for the time being. After Li Peng issued a directive to the Railway Ministry to stop students from flooding into Beijing, many trains into Beijing from other major Chinese cities had been canceled. Even so, more and more students managed to find their way into the capital. As the intensity of the movement died down a bit and local Beijing students began to drift away out of disillusionment or fatigue, these provincial students formed the main student presence on the Square. Many were in Beijing for the first time. I heard reports that during the day, some of these students walked the Great Wall, toured the Forbidden City, circled the Temple of Heaven, and then returned to the Square at night to eat free food and sleep.

Our new leadership committee called a meeting of roughly 400 student representatives from 319 schools nationwide to decide how to proceed. Li Lu conducted the meeting, as he usually did. Out of the innumerable ideas suggested, we selected four options and put these up for a vote. Of the 288 valid votes, 162 were cast in favor of staying on the Square and launching frontal attacks to pressure the government. Specifically, the majority wanted to surround the central government compound in Zhongnanhai, seize key government organs, such as the Central Television station, and launch another hunger strike and a worker's union strike. Of the minority, eighty voted to stay on the Square but pursue discussions and withdraw once certain progress had been made—such as the lifting of martial law; thirty-eight voted to preserve the purity of the student movement by not engaging in any power struggles with the government; and eight people voted to leave.[1]

The Beijing Students' Autonomous Federation was reorganized, with Yang Tao as its new president. Yang was a close friend of Wang Dan's. He'd been actively involved in the democracy salon in the early days of the movement at Beida. We were all happy to see him at the Square. He had some new thoughts about how to deal with martial law. In order to hear his ideas in a relatively quiet setting, Feng, Boli, and I got into a taxi with Yang and Shen Zeyi, an older Beida graduate, and held a meeting while the cab slowly drove around the Square and the Forbidden City. Yang revealed his plan to us, which he called "empty campuses." He thought students should vacate their college campuses and the Square and retreat to their home cities and towns. This strategy, Yang asserted, would rob the government of any excuse it might have to send in the troops. More important, Yang said, students would spread word of democracy to the far corners of the country. Every city square would become a mini Tiananmen Square.

Yang Tao was only twenty years old, but he carried himself with poise and deliberation. By now the mass movement was running out of emotion, and his idea was very intriguing. If we sent students back to their home provinces equipped with a mission, they just might push the democracy movement into a new dimension. I felt the stress and fatigue begin to lift from my shoulders as I envisioned democracy spreading to all corners of China.

The warm afternoon sun reminded me of our campus and how beautiful it was around the lake in springtime. "It would be so nice to go back to school," I said. All of us in the taxi were simultaneously struck by nostalgia. Our driver stepped on the gas, and soon we were flying west through the city.

Beida—the birthplace of modern-day student movements; the place that nurtured our youth, cultivated our love, and enriched our minds. Its beauty and serenity were pervasive.

As we drove through campus, Shen Zeyi, who had been prosecuted for challenging Mao and had spent many years in prison, spoke passionately against the "empty campuses" idea. He said it could be a trap that played right into the hands of the government. "When all of us go back to the countryside," he said, "the government will mobilize the local police and military, and the local Party machine, to catch us one by one. Then the entire movement will be crushed, disappear, and vanish in silence. The Square is our battleground. We cannot give it up by leaving it."

His words brought an air of heaviness into our moment of joy and relief. Even Yang Tao, who only a minute ago had been excitedly championing the idea, was brought to silence.

The driver seemed to know how we were all feeling. He steered the car toward No Name Lake, driving slowly to let us enjoy the setting sun over the water. No one spoke. We knew it would be a long time before we would all come back to this spot together, if ever. This vision of the landscape formed an image in my mind that I would carry forward into the future. It was the last time I ever saw Beida in such a beautiful light. Our lives would soon be radically changed.

Back on the Square, Yang Tao's proposal went nowhere. Li Lu was the first one to shoot it down. He argued persuasively that if we left the Square without achieving our initial goals, we'd lose the support we had accumulated. He seemed unhappy with me for even considering the "empty campuses" idea.

A day later, Yang Tao, like many of his predecessors, resigned from the Beijing Students' Autonomous Federation. The pressure of leadership on the Square demanded a high level of physical perseverance and sheer willpower.

Among our pressing concerns, the most immediate and urgent problem involved food and shelter. Fifty thousand students were living on the Square, and our headquarters provided bread and water from a fund of donations at a cost of 40,000 RMB per day. This meant each student could count on only one piece of bread per day. And though the good people of Beijing donated whatever else they could, the influx of donated food had begun to dwindle. Many students held out boxes inscribed with the word *donation*, but they managed to collect little, if any, food this way. As for shelter, most of it consisted of flimsy lean-tos made out of plastic. Two days earlier, a professor from Hong Kong University had responded to my suggestion and volunteered to acquire tents for the Square.

The next morning, May 27, I came to our Headquarters tent, where the broadcasting center was. I remember sitting along the outer edge, where part of the fabric had been lifted up to let in some fresh air and light. There was a bit of tension between Li Lu and me, which might have been due to the fact that I had agreed with Yang Tao's idea the night before. We were sitting two or three people away from each other, and there was an awkward silence.

Then a student sitting across from us asked a question.

"So what are we hoping for? What can we achieve?"

I had been thinking about that myself.

Li Lu responded calmly and quietly, "What we are actually expecting is a crackdown." (In that context, I assumed he meant *in public*.) "When the government runs out of tricks, like a dog trying to jump over a wall, and has to face the people with a butcher's knife—when the Square is awash with blood—only then will the people of China be awakened and united to overcome this government."

I saw the student's face light up at this shocking and powerful insight. Now I understood Li Lu's reason for rejecting the "empty campuses" idea. Both he and Ren Wanding shared a strong conviction that if the government were able to move the students away from the spotlight, the same kind of crackdown would take place in the darkness, out of the public eye, and the truth would be covered up. That would be a tragedy, because all the sacrifices the students and citizens had made to this point would be lost. That morning was the first time I realized what some of the scholars had been saying about the April Fifth movement, in 1976, when the government had sent plainclothes police into the Square at night to beat and arrest people who had gathered in memory of Zhou Enlai.

Phrases such as "dogs jumping over a wall," "butcher's knife," and "awash with blood" may sound horrible to an English-speaking audience (I felt the same way as a Chinese speaker when I heard the English phrase "drop-dead gorgeous"), but these were common phrases when we were growing up in the Communist Chinese culture. Still, I was shocked by what I had just heard. For the first time, I began to realize that our hope for a dialogue with the government and a reversal of the *dong luan* verdict was gone and we were now facing an inevitable crackdown. Even so, I did not think Li Lu was talking about a massacre.

Before I could process it any further or ask any questions or discuss it, a man poked his head into the tent and changed the subject. It was one of the tall representatives from the intellectuals.

"Here you are, Chai Ling, Li Lu. I've been looking for you guys all morning. We need you to come. The meeting is starting now. Come quickly."

Before I could respond, Li Lu waved his hand at me and said, "I'm not going. It's a waste of my time. But you go, Chai Ling. You should ask them for some money for the Square."

The last time Li Lu had gone to a meeting of the Capital Joint Conference, others there had offended him by questioning his identity. Li Lu was constantly singled out by various people in the movement as someone with a questionable background. After defending him repeatedly, this time I was too tired and didn't say anything.

I would not have gone to the meeting if Li had not suggested it might be a way to obtain some badly needed funding. Feng, who was in charge of finances for the Defend Tiananmen Square Headquarters, went with me.

The meeting became a marathon, with representatives from many organizations present. I reported on the situation in the Square, including the power struggles and daily coup attempts by out-of-town student groups. The "empty campuses" idea was officially vetoed, but Wu'er Kaixi proposed to go to the provinces to mobilize more students to come to Beijing. After long hours of debate, everyone present agreed Tiananmen Square had become the banner of the democracy movement, and we could not allow that banner to fall. We concurred that the student movement should remain on the Square until the National People's Congress convened on June 20, on the assumption that Li Peng's government would be overruled and martial law lifted.

When it was Feng's turn to speak, he announced we were running a deficit. Without more funding, he said, we would not be able to sustain ourselves for even one more day. This took everyone by surprise, including me. Feng had not said anything to me about a shortfall, and it was only now that I realized how serious a problem we had. Chinese Central Television had forwarded 20,000 RMB in donations from all over the country, Feng said, but it was far from enough. The Beijing Red Cross had received 40,000 RMB donated specifically for the students, but they had never forwarded the money. The Beijing Students' Autonomous Federation had raised nearly one million RMB during the week of the hunger strike, but they had taken the money with them when the Hunger Strike Committee reassumed leadership on the Square, leaving behind a bag of loose change amounting to less than 10,000 RMB. When Feng explained to those who were not on the front lines in the Square that it cost 40,000 RMB per day to provide each student with a single piece of bread, they were shocked. All eyes turned to the representatives from the Beijing Students' Autonomous Federation, who explained they had put half their money aside for the next movement—which was a clear indication they had no faith in the present movement. However, the spokesman agreed to provide 100,000 RMB for the Square, which meant the students could survive on their single piece of bread for another two days. Everyone present then agreed we would withdraw from Tiananmen Square on May 30—in three days.

During lunch, the focus of the meeting shifted. Liu Xiaobo, a professor from Beijing Normal University, proposed that Wu'er Kaixi be appointed as spokesman for the movement. Feng and I were both shocked by this idea, given the individualistic leadership style Kaixi had demonstrated.

When I asked Wang Dan, whom I tended to trust, what was going on, he said, "Look, all these people have their own interests and agendas. They're not like the students at the Square, whose motives are pure."

I was taken aback by his response. "What would you do if you were me?"

"If I were you, I would either leverage what they are interested in achieving in order to accomplish my own goals, or I would withdraw from the alliance."

"Why are you still here?" I asked. "What's your interest?"

Wang Dan looked me in the eye and said, "I may be interested in a little bit of fame."

I was moved by his honesty and felt I could continue to trust him. Still, Feng and I decided to resign from the Capital Joint Conference on behalf of the Defend Tiananmen Square Headquarters.

When we returned to our headquarters, Feng went off to get ready for a press conference. Li Lu was inside the Headquarters tent, and he seemed to be in good mood.

"So what did you guys decide after such a long day?" Li Lu asked with a smile. "Did you get some money to feed the people?" He seemed ready to be amused by whatever news I had brought back from the meeting.

I told him we had managed to scrape together a few renminbi. Before I reported the shocking proposal to make Wu'er Kaixi spokesperson for the movement, I mentioned that at the meeting we had agreed to withdraw from the Square on May 30.

Li Lu exploded.

"What a stupid idiot you are!" he screamed. "Don't you have a political brain at all? What an idiot! To *withdraw*? Don't you realize this is exactly what the government wants but couldn't purchase for millions of renminbi? Don't you know the government has been buying off people on the Square with promises of riches and power if they can help bring the students out of the Square? And you guys just handed it to them on a platter. Who were these people at the meeting to make a decision like that? Do you know their background and their motives and their connections? Who are these people?"

As Li Lu stormed back and forth inside the large tent, my bodyguard, Ma Bin, looked at me as if I had just done something to bring down the entire movement. I was so embarrassed. Of course, I had no way to verify that the government was trying to bribe student leaders and scholars to get the students out of the Square. I trusted Li Lu so much I did not even question the validity of his statement. At the meeting, the decision to withdraw had centered on the funding issue and had not seemed so momentous. Now I felt horrible that I might have missed something profoundly important.

Li Lu continued to walk back and forth inside the tent. This was the first time I had seen him really lose his temper and self-control. The pacing seemed to help him get hold of himself, and he started sounding rational again, though he was still clearly upset.

"Where were they all those days and nights when we were busting our tails to get the Square in order? Where were they hiding when the Square was about to be cleared out? Don't you know that the decision to stay or leave should be made by the representatives at the Square? We can find a way to get money. I knew nothing good would come from that meeting."

He stormed off, leaving me on the verge of tears. Never in my life had anyone spoken to me like that.

From day one, I had trusted Li Lu. I had defended him and fought long and hard for his right to be one of our leaders, even as others attacked him viciously and accused him of being a government spy because he didn't have a student ID. So many times, when people questioned who he was, I had defended him unconditionally. Now he was questioning other people's motives and identities. I had supported him and stood with him through the most difficult times because I believed in him and in the fundamental fairness and rights of all participants, not just the Beijing students. But if all this time he had thought of me as an idiot—someone to be manipulated, someone easy to control—then I couldn't possibly continue to work with him. I was hurt and humiliated by his insults. After how calm he had been through much of the chaos, Li Lu's crazy rant now shook my trust and sense of judgment to the core. Worse yet, I found myself thinking he might be right and I was wrong. If the government truly wanted us to leave the Square, had I been deceived into agreeing to the May 30 withdrawal on behalf of the students? Li Lu's point was valid that only the students at the Square should have the right to vote about whether to stay or leave.

The organizers of the Capital Joint Conference had scheduled a press conference for half an hour from now to announce the results of the meeting—including the decision to withdraw. But if that was the wrong thing to do, what should we do now? I was torn and tormented, but there was hardly any time to think it through.

Just as I was about to step out of the tent, the communication liaison from the conference crashed in and started shouting at me, "Chai Ling, how could you do that? Li Lu told us you changed your mind about announcing the withdrawal decision now. Our press announcement was already written and printed out. How dare you change your mind and play us like that!"

After Li Lu's outburst, I did not have enough energy to calm down another angry man. So I said, "You should go ask Li Lu to explain it to you." He looked at me with daggers in his eyes and left. Only later did I learn that he and another man from the conference were threatening to drag me out and beat me up for what they'd heard I had done.

I was still trying to collect myself when a student marshal came to me with a complaint. He told me he was the head of the picket line guarding our headquarters, and for this task he had been rewarded with a pair of toy binoculars—but the guys guarding the Beijing Students' Autonomous Federation had been given walkie-talkies. In the midst of all the chaos, you can imagine how astounded I was by this petty concern. I didn't say a word. I just looked at him. This kind of thing had driven me to the edge of exhaustion. As the commander in chief, I was at the center of every conflict, large and small.

Ma Bin came to the rescue this time. "What are you guys here for?" he said. "Are you here for these toys or to find a better future for our country?" The embarrassed student marshal returned to his post.

Seeing me in a moment of calm, another student approached. He was from a maritime college in northern China. When he and his fellow cadets first appeared on the Square, they immediately stood out in their eye-catching white uniforms. They were tall, well built, and clean cut, impressively military in their bearing. After martial law was declared, they were recruited to guard the broadcasting station. "We have been standing here day and night," he told me, "watching your leaders come and go without doing anything. We were disappointed, and most of us went home. Originally several hundred cadets from my school were here, but now only ten of us remain." Tears welled in his eyes. "I'm still here," he said. "I just want to see if there is still any hope for us and for our country."

Deep down I felt the same way. I was disappointed by all those in the movement who seemed to care only about grabbing power and fame. The country was in crisis; the ruling party was split; the government stood against its own people; the capital was under martial law; troops surrounded the city; tens of thousands of students from out of town occupied a square that was growing ever more squalid and filthy; rumors circulated about blacklists being compiled or that so-and-so had been arrested; many familiar friends had said farewell and disappeared. Yet students like this cadet looked to me for strength and advice. How could I possibly tell him I felt the same way he did? I had been appointed commander in chief of the Defend Tiananmen Square Headquarters, and I had led the entire Square in an oath to fight to the very end. Now, in my worst moment of humiliation by someone I had trusted, I still needed to be a source of encouragement for the many who looked up to me as a leader.

"We'll figure something out," I said. "Don't give up."

"I won't," he replied. "I'll never give up."

21

LAST WILL AND TESTAMENT

AT THE PRESS conference to announce the decision to withdraw from the Square on May 30, Wang Dan, Wu'er Kaixi, and I were portrayed as the three main student leaders. I felt neither joy nor relief. I felt I had made a mistake to agree to the withdrawal without a vote by the students at the Square. I had led the students in an oath to hold our ground in a stand for democracy. As commander in chief, I bore a responsibility to those who had invested their trust in me. To conform to an arbitrary retreat without giving the students a chance to vote would violate the same democratic principles the movement was striving to achieve.

At the press conference, I dissented from the official announcement and declared the students on the Square would first have to sanction any such decision. After the announcement, the students held another congressional meeting, and the majority voted to stay at the Square.

Bai Meng, the poet from the Beida writing class, found me after the press conference. He had been with us since the launch of the hunger strike and had taken charge of the broadcasting center, which was always the first object for takeover by those who unendingly tried to seize power on the Square. Bai Meng told me that given the deteriorating conditions on the Square, I should consider the plan to withdraw. It was obvious, he said, the government was waiting for the movement to die out on its own. If I did not agree with him, he said, it would be time for him to resign and leave the Square.

By then I had had it. I was tired of people using personal pressure, charm, or threats to get me to announce that we were staying or leaving. I was upset that someone so trusted, a friend so passionate and endearing, the same friend who had bought us a bowl of steaming dumplings to eat after my hunger strike speech, would think of leaving and in the process try to persuade me to take the students out as well. Those who chose to stay on the Square nurtured resentments against those who left—calling them cowards and traitors who had been bought out by the government. As I gazed at Bai Meng, I could not believe that he, too, had lost hope and changed his mind.

By the end of the day, I was completely exhausted. I had endured a seven-hour meeting of the Capital Joint Conference, Li Lu's tongue-lashing, a grueling press conference, and the resignation of yet another close friend. That night I wasn't sure where Feng had gone to rest. When my bodyguard asked for time off because his girlfriend had come to visit him, I realized I had no place to sleep. In despair, I went to our supply division, where mountains of new tents had recently arrived from Hong Kong. However, the young student in charge insisted on equality and would not allow me to be the first to set up one of the tents, even though, as commander in chief, I had gotten the tents flown in in the first place. After some negotiation by my bodyguard, Ma Bin, the student agreed to let me sleep in one of the large enclosures housing the bags of tents that had not yet been set up. I fell asleep amid a pile of unused resources.

With the morning sun radiating through the fabric of the tent, I woke up sweaty all over. The fumes from the new tents made me dizzy, and my back hurt from sleeping on an uneven surface all night.

As I thought about the events of the previous evening, I realized my trust and fellowship with Li Lu was broken. I could no longer depend on him for support or guidance. This time I searched my own heart and asked, "What should I do as a commander in chief for the Square? What is the right thing?"

I felt a deep conviction that the real battle was not at Tiananmen Square or in who would be the people's spokesman. The most important thing was to reach the army and convince them not to execute martial law. If we could accomplish that, we could achieve real and prolonged peace and success. But that was a dangerous job—stepping out of the protection of the limelight and into the darkness of the unknown. Tiananmen Square, contrary to general assumptions, had become the only safe place in China by then. As the darkness was marching toward us, we all knew that anyone who left the Square could easily be apprehended or disappear, as had happened already to a few key leaders.

Who should be the one to try to contact the army? What would be the duty of a real commander of the movement versus just a figurehead on the Square?

As I began the day, I felt convinced about this new direction. But before I tried to contact the army leaders, I thought about what would happen if I were arrested and disappeared. What would be my last will and testament? I wanted to leave a record of my experiences and my thoughts about the movement so others could pick up where I left off if something happened to me. But amid the chaos of the Square, I didn't have time to write everything down. That's when the idea of quickly taping something came to mind.

I saw a young student named Wang Li, whom I had met once or twice during the movement and who had mentioned he might know some Americans. I wanted to find a safe place to record my thoughts, and I didn't want to talk to the media. I wasn't intending to conduct an interview. I just wanted to make sure that what I had experienced during the movement wouldn't be lost.

When I asked Wang if he knew of anyone who could tape my statement for me, he said he knew an American student who might be able to help. He took me to a hotel and introduced me to a tall, Caucasian man named Philip Cunningham. Philip's Chinese wasn't very good then, and I wasn't certain how much he understood what we were talking about. I explained that I needed to find a quiet place to tape my thoughts before I went on a dangerous mission. He said he knew someone who could help us. He didn't tell me he was working for a media outlet during the Tiananmen crisis.

While I waited for Philip to be ready to go, a female reporter from Hong Kong saw me and insisted on joining us. Wang Li made it clear this would not be an interview, and she agreed. She just wanted to be part of the action.

Along with the Hong Kong reporter, Philip Cunningham and I took a taxi to the apartment of one of his friends. When we arrived, he made room for me to sit on one of the beds while his friend set up a video camera. Then I started talking.

"My name is Chai Ling. I am twenty-three years old. Isn't it strange that my birthday is on April 15, the same day Hu Yaobang passed away?"

Speaking rapidly as the words flowed from my heart, I told the story of how I became involved in the student protest movement and the circumstances that led me to become commander in chief of the Defend Tiananmen Square Headquarters. As I relived the events of the past six weeks, I became emotional and started to cry. I had an overwhelming sense we would not be able to achieve our fundamental goals, to convince the government with our peaceful requests for reform. And this made me sad. Still, we had made vows to persevere until the very end and to continue to put forward our requests with integrity and peace.

I thought of what it might mean to my family if something happened to me; about whether my dad would be able to console my mom and younger siblings. I thought of the moments of joy and unity in the early days of the movement, and the recent friction and infighting, the ugly side of human nature. I hoped that in a new free and democratic China, the people's eyes would be opened, they would be cleansed of the friction, and they would be truly united once and for all to change the nation for peace and a better society. What would this mean for China as a nation? Was it worth our sacrifice? I promised myself that if I sur-

My young parents in their People's Liberation Army uniforms during the 1950s. My dad, who had already enlisted in the army, was inspired by my mom to go to medical school. My mom, as a young medical college graduate, was inspired by my dad to join the army.

Mom and Dad came to visit me during my junior year at Beida, in 1986. The Palace of Heaven is in the background.

Late May 1989, after the declaration of martial law. I was speaking to the students as commander in chief of the Defend Tiananmen Square Headquarters. Other student leaders present: Li Lu (second from left, hand on chin); Feng Congde (front, reaching upward); Zhang Boli (white shirt, behind Feng); Wu'er Kaixi (right foreground); and Wang Dan (partially hidden behind Kaixi).

vived, I would devote my life to raise up a new generation of Chinese. I was not sure whether I would be given that opportunity.

Still fresh in my mind were Li Lu's words about the government coming after us with knives and the Square awash with blood and his tirade about abandoning Tiananmen. At one point in my statement, I repeated what Li Lu had said, and these words later became a source of confusion and misunderstanding.

What I meant to communicate was my concern that while many on the Square seemed to have an unrealistic sense of optimism because major foreign media outlets were covering the protests and others had started focusing on certain individual gains, I felt an inevitable crackdown was getting closer. That's why I had the idea to try to contact the army, to somehow forestall their enforcement of martial law.

When Li Lu told me on May 27 that allowing the students to withdraw from the Square would hand the government a victory, I felt terrible about initially going along with the decision to leave. And when Wang Dan told me that the motives of the people who attended the Capital Joint Conference were no longer as pure as those of the students in the Square, I put those two things together.

I was led to believe some people were selling out the movement by trying to move the students out of the Square so the crackdown could happen under cover of darkness, as it had in 1987, when plainclothes security officers came into the Square at night, beat up some people, and arrested the leaders of a tribute to Zhou Enlai. If that happened again with our movement, no one would know about it, and the government could imprison or kill all the key leaders, making it hard or impossible to start another successful movement. So, for me, it was important for the true face of our government to be known to the Chinese people and shown to the world. However, even in my worst nightmares, I was not prepared for the extent of the crackdown. I didn't know that words like "blood running like a river" could become so close to reality.

When I heard the phrase from Li Lu the previous morning at Tiananmen, I thought it was insightful, powerful, and moving rhetoric. It might be compared to how some people in America seem to idealize warfare, even though anyone who has been in combat will tell you that war is neither glorious nor glamorous, but brutal, ugly, and cruel. In

today's China, we still find banners in support of the one-child policy that say things like, "We would rather have blood flow like a river than one extra child to be born."

As I processed my thoughts during the taping, I started realizing what it might mean to ask the students to stay at the Square and face the crackdown. I felt I couldn't ask people to sacrifice their blood as we had asked them to volunteer to burn themselves during the hunger strike. At that time, more than ten students had stepped forward to volunteer. But this time I did not feel right asking them to make that kind of sacrifice. We each had to make our own decisions.

In speaking to Philip Cunningham, I was far too trusting. I really had no idea who he was. He kept the tape of my statement, as we had agreed, to be released to the public if something bad happened to me. Several years after the massacre, and without my knowledge or approval, he gave the tape to a group of people who were making a documentary about Tiananmen Square. That's how my statement came to be used, out of context and selectively edited, to brand me as a leader who had deliberately exposed her student followers to bloodshed and death at Tiananmen Square, a notion the Chinese government quickly adopted. This distortion of reality caused me immense pain, especially when the filmmakers minimized the fact that I stayed at the Square until the last hour. My statement was presented in the worst possible light, as if I had somehow twisted the government's arm to provoke the massacre and had hypocritically called others to sacrifice their lives while I ran away to save my own. Neither of those inferences is true.

For the past twenty years, I have shouldered much of the blame on behalf of the students. To my great disappointment, Li Lu, the one who scolded me for agreeing to take the students out of the Square, has never owned up to anything he said or did at the time. He has even been back to China several times, as if nothing ever happened. Feng, on the other hand, has devoted time over the past sixteen years to write books and articles defending my actions and my reputation. He told me he did this not out of personal affection, or because of our past relationship, but

out of passion for the truth about Tiananmen and to honor the sacrifices of the entire Tiananmen generation. Zhang Boli, another deputy commander, who later became a Christian pastor, stood side by side with Feng when the time came to sign a letter of truth and support, along with more than 160 other students and scholars from Tiananmen.[1] So did Zhang Jian, the head of the student guards at Tiananmen, who suffered a gunshot wound to his arm on the night of June 3. During the dark nights and days when I felt most sad and betrayed, I was always grateful for their trust and support.

This is the first time I have told my side of the story about the last days at Tiananmen. Back then, I thought I was responsible to speak for the student body at large. But now I realize I can only represent myself. The other student leaders and I may have been misled, or we may have done exactly the right thing in staying at the Square; I don't know. But even though I was concerned for my safety and my future, none of my decisions were made out of cowardice or to try to make all the students suffer for what might have been my punishment as one of the leaders. I don't believe I can speak for Li Lu anymore, but a few of the other student leaders with whom I was closest operated in good faith, and we tried to do the best we could for our country and our people, including the sacrifice of ourselves and our families.

Some of the victims' families may feel that if the students had left Tiananmen Square sooner, their family members might not have been killed. As a mother now, and as one who has lost loved ones, I understand the deep pain. I hope you will forgive my limitations in not foreseeing the massacre and my inability to follow up with my plan to try to persuade the military officers to abolish martial law. There was never any intention in my heart for anyone to make the ultimate sacrifice. We all wanted to live—and live in freedom. I know the irony that I am still alive while your loved ones are gone. I am so sorry. This is one thing that has tormented me for the past twenty-two years, and only recently have I had a measure of peace. I pray that one day you will receive peace and healing, and be given renewed hope and joy, as well. And that one day you will know there is a higher force who knows all truth and all hearts and deeds. Through him, true justice will be served.

After giving my statement to Philip Cunningham, I went back to the Square to find Feng to go with me to contact the army. But he was too deeply immersed in other things. When I told him my idea, he said plainly and firmly, "That is an important task, but as the commander, you have become a symbol for the Square. You can't leave. Find someone else to do it." Then he walked away.

I sighed and thought to myself, *If I cannot persuade my husband to agree with the importance of this job, who else can truly understand me?*

That night at a meeting with movement representatives, I offered to resign. The students kindly gave me one day to rest before making my decision. Feng took me home, and I slept all night and most of the next day. The rest restored my energy and clarity, and by evening I was back on my feet, determined to live up to my pledge to defend Tiananmen Square to the last person. Li Lu made an effort to repair the breach in our relationship, and that rebuilt some of my confidence, though I was no longer able to trust him unconditionally. After May 29, I never left the Square until the end, when the students voted to leave on the morning of June 4.

The support we received from Hong Kong at this time was crucial. Our supporters in Hong Kong, which in 1989 was still a British colony, held a marathon concert and raised twenty-six million Hong Kong dollars in support of the democracy movement. When they sent the money, they also sent tents. At last, a much-needed order reasserted itself on the Square. The infusion of money provided renewed energy. Tiananmen Square was transformed overnight into an orderly tent city.

Early on the morning of May 30, students from eight art schools unveiled a thirty-foot-tall statue of the Goddess of Democracy near the national flagpole directly facing the giant portrait of Chairman Mao on Tiananmen Gate. The presence of the Goddess drew new waves of support to the Square and buoyed the spirits of those who had been at Tiananmen since the beginning.

A student from Beida arrived with a thick envelope addressed to Feng. It was a letter of acceptance from Boston University, granting Feng a full scholarship to BU's doctoral program in remote sensing.

Feng and I sat in the headquarters tent and perused these pages. Paperwork was included for visas we'd both need. It was the next step in our American Dream. We looked at each other and realized how much our lives had changed in the past fifty days. Our Chinese Dream now took priority.

That night we arranged to occupy a small tent of our own. We had not spent the night together for a long time. I was very tired and fell asleep quickly. At four in the morning, a hand choking my throat woke me up in terror. It reminded me of the time when I was drugged and gagged at Beida. A few men, led by Wang Wen, were twisting my arm and forcing Feng and me to get out of our tent. When they began to bind us and gag us, I thought they were assassins sent by the government to kidnap us. I asked them to let me put on some clothes, and they agreed. As I was dressing, I screamed at the top of my lungs, "Help, help, the commander in chief is being kidnapped!" That brought some other students to our aid.

When help arrived, Wang Wen raised his voice and claimed he wanted to investigate us for embezzlement. This came out of left field. I couldn't believe this boyish-looking young man, with whom I had sat on our first night at the Square watching over the students, could harbor such a deep and violent hatred for having been excluded from the leadership group and could direct all his anger and resentment toward me.

After Wang and his cohorts managed to flee the scene, we held a press conference to disclose the attempted kidnap and call for greater vigilance and unity, which had become increasingly difficult to maintain.

That day was June 1, the Children's Day holiday in China. The students made an effort to create a festive mood for the kids who visited the Square. We cleaned up the trash, and it helped to have the colorful tents and the Goddess of Democracy as points of interest. Nevertheless, the steam had begun to run out on the movement. The local students had almost all packed up and gone home, and out-of-town students began to leave. Toward the end of May, the railway system added more outbound trains, and railway workers handed out free tickets to get students to leave town. During the first ten days of martial law, four hundred thousand students reportedly boarded trains in and out of Beijing.

Because Li Peng had canceled many inbound trains, most of these students must have been leaving. On May 29 alone, thirty thousand students reportedly left Beijing by rail.

The *People's Daily* published a letter written by eight Peking University professors calling on students to return to school. The *Beijing Daily* ran an article titled "Tiananmen, I Cry for You" about chaos on the Square and disillusionment within the movement. The student author called on the remaining students to withdraw. Then, late on the night of June 2, an army vehicle speeding down Chang'an Avenue struck several pedestrians three miles west of the Square, killing three people. Thousands of angry students and residents rushed to the scene under the impression this was an intentional killing by martial law troops. Meanwhile, also on Chang'an Avenue, people discovered buses and trucks loaded with helmets, rifles, and bayonets.

It appeared all hell was about to break loose.

22

THE LAST STAND

One hundred years ago on a tranquil night,
in the deep of the night before enormous changes
Gun and cannon fire destroyed the tranquil night,
surrounded on all sides by the appeasers' swords[1]

ON JUNE 2, pop singer Hou Dejian and three intellectuals, Liu Xiaobo, Zhou Duo, and Gao Xin, came to the Square and began a hunger strike in support of the student movement. Together they became known as the Four Gentlemen.

Hou Dejian's presence attracted new waves of people to the Square. The students began to chant for Hou to sing his hit song "Heirs of the Dragon," and the entire Square seemed to hum along as he sang. It was an interesting song. The lyrics echoed the sentiments we had been taught while growing up in China. The "gun and cannon fire" that "destroyed the tranquil night" refers to the Eight Alliance Army of foreign troops that invaded our ancient capital in 1900 to relieve the siege of the Legation Quarter by the Boxer rebels. That was the last time gunfire had brutalized the city. When the Japanese occupied Peiping, as the city was called in 1937, it was accomplished without gunfire. In 1949, not a single shot was fired when Mao's People's Liberation Army took possession of the capital. Who could have known that the same PLA that had peacefully liberated the city forty years ago would one day roll through the streets in tanks, firing machine guns?

"Mighty dragon, mighty dragon, open your eyes, forever and ever, open your eyes."[2] The final refrain of "Heirs of the Dragon" reverberated in the air above the Square throughout the day of June 3, and only years later did I finally understand the song's full impact and its spiritual meaning at that critical time of history.

The next morning, the gentle voice of a female student volunteer greeted the day with the morning broadcast from the headquarters on the Square.

> *The sun has slowly risen from the east. Today, June 3, 1989, our peaceful sitting has entered its twentieth day, and there are twenty more days to come before the National People's Congress meets. We hope the people's representatives will give assent to our request and lift martial law as a matter of constitutional right. We believe liberty will rise like the morning sun and arrive in the long-suffering land of the East. History will remember these many days and nights of 1989. History will remember the contributions students made toward the building of democracy.*

The students woke up in their tents to welcome another day on the Square. A line of soldiers marched out of the Forbidden City, crossed the Golden Bridge in front of Tiananmen, the Gate of Heavenly Peace, and advanced toward the Square to raise the national flag. The national anthem sounded from the government loudspeakers while the five-star red flag slowly ascended. All the people in the Square stood to salute the flag as it rose. It was a moment of harmony, as the soldiers, the students, and the Goddess of Democracy all stood facing the ancient Forbidden City and our nation's flag. The early days of summer in Beijing were beautiful and serene, even during that chaotic time on the Square. As we opened our hearts to the morning sunshine and the music of the national anthem, no one could have foreseen that all this would come to a brutal end that very night.

We knew that for the first time in the two weeks since martial law had been declared, the army was seriously pushing into the city toward the Square. People began to set up barricades on Chang'an Avenue near the Square to block all traffic.

Around eleven o'clock at night, after an otherwise peaceful day, a young man burst into the headquarters tent, shouting, "They're really shooting!"

He instantly had our full attention. "We were all in line," he continued, "holding each other's arms. Ping was standing next to me. He was telling me how tired he was after several days without any sleep. I saw a flash. Then I heard a crack over where the soldiers were. Ping fell down. I kicked him, laughing. 'Don't fool around like that,' I said. 'You can sleep *after* tonight.' He didn't answer."

The young man's mouth was wide open. His face was wet with tears. "I reached down to get him up, and"—his hands formed a big circle—"he was dead. He had a huge hole in his back."

Around midnight, news of casualties in other parts of the city became more frequent. One worker broke into the tent and pointed a gun at me. "Chai Ling," he shouted, "so many of my fellow workers have died to protect you students. If you withdraw from the Square, I'll shoot you. And I'll shoot you if you don't ask students to arm themselves and join the fight too."

No sooner had I calmed him down than another student came in. This one had a knife, which he pointed at me. "Chai Ling, so many students are being killed. . . . I'm going to cut your throat if you don't order the students to leave."

Growing up, I was trained to speak softly and treat people gently, as befits a humble Chinese woman. But I was fed up with taking this kind of abuse. I stood up and pressed my body against his knife. "Go ahead," I said, "cut my throat now." This surprised him and he paused for a second, looking into my eyes. Then a weird grin stole over his face and he fled.

In the distance, I heard the crack of rifle shots and the intermittent, staccato bursts of automatic weapons. It unnerved me to realize we were in the midst of a battle.

As the commander of the Defend Tiananmen Square Headquarters, however, I had to remind the students our movement was nonviolent. "We cannot—we must not—resort to force or the use of weapons," I said. "And if you choose to do so, please leave the Square."

Feng came back and reported that a second broadcast center had been set up on the steps of the Monument to the People's Heroes. He said we should abandon our current headquarters and move to the monument.

By two o'clock in the morning on June 4, the army had surrounded the Square, and the sound of gunfire had died away. The moonless night was so dark I could not tell how many soldiers, tanks, and weapons were assembled along the edge of the Square. Beyond the flickering lights on the Square, the city was a sea of darkness.

Death is an abstract concept to people in their youth, but in that dark hour, it became suddenly, inescapably real.

Out of the pitch-black night, the first row of tanks began to roll toward us. Fear and anger erupted all around me on the Square. A feeling of futility overwhelmed me. In that initial moment of panic, I knew for certain, and perhaps for the first time, that I was powerless. I could not believe this was really happening. We had wanted a dialogue with the government, and now the government was going to kill us, along with all the other unarmed people on the Square.

Within minutes the army had encompassed us on every side. As we clustered together around the base of the monument, I tried to imagine what my parents would feel when they heard I was dead. Would Mom make it? Would Dad also collapse? If Dad collapsed, what would happen to our family? How about my own little family? It was probably lucky Feng and I had no children, because they would have grown up as orphans whose dead parents were labeled "enemies of the state." This line of speculation was too frightening to pursue. I had made a pledge to protect the Square, and I intended to keep my promise.

A female voice began to sing the words of a popular song that had been composed for PLA soldiers sent by Deng Xiaoping to fight a border war with Vietnam in 1979—a catastrophic effort that reportedly cost two hundred thousand soldiers their lives, though the official government report placed the number at twenty thousand.

Perhaps I take leave, never to come back again,
If it were so, would you forgive me?
Would you understand?
Perhaps I would fall down, never to open my eyes again,
If it were so, please don't grieve,
For where you look at our national flag,
You will see its glories have been written by my blood.

This song reflected how we felt at the last hour, as soldiers of the PLA marched toward us.

The safety of the students remained my utmost concern. It was a foregone conclusion that as student leader, I was doomed to be captured or killed; but the students did not have to be part of this sacrifice. What could I do to protect the holdouts, the last of the students who had remained on the Square?

"You cannot let the students leave," a worker from Beijing had told me earlier in the night. "Your departure would be an insult to the sacrifice the citizens have made on Chang'an Avenue."

Those words tore at me as the night wore on, as new information continually came to us.

"Stay until 6:00 a.m., Zhao Ziyang's army will rebel."

"Hold on until morning. The U.S. government is going to intervene."

Meanwhile, two hundred yards from where I was sitting, I could see glimpses in the dark of machine guns and tanks.

Then I heard voices from the south side of the monument. The Four Gentlemen were talking to the remaining students and urging withdrawal. I listened in silence for half an hour while they talked.

"Those cowards," I heard Li Lu say in a low voice. "In peaceful days, they staged a hunger strike to show off. Now, in a time of real danger, they're afraid of death, but they can't just run away in full sight of all the students."

I did not reply. I was thinking about what he'd said earlier: "We will just wait here. If they really dare to open fire on the students, so be it. Let our red blood pour over the People's Monument. Let the whole world know what really happened."

Some students used the loudspeakers to encourage people to stay on the Square.

"Citizens have risked their lives to block the tanks and troops so we can stay on the Square," one student said. "To leave now would render those sacrifices meaningless."

Another said, "If we hold out until sunrise, two million Beijing citizens will come to our support. If we leave now, we'll never get back onto the Square."

Hou Dejian came to see me. "What do you think, Chai Ling?"

I told him we had received information that if we held out, Zhao Ziyang's army would come to our side.

"Is that so?" Hou said. He seemed surprised.

He returned to his colleagues and came back in a few minutes. The Four Gentlemen thought the student leaders should consider negotiating a withdrawal with the troops. But that was out of the question. The leaders would never take a position that might involve surrender.

"You are free to do whatever you want," Feng said. "If you go to negotiate with the army as a third party, you have my personal respect. But you cannot tell them you represent the students. The students must give their final approval to any deal you arrange with the army before it can be effective."

As Hou Dejian departed with another gentleman and two doctors, Li Lu came to where I was standing. "Let's go," he said. "You've got to pay a visit to your students at this final hour. They want to see their commanders, and we should let them know the leaders are with them before the last moment arrives."

Three or four thousand students were seated on all four sides of the monument. They looked calm, yet helpless. Obviously tired, their faces showed the same emotions of farewell and defiance that I was struggling with. Girls and boys leaned against each other for support and warmth, like lambs awaiting the chopping block. No rah-rah rhetoric would work with a crowd that now faced its last hour. I was glad Li Lu spoke first as I gathered my thoughts.

"We members of the headquarters have spent so many days with all of you," Li Lu said. "Today is the last time we will be together. I hope

everyone will face the last moment calmly. We will stick to the principle of nonviolence to the very end."

I tried to think of something to say that would bring them—and me—courage for the next, darkest hour. A story I'd heard about ants came to mind.

"A colony of ants lived on a tall mountain," I began. "One day, the mountain caught on fire. The ants in the colony realized their only recourse was to roll downhill. All the ants formed a large ant ball and rolled down the mountainside. The ants on the outside burned to death, but the ones inside survived. Tonight," I declared, "we are the outside ants. Out of our sacrifice will be born a new China."

A loud and genuine applause arose among the students. At that moment, I felt a warm flood of emotion come into my body, a feeling I can only describe as *love*. As I looked into the darkness, I said to myself, *I wish they would know, including the ones who were sent to kill us tonight, how much we love them.*

Hou Dejian's delegation returned around 4:00 a.m. with an announcement. The army, they said, would not open fire if we all withdrew before six o'clock.

Liu Xiaobo came to me and said, "Chai Ling, at last I understand. Wu'er Kaixi was not the right person."

He was referring to the meeting on May 27, where he had advanced the proposal to appoint Wu'er Kaixi as student spokesman. Feng and I had walked out of that meeting in protest.

I was touched by Liu's comment because he finally understood what was happening on the Square and the leaders who had stood by the students during even the most dangerous hours. To me, his words conveyed that the intellectuals and the students had at last achieved unification on a deeper level. The Tiananmen movement was not based on lofty ideals for democracy and freedom. It was rooted in a simple demand that all people be treated with justice and dignity. Liu gave me a big hug and went on with his preparations for the final hour.

It was time to vote for the last time on the question of whether we

should stay or go. Soldiers at the edge of the Square fired their guns in the air to press us to leave. The bullets whistled over our heads. One bullet hit the loudspeaker next to me. There was no time, but we had to take the vote of all the students who remained on the four sides of the monument. We took a voice vote. Feng told the students to shout out in a clear voice in the order we enunciated either the word *leave* or the word *stay*. It was impossible to determine from the responses which one was the majority preference. We all turned and looked at Li Lu, who usually counted the votes and announced the verdict. But this time he stood in silence, looking down at the microphone in Feng's hand. (Feng was kneeling on the ground.) I wasn't sure what was going through Li Lu's mind. His silence and inaction seemed to last a very long time.

Just as this historic moment of deliberation reached its climax, several gunshots blasted nearby, and I heard bullets whizz overhead and strike some part of the monument. Then a strong human wave surged around me, nearly pushing me backward.

"Soldiers!" someone shouted with a mixture of anger and fear. "The soldiers are here now!"

Immediately, a contingent of fully armed soldiers pushed aside the crowd and rushed to the top of the monument steps. I felt the blood rush to my face, and for a moment I thought that perhaps there had been no cease-fire agreement. Maybe this was how the final moment would arrive, with the soldiers coming up to take us all. I felt we should hold up each other's arms to resist peacefully, just as we had planned.

In the midst of the commotion, Feng knew instantly he had no time to lose. With one final look at Li Lu, who still looked downward in silence, Feng shouted decisively into the microphone.

I couldn't hear what he said. The gunshots had destroyed our loudspeakers. But immediately a wave of students who were standing nearby rushed down toward the bottom of the monument. By then, I had been pushed farther away from Feng and could no longer see him in the crowd.

As the surge continued downward like an outgoing wave, I heard Feng's voice amid the roar.

"Where is Chai Ling? Get Chai Ling!"

An instant later, he was at my side. "Oh, here you are," he said. "Let's go."

Feng and others grabbed me by the arms and rushed me down the stairs from the monument.

"Why are we leaving?" I asked.

"We voted to leave."

"Really? If that's so, there must be other students who did not hear this decision," I said. "Let's make sure all the students know."

I started grabbing the shoulders of students who were still sitting on the ground as I went down the steps. They looked at me with fatigue and confusion.

"Let's go," I shouted. "We've decided to leave. Tell the others behind you."

More students began to stand up and follow us.

"You go ahead," Zhang Lun, the leader of the student marshals, said to me. "We'll take care of everyone."

He immediately set about lifting students off the ground, one by one, and sending them off on the withdrawal march.

Li Lu said that as commanding officers we should walk in front of the students because the soldiers might decide to fire at us as we left the Square. I thought that made sense. We were the ones who should die first. Together we sped up and reached the front row of retreating students. With arms locked, we walked along the narrow path formed by the soldiers and their bayonets.

Dawn was breaking as we reached the edge of the Square. The streets along that side were littered with rocks and debris. After a short while, we realized no troops had been stationed up ahead to ambush us on our retreat.

"This is bad," Li Lu said. "This is bad. Someday they are going to ask us to take responsibility for this moment in history."

"Who's going to ask us to do that?" I said. "Who's going to ask us to be responsible? We aren't the ones who killed people."

Li Lu did not reply to my questions, as if they were too naive to merit a response.

"It's bad," he said. "Very bad. No student leaders died."

I wasn't sure what he meant by that. Why should student leaders have died?

"Let's go back to the Square," Li Lu said as he tightened his grip on my arm. "None of our commanding leaders died."

His statement cut short my feelings of relief that I was still alive. Still, I did not resist as Li Lu pulled me into an about-face and headed back toward the Square against the tide of retreating students. Almost immediately, however, residents and students began shouting at us. "The Square has been completely sealed off!" someone said. "They are aiming their machine guns at incoming people. Going back there is just going to waste lives for no reason. Get these students to safety. That's your responsibility now—as leaders."

Li Lu got the message. We reversed course once again and continued our march along Chang'an Avenue. As we approached an intersection just west of Xinhua Gate, we heard the blast of explosives. Soon we could smell tear gas, and yellow smoke began to cloud the air. We were forced to unlock our arms and cover our mouths and noses. Pressure from behind forced us to move faster. Students ran and screamed.

"They're coming! They're coming, and they are killing the students!"

We were marching in front of the retreating students, so we couldn't see what was happening at the rear of the procession, which stretched out behind us along the bicycle lane. A metal fence ran between the bicycle lane and the pedestrian sidewalk. Eight vehicle lanes lay open and empty along Chang'an Avenue. In a panic, some students ran up to tell us the tanks were running along from behind and the soldiers inside were firing tear gas. We heard that one tank, in the bicycle lane, had rammed into the procession with no sign of slowing down. Dozens of students had clung to the metal fence, and others were killed instantly. The tank crushed their bodies to an unrecognizable pulp and rumbled on like a speeding beast. Fang Zheng, a strong and athletic student from Beijing Sports College, pushed to safety a girl who had frozen in the path of the oncoming tank; but in his heroic moment, Fang lost the precious seconds necessary to evade the tank himself. His legs were caught in the tracks and his body was dragged forward. Fang grabbed the metal fence with both hands and the tank roared on, severing parts of both his legs.

This news made our blood boil. But once again, when we turned back to rescue students at the rear, other students stopped us and kept us moving westward, toward the Beida campus. Along our route, the streets were littered with debris, and the air was thick with smoke and the smell of gunpowder.

As we marched arm in arm, we sang "The Internationale" and other songs, but no words could express our feelings at that time. We were powerless and we grieved, but without tears. We did not have the strength to weep. We wanted to shout, but we had no voice. We wanted to fight, but we chose to use no weapons. We were diminished to a sense of smallness, of utter insignificance. We were nothing. We were zero.

It was almost noon when we finally reached the south gate of Beida. A mere three weeks had passed since we had marched out of this gate to launch the hunger strike on May 13, but it felt as if we'd been gone an entire lifetime. I knew this: The world for me would never be the same.

FAREWELL
TO BEIJING

23

ON THE RUN

When Feng and I finally reached the dormitories, my body gave out. I fell asleep the moment I put my head down. I don't know how long I was submerged in deep slumber before Feng's urgent voice awakened me. I opened my eyes just as Li Lu and his bodyguard waved good-bye and disappeared through the doorway.

Over the loudspeaker, I heard the voice of a female student: "Students! Pay attention! A line of tanks is approaching Beida. Our campus will soon be surrounded. We urge all students to move to other locations."

"But where can we go?" I said. I looked at Feng and his bodyguard, Liu Guang. At almost the same moment, we all said, "Let's go see the president of Beida."

Ding Shishun had committed himself to promoting reforms at Beida, and this had earned him the love and respect of the students. Ever since he had secured the release of Feng and the other students arrested in 1987, he had enjoyed a reputation as the protector of students.

When we reached President Ding's house, his wife opened the door and led us into the living room.

"Did you leaders bring all the students back from the Square?" she asked with concern.

"Yes, most of them are back safely," Feng replied, "except the ones lost during the tank attack."

"That's good," the president's wife said with evident relief.

When Ding appeared, he looked exhausted. "I have just received an emergency call," he said. "As president of Beida, I cannot promise how long I can guarantee your safety on our campus. You probably know better than I do what's going on out there. As to what you should do next, I don't think that's going to be a difficult decision. I'm sure you've read books about what happened to Communist Party members who fought the Nationalists."

He paused to regain his composure.

"Forty years ago," he said, "when my wife and I were students, we demonstrated and boycotted classes to convince the Nationalists to stop the civil war. The soldiers pointed guns at us and forced us to go back to school to take exams. I can't believe that forty years later the Communist Party is using their guns the same way."

President Ding was obviously pained. We decided to leave before we brought more trouble to his doorstep.

Outside, we realized we had no place to go. The advancing tanks seemed to have stopped before entering the campus, perhaps awaiting new orders.

Just then we realized how hungry we were. We could not recall the last time we had enjoyed a decent meal. The only restaurant on campus happened to be open, so we went there to fill our empty stomachs. The food looked delicious, but I couldn't eat much. Liu Guang asked Feng what he planned to do. Feng didn't want to run. "I've decided to stay on campus."

Liu was surprised. "If something happens," he said, "I don't think I can be of any help. Maybe it's time for us to go our separate ways."

"I think you're right," Feng said, after a moment of silence. "How much money do you need?"

Feng gave him money for the road, and Liu gave us a Bible he was carrying.

"May God bless you," he said.

After Liu Guang left the restaurant, I asked Feng his plans. He turned his back and said, "I'm not going anywhere. I'm just going to my dorm to sleep for the night."

I was shocked. I knew staying at Beida would lead us straight to prison. Surely our names were on a blacklist, and the government would not show mercy to the student leaders. But how could I leave my husband and run for safety on my own? I had stood by his side from the day we married. I had stood by his side throughout the movement. And I knew I would stand by his side under any circumstances, like the good wife my mother had raised me to be. I walked behind him, slowly and sadly.

Out of the blue, a little white rabbit hopped across the pathway in front of us. Paying no attention to our troubles, it stopped to nibble some grass before continuing on its way.

I let out a sigh. "Oh, how much I wish to live."

The sight of the little white rabbit transformed my thoughts from the craziness of our life-and-death situation to the memory of the time when Feng and I first fell in love.

Feng stopped walking. He turned toward me and broke into tears. "I've been a lousy husband," he said. "I'm so sorry. I didn't prepare anything for our escape. Here we are, and I have no idea where to go."

"Oh, that's why you wanted to go back to your dorm to sleep," I said. "That's okay." I patted his back, trying to comfort him. "Let's promise each other we will try to survive, try to live on."

"Let's promise," Feng said.

We had survived the massacre, but we had nothing left of what had once been ours—no home, no school, no dreams of studying abroad, no movement nor the million students who'd been part of our lives.

All we had was each other and our determination to survive.

Our promise to each other cleared our confusion and provided a new focus. But as the afternoon waned, Feng and I walked around campus

like two caged animals trying to find a hole in the fence. When we ran across some leaders from the old Preparatory Committee, they were shocked we were still in Beijing. They immediately procured two bicycles for us, gave us money, and sent us out through the West Gate to meet up with a friend who would accompany us to the train station.

As night fell, we rode furiously across the city on our bikes. Before long, it was pitch-dark and the air was thick and heavy with the smell of smoke and death. In the occasional lamplight I glimpsed helmets, rifles, and bayonets. We rode with all the energy we had left, not knowing how far we'd gone or how much farther we would have to go. Sporadic bursts of gunfire punctuated the night. I rode with one idea in mind: *to live.*

Suddenly, a sharp pain shot through my knees and up through my entire body. I found myself facedown on the street with my bike on top of me. I thought I'd been shot. It turned out I had fallen asleep riding. The past fifty days of constant activity and anxiety had taken a toll. My body just wanted to curl up in the middle of the street and sleep. Yet, if I were captured and interrogated, I might never have the chance to sleep again. It took everything I had to gather my strength and climb onto the back of Feng's bicycle for the remainder of the trip to the train station. Along the way, we and many others on the street had to duck and dodge to avoid random gunfire by soldiers who were trying to deter people rushing to the train.

At the station, our friend shoved us onto the train. It was like a war zone, chaotic and confusing. We could hear more gunshots in the streets.

"You've done your work," our friend shouted to us. "We'll take over from here. You'll see."

This friend, usually so calm and even-tempered, was suddenly overcome with outrage.

"This government will fall within weeks, if not days," he shouted. "They are out of their minds."

The train released a long, solemn whistle as it slid away from the platform. Feng and I put our heads down on the table between us and fell into a long, deep sleep. When we awoke, it was ten o'clock in the morning and the train was stopping in a city south of Beijing.

Feng got off the train and dashed to a store to buy new clothes so we could change out of the ones we'd been wearing—notably the green-

and-white, short-sleeved sweater in which I had been photographed many times at the Square. Feng also managed to purchase a small radio so we could try to pick up news and maybe tune in to Voice of America or the BBC.

I changed clothes in the ladies' room. When I came out, I saw a group of young students sitting outside the train station on a dirt road. Their clothes were caked with dirt and some were even bloodstained. They sat silently, with their heads bowed in what looked like terrible grief or pain, as if no words could relieve the horror they'd seen. My heart ached for them. How much I wanted to walk over to hug them and offer comfort; but seeing some policemen nearby, I walked back to the train instead.

"I am just a married student on summer break with her husband," I told myself. In my heart I said to the students, *Be strong, my dear friends, be strong. There will be justice; someday, there will be justice.*

Feng and I changed from train to boat, from boat to bus, and from bus back to train again. We did our best to play the part of students traveling for leisure. From a distance, we nonchalantly observed the demonstrations we encountered each place we stopped. On one leg of the journey, after the police had scattered demonstrators who blocked our progress, a passenger suddenly turned to me and whispered, "Miss, there's fire in your eyes. You'd better be careful. If those two men on the other side of the car see you, it could be trouble." I looked at him and forced a smile as I buried the fury I had so carelessly exposed.

We finally reached Wuhan, the city where the government's Second Command Center was situated. Many angry citizens blocked the train and forced it to stop. We got off and made our way to Wuhan University. There, in the dorm room of one of the student leaders, after watching a government spokesperson openly deny the massacre to the world, I was asked to record a statement telling the truth about what had happened.

"My name is Chai Ling," I began, "commander in chief of the Defend Tiananmen Square Headquarters. I am still alive. Today is June 8, 1989, and I want to tell the truth about the massacre at Tiananmen."

That's as far as I got. My mind went blank. The sound of the tape recorder clicking off seemed to ricochet off the walls of the dark room. On my forced flight, I had suppressed all the painful memories and they wanted to stay buried.

The leader pleaded with me. "Can't you just try?" he said. "We need to know the truth about June 4. Voice of America and all the other foreign reports are so limited. Yesterday at a rally a classmate who came back from Beijing described the terror of seeing the soldiers slaughtering students. Some students want us to arm ourselves."

"*Arm* yourselves?" I said. "Are you out of your mind? The students can't get weapons. And even if you use chains and clubs, how can you fight against armed soldiers? We cannot invite more sacrifice, and we cannot lose more people." I was once again filled with fire. "This movement," I said, "has always been peaceful. It has always been nonviolent. At Tiananmen, we didn't violate this principle, even at the last hour, because we didn't want to give the government any excuse whatsoever to carry out more repression."

"That's the point," the Wuhan student leader agreed. "That's why you have to speak. You have to explain that to the students here. They never had the chance to go to Beijing, so they don't know what happened. They have no idea. Everyone was furious about the massacre and wanted to arm themselves so they could take revenge for all the dead."

"Revenge? The most important thing to do now is get the truth out." With renewed resolve, I pressed the record button on the tape recorder and once again began to speak.

"It is now four o'clock on June 8, 1989," I said. "I am Chai Ling, commander in chief of the Defend Tiananmen Square Headquarters. I am still alive . . ."

After I finished my statement, Feng and I continued our journey. We had no idea where to go or how to travel; we just knew we had to go south—the farther south the better.

Two mornings later, Feng shook me awake in the small bedroom we occupied in the home of a stranger who had taken us in. He wanted me to hear something. A voice, vaguely familiar, penetrated my sleep-logged brain.

"My name is Chai Ling. I am commander in chief. . . . I am still

alive." I shot up in bed, fully awake. Feng had tuned in to Voice of America on the little radio he'd bought. "Oh, if they catch me, they'll torture me to get me to change my story," I told Feng. "I'm not afraid to die for my own sake, but what if they threaten my family?" I was in a state of panic. The full consequence of the words I'd put on tape hit me like a jet of freezing water. "We've got to survive," I told Feng. "Being captured is not an option."

My resolve to escape became a single, overpowering drive.

———

We traveled by bus to the edge of the South China Sea. I had never traveled this far from home. When we stepped off the bus, the sun was high in the sky and gleamed on the water. The gentle breeze smelled of the ocean. People wore summer shorts and shirts and sandals. Palm trees rustled in the breeze. It was heavenly. We really felt like students from the North on summer break, which was how we described ourselves to people who offered us places to stay. In our thick spring jackets and long black trousers, we looked like northerners, out of place among the locals.

By sundown, we had found a place to stay, and I was able to take my first shower in days. I was relaxing under a flow of warm water when Feng burst into the bathroom and told me to come out right away. He and our hosts had been watching Hong Kong TV, and Feng had seen an image of my face on the screen, accompanied by the audio of my June 8 statement. This was followed by scenes of the massacre, most of which were new to me because I had been on the Square when the killings on Chang'an Avenue took place. I watched in horror as the cameras showed people rushing a flat cart with a bleeding body on it to the hospital. I shook involuntarily. I wanted to cry out, but I forced myself not to scream.

That night, I was filled with pain and agony for the families of the dead and injured. The pain found its expression in an old toothache that flared up and vibrated like a drumbeat in my head, keeping me awake all night long. By the time dawn broke, a stubborn question had emerged: *Why am I still alive?*

It was a Sunday, and our host couple was still asleep. Their son, who looked to be in his late twenties, had arisen early and was seated in the middle of the living room floor, meditating. When we came in, he stopped what he was doing and engaged us in conversation.

"How was your sleep?" he asked me. "You looked troubled last night. Is everything okay?"

This young man radiated a peaceful calm, and I sensed I could trust him. I sat on the bamboo sofa, shook my head, and briefly told him what was on my mind. It felt so bad, I said, to be a survivor after what I'd seen on TV. Now that I knew how many people had died, I felt so guilty. "Why did I get to live?"

"I understand why you might feel that way," he said, looking at me with a spirit of tranquility. "In the Buddhist world, we are all born with a special mission. The people who died may have finished their mission in this life, and they are now in heaven. Your job is not yet done. That is why you are still alive."

His words soothed my aching heart. *Your mission is not yet done.* With one sentence, he lifted me from utter confusion and grief to a new vision. Buddhism opened a new world to me.

"Please tell us more," I said.

"In this world, we believe in reincarnation. All material things are fabrications. They do not last, and they are not of any importance. Money, material stuff, our flesh, our looks. What is truly lasting, what endures, is our souls, which are our real selves. We have to nurture our souls every day through meditation and care."

"That is so different from what I learned when I was growing up," I said. "We were encouraged to study matters having to do with the real world, like physics. We were never educated in matters of the soul. How is this different from Christianity?"

"That's a really good question," he said. "I'm not qualified to give you an answer. I believe that somehow Buddhism and Christianity become one and the same at the highest level of understanding."

As I looked at his serene expression, I marveled that he was so tranquil. He knew the kind of trouble we were in and that it could affect him and his family if we were caught.

"Why are you doing this?" I asked him directly. "Why are you risking your safety to protect us?"

"Oh, that," he said with a smile. "I watched you students on TV during the demonstrations. If I had been the person I once was—in the world—I would have joined you on the streets. But I am committed to the world of the spirit now. I have decided never to marry or have children. Worldly things such as politics are no longer my concern. Buddhists don't involve themselves much in the real world. But you came under my care, and it is my responsibility to save you. There is a reason why we met. Perhaps, in one of our past lives, we shared a long journey, perhaps something else. Either way, we are bound together by this unusual situation. In our world, saving one life is the highest form of worship."

"I want to know more about your world," I said.

"Well," he continued, with a certain excitement, "each life is an independent spirit. After the body dies, the spirit goes on living. It leaves the body, finds life, and is reborn. It may be reborn as a cow or as a person. It really depends on the situation."

I was drawn to this new realm of the spirit, as if it were touching a hidden part of me.

Feng, too, was interested, and we came to call this peaceful young man Big Brother. He became our spiritual master, teaching us how to sit and meditate, how to practice tai chi, and how to take in the energy of the sun, the wind, and the universe and put it into our bellies. Soon Feng, Big Brother, and I were chanting together in unison, "*Wong ma ni ma mi hong wong ma ni ma mi hong*" (in English, "May all the evil stay away").

24

CHINA'S MOST WANTED

On June 13, we were eating lunch and watching the news on TV when we saw a broadcast of the government's most-wanted list—which included pictures of Feng and me. Though we'd been expecting this, it had a powerful impact when we finally saw it on the screen. The blood drained from my face as they showed the police accosting Xiong Yan, one of our close friends. His hands were twisted behind his back as two policemen pushed him along. Even so, our friend wore a smile on his face. I admired him for that.

The older couple with whom we were staying recognized our faces on the TV. After lunch, they told us they had decided to protect us. As our guardians, they locked us in a small room during the day and ordered us not to make any noise. At night, we prepared ourselves for potential interrogation by the police. In the distance, we could see the lights of Hong Kong, which fueled our hope of freedom. But those lights were a goal beyond our reach. We could, however, watch Hong Kong TV, and that's how we learned that Li Lu and other student leaders had escaped China. We looked forward to the day when we, too, could leave.

I woke up every morning with the realization that I was not free. I was a wanted criminal. Yet each day as I watched the sun come up, I hoped some good news might reach us. Big Brother was working on a plan to get us out of China with the help of some of his friends. Days went by. Every evening, I watched the sun go down knowing we remained in peril. We had no idea how long we would have to wait; we only knew we were trapped. All we could do was sit in our room and wait.

Two months passed. Finally Feng decided he could wait no longer. We were putting too big of a burden on the couple protecting us, he said. He gathered Big Brother and his friends to form a plan to cross the border to the New Territories. These brave comrades put together all the items Feng needed to make his escape to freedom, except for one key item—an ID card, which Feng would need as a pass on the road.

Nevertheless, Feng left with his companions the following night. Before we parted, he told me he would make arrangements for my escape once he got to safety. I waited all the next day for Big Brother to return with news of Feng's escape. My toothache flared up once again, and I spent the day in double agony.

Looking serious and troubled, Big Brother and his friends returned just after sunset. I could instantly see that all had not gone well. Big Brother broke the bad news. "We're worried Feng might have been arrested."

I was stunned.

They had taken a tested route that should have been clear. But out of the blue, two security guards had appeared. Big Brother, ever calm, had spoken to them in the local dialect. They said they'd been sent south to look for students from Beijing who might be trying to escape along the narrow route to the border. Feng was standing right in front of them. If he'd opened his mouth, his Mandarin would have given him away. But he was spared; the guards let them pass without asking for his ID.

Big Brother had a bad feeling as they proceeded. He wanted to change plans and organize another approach. As they returned along the same path they'd taken, a farmwoman in a field asked if they were helping students from Beijing. She pointed to a shed on the side of the road ahead and warned them that security forces were waiting there.

Big Brother and his companions chose another route.

As the group pressed on toward the border, Feng became weak. He hadn't accounted for how much two months in hiding had weakened his muscles. He kept falling as they climbed a mountain along the way.

Finally they reached the river separating the People's Republic of China from the New Territories. Feng had planned to swim the river to safety, a fantasy that evaporated when he saw armed police stationed up and down the riverbank at one-hundred-yard intervals. The men quickly realized they'd have to postpone Feng's escape until they could formulate a new plan. They split up and agreed to meet at a secure location.

When Big Brother got on the bus, he realized the police had intensified their inspection process. He knew Feng was on another bus without an ID and with no command of the local dialect. Feng was clearly in grave danger, and Big Brother was powerless to help him. He reached the agreed-upon meeting site and waited for a long time, but Feng never showed up.

Their message for me was urgent. If Feng had been caught, his captors would soon find out where I was hiding and come for me. We had to leave at once for a new location.

"Gather your stuff quickly," Big Brother said. "We don't have any time to lose."

As I packed, I began to weep. I picked up Feng's clothes and could still smell his scent. My tears fell on the pages of the book he had just been reading. Never in a million years had I thought he'd be captured or killed almost immediately. He'd told me he would send for me once he reached freedom. Now he might not even be alive.

I heard a soft knock and Big Brother's voice through the door. "Let's go," he said. "No time to mourn."

When he saw me, his face sank. I guess the sight of my puffy red eyes and tear-streaked face aroused a sense of guilt.

"I am very sorry. I have underestimated the danger," he said quietly.

"Oh, no," I said, trying to be brave. "You did everything you could. I am deeply grateful."

Big Brother put me on a bus headed north and told me where to find my contacts at the other end. I took one last look at the lights of freedom across the water.

For the next several weeks, I shuttled from one home to another within a network of devout Buddhists. I was in such emotional turmoil that my mind and heart were open to their spiritual nurturing. On the run, it was easy to break my attachment to material things such as money, beauty, fame, power, and emotion. The only thing that still held an attraction for me was love—my attachment to my beloved Feng, my family, and my friends. It grieved me not to know whether Feng was alive or dead. And I was unable to contact my family to find out what had happened to them. I had no idea it would be this hard.

I prayed for enlightenment to a statue of the Buddha and promised to forsake everything I once loved, except my family. I missed them, and I couldn't help it. "Is this what you intended?" I asked. "For me to live in the present without attachment to any worldly things?" When I opened my eyes, the smiling statue of the Buddha was silent.

"Should I cut my hair," I inquired, "and become a Buddhist nun and serve you in the temple?" The Buddha was still silent, still smiling.

My last stopping place was with a family of simple peasants. They were gentle and kind, free from anger and gossip. They found joy in the small things of life. Their kindness worked on the grief I felt for the loss of Feng. Gradually I achieved a state of peace. I decided that if Feng had indeed been captured, I would either turn myself in or join a temple and become a nun. With that, I passed a milestone I had not known existed.

Two weeks later, word reached me that Feng was safe.

Though I was overjoyed to hear the news, for reasons of safety, I was not allowed to join him. Pictures identifying us as a couple had been sent out all over China.

Mug shots of me had been posted everywhere. The authorities were searching for me high and low. Ten girls who looked like me were locked up and interrogated. According to one rumor, Wang Zhen, an old crony of Deng Xiaoping's, had declared, "Until we find Chai Ling, the Tiananmen incident will not be finished." It was vital for me to avoid capture.

With the help of Big Brother and other rescue workers, I came up with a plan to change my appearance. A small bit of plastic surgery on both eyelids added an extra fold that gave me a distinctly different look

from the person in the mug shots. Big Brother also sent a trusted friend to visit my parents to tell them I was alive and well in hiding. I was particularly grateful to him for that.

One afternoon there was a knock on the door of the house where I was staying. I immediately went to my hiding place. A few minutes later, my host brought me out, and I beheld Big Brother with Feng. They were in the process of transferring Feng to another location. I was thrilled to have him back in my arms, even if only for that one afternoon. He told me about his adventures and how he had been studying Buddhism and practicing meditation every day.

When evening came and Feng had to leave, he saw the tears in my eyes. He gave me a hug and promised he would come for me no later than the Spring Festival, which is Chinese New Year, when we would once again try to escape. He said this with such conviction that I had no doubt he would make it happen. From that time on, I dreamed about how happy we would be when we were finally free. It kept my spirits alive.

To prepare for the long journey, I was determined to get my body in shape. Every morning, I got up early and practiced tai chi, then took a cold bath and rubbed my skin with a wet washcloth until I was pink all over. When I emerged from the tub, my blood was racing and I was ready to face the day.

I also began to pray furiously and devoted myself to reading Buddhist scriptures. This kind of learning was so different from all the studying I had done from childhood through college.

When your past has been stolen and you don't know what the future holds, you can only concentrate on the present moment. Yet the present, too, was filled with questions. I never knew when the authorities might discover where I was or what they would do once they found me. Sometimes I would gaze out the window at the crisp, white clouds and imagine spirits were waiting to lift me from my entrapment. At other times I imagined myself as a Buddhist nun living a life of worship and solitude. Once upon a time, I had lived a life according to a crazy schedule with hardly any time for sleep or rest. To contemplate a life of solitude and nothingness was a great and difficult change for me. Was this the Buddha's idea of living in the moment?

Each day, I had to find a way to prevent the nothingness from driving me insane. That was the challenge in my life that renewed itself day by day. I had to concentrate my energy to prepare for a remote and unknown world. Each morning the sun came up; each evening it went down. Then, after a long, difficult night, the sun rose again on another day of waiting for something to happen.

Spring Festival is important to the children of China the way Christmas is to American children. It is *the* big celebration, ushering in the new year. It is the time when parents provide their children with a new wardrobe for the entire year. My siblings and I would ask to go to bed early so we could put our new clothes under our pillows all night.

Firecrackers often go off before dawn and wake everyone. They are intended to scare away the ghosts. My father was superstitious about Chinese New Year and always took the day off, believing that if he did, he wouldn't have to work as hard during the coming year. Invariably, however, he'd be called to the hospital to treat people with firecracker injuries.

The army used to provide each family with either a half or a whole pig's head, and the tongue was a special holiday treat. During this time of celebration, we were not supposed to do any work or perform chores; we were only supposed to eat and socialize. Now that I was far from my home and family and unable to communicate with them, all I had were the memories of our Chinese New Year celebrations together.

Even though I was a fugitive, I refused to give up and let the Spring Festival pass me by—especially since I was expecting Feng to return, as he'd promised. At the risk of being discovered, I slipped out of my hiding place to shop for the ingredients I would need to cook a great feast for Feng.

In a store where I'd stopped to purchase fish and meat, someone who looked like a soldier in civilian clothes came in to buy matches. Something clicked in his mind when he saw me, and I had to fight my instinct to run. My heart pounding, I paid for my purchases and sauntered past him as if everything was just fine. As soon as I stepped out the

door, however, I started to run. I ducked into an alley and then peered out and saw the man calling to some colleagues to search the area. I crisscrossed a few streets and made my way back to my hiding place via a circuitous route. Only now, as I write about it, do I realize how foolish I was.

The people who were protecting me prepared the meals for Feng, though one of my hosts laughed at my stubborn determination.

"I can't believe you really think he will come for you in this situation," she said.

Her casual tone upset me.

"He said he'd come, and he will," I said. "You'll see. I'm staying here until he does."

Reluctantly my hosts left and went away to spend the holiday with relatives. They wanted to take me along, but I didn't want to miss Feng when he came, so I chose to stay behind. This time I was completely alone. My hosts were afraid their neighbors might realize there was someone still in the house, so they insisted I not turn on any lights or do any cooking.

I changed into traveling clothes, packed a small bag for the road, and sat down to wait for Feng. New Year's Eve came and went. In the evening, I heard the neighbors laughing and imagined the television shows they were watching. I tried not to fall asleep, so I wouldn't miss the knock on the door when Feng came for me. At dawn firecrackers began to explode, and the noise went on for most of the morning. I still waited and prayed for Feng to arrive. Perhaps he had been forced to take a longer route.

On the third day of New Year's, my hosts returned from the country. They said nothing about the discussion we'd had before their departure. They knew how embarrassed I was about my misplaced trust.

Feng never came.

25

ESCAPE TO HONG KONG

AFTER ANOTHER MONTH had passed, the rescue network transferred me to a new hiding place. Though I was still worried about Feng, I was grateful. As the network continually expanded, my protectors enlisted the help of someone who worked in the security department and managed to obtain an ID card for me. Now I would be able to transfer between locations by taking the train. I felt I had survived the worst of my ordeal and that freedom outside of China was only a matter of time. Still, one could never be too careful.

They transferred me back to the city, where once again I was by myself. One day a rescue worker arrived to take me to a Buddhist convention. I donned a quick disguise and soon was walking city streets for the first time since my flight south. The convention was held inside a massive, open sports arena, with tens of thousands packing the grandstands. No one paid the slightest attention to me, including the guards. Having the ID was a great boost to my confidence.

The Buddhist master leading the conference spoke to the huge crowd as if he were engaged in an intimate conversation. He urged us to relax and to practice our systematic breathing.

"The key to life," he said, "consists of three words: truth, kindness, and endurance. With those three words, we can create a world of peace and kindness. We must let go of all the bad emotions, such as greed and hatred, which only poison our real selves. We must let them go and let our pasts go."

He led us through an exercise of releasing the past and encouraged us to let everything go. When I closed my eyes, all the images of the soldiers' advance at Tiananmen and the ensuing chaos flooded in. Around me, people began to cry, laugh, and scream as they faced their own issues. I opened my mouth, but nothing came out. As more voices joined the screaming and loud cries, I was silent, but my body was shaking with grief.

The master encouraged us not to be afraid to let all the hurt, resentment, anger, and hatred go. His calm words were reassuring, and I felt a gentle wave of energy begin to move my body back and forth. As I swayed rhythmically, I felt the pain in my heart was healing and some internal blockages were breaking down.

"Open your heart," the master said. "Let your heart fill with truth, kindness, and endurance."

When he encouraged us to make a wish for the future, I wished I would make a successful escape and achieve true freedom.

By the time we left the stadium, it was dinnertime. The day had passed in a blink. My body felt healed, full of energy, and in a state of harmony.

With the spring came renewed hope. When Big Brother dropped in for a surprise visit, I was almost expecting him. I was no longer the same girl who had begun this journey ten months before. No longer regretful, frightened, or full of sorrow, I was calm and at peace with my destiny, even though I had no idea what that destiny might be.

I was sequestered at a location near the border with a couple who had a sweet teenage daughter. She and I soon became close.

One afternoon I heard a distinctive knock on the door, which I recognized as the rescue network's special code. When I looked through

the peephole, I saw Feng on the other side. Even though my heart was pounding, I didn't open the door. I was upset with him for breaking his promise to come for me during the Spring Festival.

Soon my hosts returned and invited Feng inside. Big Brother, who accompanied Feng, gently told me I should not be playing games at this particular time. Feng could have been exposed and captured. I was embarrassed by my childish behavior.

When I asked Feng why he didn't come as he'd promised, he looked at me with surprise.

"Did I really say that?" he asked. He had simply forgotten.

Big Brother explained that our opportunity to flee China was near. "The odds of success are fifty-fifty," he said. "If we succeed, it will be very good. If not, it could be disastrous. What do you think?"

What did I think? After almost a year in hiding, most of it separated from Feng, all I needed to hear was that there might be an opportunity to leave. I was more than ready to stop depending on the care of others and to stop putting others in danger.

"We'll take it," I said.

Feng seemed to agree, though I wasn't entirely sure. I couldn't put my finger on it, but he seemed different. Gone was most of the warmth he'd expressed when we'd sworn our oath to go on living. He seemed detached and a little lofty. I thought this might be the result of meditation and our long separation. He returned to his own hiding place to await final preparations.

The night before our escape, I couldn't sleep. I kept imagining how Feng and I would soon be reunited. Together we were going to reach a world of freedom. No longer would we live in perpetual fear.

When Feng and Big Brother returned, we were led down to the harbor. The evening breeze carried a salty, fishy smell, reminding me of home in Rizhao. The breeze drove away the humid daytime air and evaporated our anxious sweat. For a moment, it felt refreshing.

The time came to say farewell to Big Brother and the many others who had faithfully risked everything to protect us. As always, Big Brother was calm and in control, but his sweaty palms revealed the tension underneath. He wished us well and told us the last step in our journey would be in a *wèng*, or "jar," a small space of confinement.

He warned us that the success of the voyage was uncertain and would depend on our strength and preparation.

In the darkness we were led onto a boat, the kind that regularly plies the waters between the mainland and Hong Kong, and were quickly spirited into a large cargo box below deck. If all went well, by the following morning we would be in a different world. For the crossing, we were supplied with two bottles of water, a loaf of bread, and a small box of matches.

When the cover of the cargo box was closed, darkness thicker than night enveloped us—no stars, no lights, nothing. The air was instantly hot and humid and hard to breathe. The container stank of dead fish. Using our matches judiciously to light up the space when we grew claustrophobic, we saw the bottom of the box was full of water. Every two feet, wooden boards stuck out on which we could place our feet. To rest and conserve energy, we sat on one piece of wood and put our feet on another.

Comfort was not an option. The lid of the cargo box was tightly shut. There was no way back. I had been separated from Feng for such a long time that my heart leaped with joy that we were finally alone together. But I had to suppress my feelings and emotions to conserve my energy and maintain my composure. With one quick touch of our hands, Feng and I sat down and began meditating as we'd been taught.

I tried to visualize a peaceful body of water bathed in clear moonlight shining from high in the heavens. As willow trees and long branches moved gently in the breeze, I imagined myself on the top deck of the boat, in harmony with my surroundings. I realized that when we change how we perceive our situation and the world, we can alter our perspective from confinement to unlimited freedom and equip ourselves to adapt to any circumstance and survive.

Inside the blackness of the box, Feng and I had no concept of time. We had been told the voyage would take eight hours, but we had no idea how long it would be until the boat set sail.

As I continued to meditate, a hideous image of bones and skulls and rotting flesh suddenly appeared in my mind. A wave of fear swept through me, but Feng grabbed my hand before I could say anything.

"Did you see something?" he asked.

"Yes, did you see it too?"

When he described the same image I had seen, we were both shocked and frightened. The spirit of death had moved in on us. Feng struck a match. The flame illuminated the entire box. We saw nothing except the bare wood sides, the stairs, and the hatchway, which was tightly shut. Under the boards we sat on, the water was dark and dirty, and it was hard to see beneath the surface. As we gazed at the water, the flame reached the end of the match and died out. Darkness again enveloped us.

Feng and I gripped each other by the hand and began to chant the mantra we had learned from Big Brother: "May all the evil stay away." As we prayed, another teaching of Big Brother occurred to me. In the Buddhist perspective of the world, our spirits must go through many levels to be born again, that is, liberated from earthly bondage: the level of hell and ghostliness, the level below the earth and the insects, the level of four-legged animals, the human level, the level of heaven, and the level of the Buddha. I had the feeling that before Feng and I could reach human freedom, we would have to be reborn to the world. At this moment, we were trying to survive hell. After intensive prayer, the hideous image vanished from our minds and the energy of sheer terror receded. As the night dragged on, our minds became blurred and we were on the verge of sleep.

Noises overhead awakened us from our drowsiness. We heard footsteps and the sound of things being moved. Afraid we might be discovered, we remained utterly silent and alert. After a while, the noises ceased, and all was quiet again. We later learned the crew had boarded the boat, but then the voyage had been rescheduled. A few crew members had remained on board and had been moving about. A member of our rescue team whom we called Little Brother had kept an eye on the situation, but with so many people coming and going, he couldn't risk letting us out of the box.

By the second day, we had no idea whether it was night or day or how much longer we would have to wait. I reminded myself I had waited ten months and could wait a little bit longer if freedom was at the other end. But it took a lot of energy to make sure we weren't losing our grip on our minds and hearts. I understood how people can go

insane during times of solitude, waiting, and darkness. I thought of my mother and all she'd been through. I could not let evil defeat me that way. I refused to give in.

After what seemed an eternity, we heard the sound of what we guessed was an engine starting up, and the box began to vibrate. Ripples of water beneath our feet gave us the impression of movement, though it was hard to detect any forward motion of the boat. In the dark I touched Feng's hand in excitement. We had survived the first great test. Finally we were on our way.

The renewed anticipation of freedom put us both in a good mood. Feng began to tell me what he'd been doing during our long period of separation. But when he told me he'd fallen in love with a Hong Kong TV star and had made up his mind to find her once he reached freedom, it was as if he had driven a knife into my heart. As it had the night we'd watched *Doctor Zhivago* two years before, his confession rocked our marriage to its foundation.

After the experiences we'd been through together and the way we'd bonded, I could not believe he would cast me aside for someone he'd seen on television. Yet we were still in grave danger. I couldn't let something like this distract my focus. I went back into meditation and ignored Feng's chatter. This prevented the pain from penetrating my heart as deeply as it once had.

The heat, the vibration, and the roar of the engine weakened my mind and will. I started to feel seasick as I drifted into sleep. I couldn't tell how long I'd been dozing when a sudden jolt snapped me awake. The engine had died, and the sensation of motion had ceased. In the dark, Feng and I couldn't tell what was happening. We heard noises overhead, both loud and muffled.

Feng had reached his limit. "I'm going crazy," he whispered. "How do we know this isn't some kind of a trick? Maybe they've left us to die. Maybe they never intended to let us out. I can't take this anymore. I'm going up. I'm going to open the hatch right now."

Feng felt sure we'd arrived at our port of destination. He couldn't

believe nobody had come to let us out. Perhaps the person who had put us here had forgotten us or passed out. He couldn't stand to wait any longer. He was going to take the matter into his own hands.

"Please don't do it," I said. "They may be just outside, waiting for us to open the hatch so they can seize us."

Feng did not agree.

"If you don't care how much time and effort we've put into our escape for the last ten months," I said, "if you don't care what might happen to us if you're wrong, feel free." My strength and resolve were fading fast.

The stubborn Feng had resurfaced. He climbed over me in the dark, and I could hear him climbing the ladder. I continued to meditate. Whoever came below would find me in a state of peace.

As the noise above grew louder and clearer, Feng stopped and came back down the ladder. For whatever reason, he did not open the hatch.

Footsteps came and went outside our enclosure. We heard some loud shouts. Finally the engine started up again, and the sense of motion returned. We had only been making a stop.

After that experience, which could have derailed our entire effort, Feng became calmer. He sat back down and announced, "This time I'll stay where I am, even if it means we have to stay here until we die." This was not a pleasant thought, but he had a point. The hot and humid box felt like a tomb.

As our bodies weakened, all we had left were our wills and our faith. Not knowing how much longer it might be or how many more tests awaited us, we were compelled to give up all pretense of control, to let faith transport us to our destiny, whatever that might be.

As the engine labored on, I dozed. In my dreams I saw an image so bright I felt it could blind me. We were bathed in dazzling sunlight, overlooking a beautiful river. Flowers bloomed on the surface of the water. At that moment, someone lifted the hatch.

"We are here," said a calm, firm voice. "You may come out now."

26

THE MEANING OF FREEDOM

It TURNED OUT the entire voyage had taken four days and five nights. One hundred and five hours. When my feet touched solid ground, I knew we had reached freedom. Unlike the sunny dream I'd had, my first breath of freedom was foggy and damp. Little Brother told us how close we had come to being discovered when the police stopped our boat out in the harbor. Apparently, they had received information that we were on the run that night. But after searching high and low for us, they allowed our boat to continue its journey.

It had been a long journey. I didn't feel thrilled or overwhelmed; I felt at peace. It was the same way I used to feel after a grueling final exam. We walked the streets of Hong Kong, totally unaware of the dangerous presence of mainland spies and operatives who might try to kidnap us back to the mainland. At the University of Hong Kong, we found someone who could connect us to the underground rescue network. The machine immediately began to move. In a matter of days, we were given the option of becoming refugees in either the United States or France. Feng chose France.

A few days later, we were given French passports and driven to the airport, where we were smuggled through the back door of a plane, accompanied by a French diplomat and his female companion. He was obviously nervous. After we were airborne, he kept glancing out the window at the land below. Finally, after half an hour, he sank back in his seat and relaxed.

"We just flew beyond the airspace of the People's Republic," he said. "I was worried. I thought someone might have leaked the information that you were onboard and the Chinese might shoot us down."

The plane cut across the blue sky and headed west, out of the endless darkness and into the sun.

In Paris, we were immediately swept off to the home of a French family, and the diplomat went his separate way. Later that afternoon, Feng and I slipped out of the house for a stroll. It was springtime in Paris, and people were in a holiday mood. Feng and I wandered hand in hand along the cobbled side streets of the Left Bank. It was the first time we could recall walking freely in public together without fear. I felt a deep, satisfying peace. On a whim, Feng took off and ran, and I chased him, like a little bird.

Free at last.

When Li Lu received word of our flight to freedom, he called from New York before boarding a flight to come see us. Over the transatlantic line, his voice sounded ebullient. Feng and I were excited to reconnect so soon with one of our close comrades. The strong bond we'd formed during the last hours at Tiananmen had erased all earlier friction.

The evening after Li Lu arrived, we were visiting with some French officials when I received a phone call from Yan Jiaqi, a well-respected Chinese scholar, who was leading the Federation for a Democratic China (FDC) in France. He wanted to meet with me. Li Lu waved his hand to signal "no." I didn't know what was going on, but I would soon begin to feel the pull of the overseas democracy movement and learn how politically complicated it had become.

When night came, Li Lu, Feng, and I all slept in one big bed like three comrades in a foxhole, indifferent to gender, just one in the purest sense.

The next morning, a tall, thin woman in her late thirties walked into the apartment and made herself at home. Li Lu's face went red. "This is Liao Da Wen," he announced, "my girlfriend." The intimate atmosphere of the Tiananmen reunion evaporated. "That ceremony I had on the Square doesn't count as a real wedding," Li Lu declared, as if reading my mind.

Feng was intrigued. He thought Da Wen and Li Lu made an interesting pair. She was clearly older than he and seemed to know a lot about various dissidents who had come out of China and where they were. She'd worked with Li Lu on his English and helped him with his school application and the book he was writing. She offered to help Feng and me as well. I just sat and listened. This was a lot of information to digest, especially for my jet-lagged brain. We were exhausted. We took a nap after lunch in separate rooms.

When I awakened around four in the afternoon, I could see Feng had been crying. Still half asleep, I heard him and Li Lu talking out on the balcony. When they came back inside, Feng's face bore a resolute expression.

"I'm not comfortable in the free world," he declared, as if making an announcement over a loudspeaker. He did not look directly at me, but it was clear he was speaking to me. "I have decided you and I and our colleague Li Lu will go our separate ways. I am going to move out. I'm leaving so I can be alone. I will let you know more in the days to come."

"Why?" I asked, still drowsy from jet lag. "I don't understand."

"He is asking for his freedom," Li Lu said. "See, it is easy to go out on the streets asking for freedom from your leaders. It's different when you are the one being asked. If you truly believe in democracy, you should let him go."

"I love democracy," Feng said. "With democracy, I can make my own choices. I love freedom," he said with boyish glee. "Long live freedom."

He walked out of the room.

Da Wen looked at me with compassion. "Let him go," she said. "Men always act like men. Let him cool off for a few days, and maybe he'll return to his senses."

With Li Lu's blessing, Feng departed. I was stunned. But I was soon to receive an even bigger surprise.

An FDC staff member brought over an extensive article from a Hong Kong newspaper by a reporter who claimed she had scooped the story of our escape. The story contained photos and details to back up her claim. Then I discovered the reporter was none other than the female companion of the French diplomat who had accompanied us on our flight to freedom. She'd heard about our escape and managed to sneak aboard the flight.

Her seemingly heroic effort won her a journalism prize but put me in a precarious position. The June 8 tape I'd made as witness to the massacre had turned me into a missing media personality, and I had been nominated for the Nobel Peace Prize. Along with the Chinese government, hundreds of journalists had been hunting for me for ten long months. The media frenzy was fueled by an award offered to the journalist who found out where I was hiding. Rumors had continually surfaced that I'd been arrested or killed. Now word was out—complete with pictures—that I'd escaped.

I was hoping for time to recover from my grueling journey, but that was not to be. Hundreds of interview requests clogged the answering machine at the office of the Federation for a Democratic China and anywhere else the media thought they might reach me. People were hungry to know what had happened during those ten months: Who had protected us? Was any part of the Chinese government involved? Where had we hidden? How did we get out? How did the rescue effort work? Who saved us? What was going to happen to China's democracy movement? Fragile in health, sleep deprived, and emotionally shell-shocked, I was utterly unprepared to face the wonders of the free-world media.

With the advice and assistance of a staff volunteer at the FDC, I decided to hold a press conference and forgo individual interviews.

"Beware of the media," Wan Runnan, the head of the Federation, told me. "They are a machine. They will tear you down just as fast as they will build you up. The higher they build you up, the steeper will be your fall." I felt I had a responsibility to represent the overseas democracy movement and restore the respect it needed for continuing support.

The burden of this duty only made it more difficult for me to rest and recover my strength.

As the hour of the press conference grew near, Feng returned, along with a former high school classmate with whom he'd reunited. Feng looked more at ease, as if he'd begun to reconcile himself to this strange new world of freedom. His friend, however, was critical of the overseas democracy movement and urged us to keep our mouths shut. He told us we were in way over our heads and should go off somewhere to study and stay out of the spotlight. Feng really drank this up, and it became the basis of how he operated.

I, on the other hand, was infuriated. How could he say we shouldn't speak up for friends such as Xiong Yan, Zhou Fengsuo, and Wang Dan, who were still in jail, others who had been killed, and those who were still in hiding? I felt we needed to show them that the rest of the world had not forgotten them. I remembered how hearing the news that others had escaped had brought me such joy and hope during my days in hiding. I spoke about this, but couldn't seem to change Feng's mind. He said he would not answer reporters' questions. A huge gulf was building between us.

The next day, Feng and I walked together into the pressroom, but I ended up doing most of the talking. After the press conference, which lasted several hours, our translator told us it was a great success. I felt relieved. I had made no major blunders. I had not let anyone down. Now I could rest and repair my health. I could finally become the ordinary wife I had always wanted to be. I could make dinner for Feng and enjoy a nice weekend with him. I could enjoy the simple things of life, of which I had so long been deprived.

It was a Friday night. I was looking forward to dinner and a movie together, like a normal married couple. But the moment dinner was served, Feng was summoned to the telephone. By the time he returned, the food was cold, but he looked happy, even excited.

When I asked who had called, he told me it was a woman he had

spent time with at Tiananmen Square. "I could tell just by her voice that she wanted me, and I wanted her, too," he said with determination.

I felt the now-familiar stab of pain as Feng went right on talking. "I'm not having dinner here," he said. "I'm leaving."

"Leaving?" I said. "Where are you going?" I wanted to say some other things, but the words stuck in my throat. Instead, I watched as Feng walked out, taking with him the rest of my dreams. Our dinner remained cold and untouched on the table.

I didn't want to sit alone in the hotel room, so I went for a walk along the streets of Paris. But it seemed that everywhere I looked, I saw happy couples hugging, laughing, and enjoying the beautiful evening. I felt completely alone in this new, unfamiliar city and this strange, new world called freedom. Just a day or two before, newspapers around the world had published happy pictures of Feng and me after our escape. Now as I listened to the sorrowful notes of a flute played by a homeless woman at a subway station, I felt I was one step away from being just like her.

A few days later, I was invited to stay with an elderly French couple in the south of France to recuperate. Feng came too, and Li Lu and Da Wen came down from Paris to join us. After eating lunch the first day, the four of us took a walk to the oceanside, but Feng immediately announced that he had to go back to Paris right away. Sorrow and pain washed over me as I watched my husband depart. While Li Lu and Da Wen drove him to the airport, I sat alone on a rock overlooking the ocean. I had finally achieved freedom, but with Feng gone, I had lost all purpose in living. My family was far away, in a place where I could not return. Big Brother and his friends and contacts who had saved me were no longer with me to protect me. I had never felt more alone. At that moment, the struggle I had gone through in the quest for freedom seemed to lose all importance. I would never have found the strength to achieve it if I had known in advance what this so-called freedom was all about. As I watched the waves crashing on the rocks below, I had a sud-

den impulse to jump in and end my life then and there. To me, all was gone. All was lost. All was over. It was finished.

A voice came into my mind: *If you die now, what will happen to your parents when they find out? You are their hope. Live for them; be strong.*

As the waves continued to crash onto the rocks, emotionless, unceasing, I could no longer hold in all the pain. Like a little child, I cried out, "Mama, I miss you! Mama, I want you! Mama, please hold me! Mama—!"

The clouds and the sky responded with silence. My mother was more than five thousand miles away—unreachable.

When Li Lu and Da Wen returned from the airport, they had decided to drive back to Paris. I had no reason to stay by myself, so I went with them. We rode in silence.

In Paris, Li Lu spoke to Feng, who sounded like his old happy self. That night, I took the Metro to visit him. The train had long since left the station before he showed up to get me.

Feng was staying with a French Chinese family, and it soon became evident he was attracted to the couple's seventeen-year-old daughter. I later learned that the mother of the family was a spy for the Chinese government—a retired spy, as she claimed. After staying overnight, I returned to my hotel convinced it was time for me to learn how to live on my own and develop my independence. Painful as it might be, I decided I would endure like a good Buddhist.

I met some interesting people, including an American diplomat who talked to me at length before a trip I planned to take to the United States for ceremonies marking the anniversary of Tiananmen. He was professional and serious. "We've been looking for a leader of the movement," he told me. "I think you may be it. The president hasn't met with any other dissidents."

I felt honored, but once again I began to feel the burden of responsibility.

May 22 was Feng's and my second wedding anniversary. I was hoping with all my heart he would remember the day and join me so we could celebrate together. I waited all morning in my hotel room, but the phone never rang, and Feng never showed up. Finally I decided to celebrate by myself, and I went sightseeing on the Seine.

My trip to the United States was rapidly approaching. I needed to obtain my visa. The day after our anniversary, I met Feng outside the US Embassy, where we were going to have our French travel documents stamped. After we'd obtained our visas, I asked Feng gently, "Do you remember what day it was yesterday?" He stared at me blankly, then turned and walked away, without a word.

Confused, I took a few steps to follow him but then decided to return to my hotel instead. I'd grown accustomed to his unpredictable ways and had settled into a routine of my own. Later, Feng called to tell me he'd be coming by in the morning to pick up some of his things. "Don't expect me to stay," he said.

"Okay." I felt I should no longer expect anything from Feng if I didn't want to be hurt by him. Still, I did have a question. "How come you walked off like that without a word?"

"I thought you would follow me," he said.

"In my heart," I said, "there are two people I live for. One is my father. The other is you. Is there anyone like that who lives in your heart?" I don't know where I found the courage to ask this question.

"No, no one," Feng shot back without hesitation, and the phone went dead.

I had tried my best to show Feng I loved him. My involvement in the student movement had been for him. During my ten months in hiding, my one dream was to get out of China and live a happy life with him. But as soon as we got to Paris, he fell in love with a teenage girl. I blamed myself for not being pretty enough or smart enough or wise enough to understand his world. But now the answer was staring me in the face: Maybe he simply didn't love me. Maybe he never had and never would.

As painful as this realization was, it was also a great relief. There was nothing wrong with me for having loved him.

27

THE NEW WORLD

I WAS UNPREPARED for the blizzard of publicity that hit me when I arrived in the United States. I wonder if any human being could remain at peace in the face of such an onslaught. For me, it was a shattering assault on my fragile state of mind and health. I arrived friendless, with a broken marriage and lingering exhaustion, to find I had been scheduled, almost immediately, for a seven-city tour of the United States sponsored by the Tom Lantos Congressional Human Rights Commission.

The tour began in New York with a series of visits and public appearances. Everywhere I went, mobs of people awaited with cameras flashing. "Here comes the Goddess of Democracy!" they shouted.

I began to vomit during the car rides after each visit. On the morning of June 3, as I flew from New York to Washington, DC, I took one look at my itinerary for the next few days and immediately threw up into an airsickness bag.

By the middle of the following day, which was June 4, the one-year anniversary of the massacre, I really felt sick. I couldn't eat. I kept having dry heaves. Liao Da Wen finally took me to see a doctor.

"You're dehydrated and have a fever," the doctor told me. "You should do no more work today. Just lie down and take it easy for the rest of the afternoon and evening."

"I can't do that, Doctor," I said weakly. "It's my responsibility—"

"Your responsibility is to take care of yourself," he said. "If you were my daughter, I would tell you not to go anywhere. Just lie down, go to bed. You'll feel better tomorrow."

As I lay in the clinic and looked up at the white ceiling, my body felt as light as a feather floating free in the air. Away from the noise of traffic and the flashing cameras, the clinic had a familiar smell and quiet calm that reminded me of home.

"No, no," Da Wen said to the doctor in a hurried voice. "She has to go. Her schedule this afternoon is full. She can't let them down."

"You are going to kill this girl," the doctor said as he walked out.

Before I left, Da Wen put a big bottle of water in my hand. "Chai Ling is a symbol now," she said. "If you use this symbol the right way, you can get a lot done for good."

The medicine I took and the water I drank made me feel a little better. I stepped into the car waiting to take me to the next place. I was on the road again.

That night, at the June Fourth memorial ceremony, I sat in the crowd with Feng beside me. The woman who had called him in Paris after our press conference sat on the other side of him. I felt sad and worn out. Just then, one of the organizers handed me a microphone and asked me to make a speech. The lights blinded me, and my colleagues and Feng disappeared into the darkness. I could feel the resentment of the people with whom I had worked on the Square and the enormous distance fame and attention had opened between us. I also heard a voice rise within me, saying, *Speak for the voiceless; it is your responsibility.* I remembered what had happened one year earlier, and I began to speak.

After the ceremony, as I waited for a car to take me to my hotel, a young Chinese man holding a baby said to me, "Do you understand why I can't join the movement? I have to take care of my wife and child. But you! You must continue the fight for democracy."

These words were like a cold knife blade cutting straight to the wound in my heart. *How about my right to be a woman?* I wanted to say.

To be a wife and a mother? To be loved and cared for? The pressure from the media and the tremendous responsibility I felt to speak for those left dead at Tiananmen Square had become a cross I would bear at the expense of my own needs.

In my interactions with the Western world, I was amazed at how easy it was to meet with American officials, especially after what the Chinese students had endured a year earlier just to have a dialogue with our government. What we got for our efforts were tanks and gunfire. In America, by contrast, officials seemed pleased when people wanted to meet with them and talk about the government.

"If I criticize the president," one congressman told me, "the worst that can happen is the White House won't give me a dinner invitation." Life here seemed simpler, gentler, kinder.

At the end of my Washington visit, I met with a national security adviser and Vice President Dan Quayle.

Da Wen was happy. For her, the trip had been like a fairy tale, and each door we'd knocked on had opened magically. Everyone seemed happy. I watched in silence.

Many people find glamour in the spotlight, but to me it was sheer torment. Everywhere I went, it seemed, I had to address the century-old question about how China was going to make the transition to a more open, modern society. And when I least expected it, people peppered me with hostile questions. "How come everyone died except you?" stands out most in my mind.

I was glad the media hadn't picked up on the trouble I had with Feng. I did not want our separation to become the focus of public attention. Several student leaders' love affairs had created scandals that seemed to have damaged the democracy movement. I could not let my failing marriage overshadow the truth about the suffering in China.

After my seven-city tour, I returned to New York, to the apartment that Li Lu, Da Wen, and many others shared. After dinner we chatted.

"In life, only a few people truly matter," Li Lu announced. "Only a

few people are worth making a sacrifice for. Most people don't matter. Do whatever you need to do with them."

I was shocked. At first I was flattered to think I was part of the small circle of people who mattered. Then I thought, *What would happen to me if I were not part of this small circle but part of a great mass of unimportant souls?*

Li Lu must have read my mind. "That's bad," he said, turning to me. "I've said too much."

I changed the subject.

"Now that the first phase of work in America is over," I said, "I'd like to talk with you about moving forward. How are we going to rebuild our leadership group to lead the overseas movement? I've also been thinking about applying to Princeton to study international relations and politics."

Li Lu burst out laughing.

"What's so funny?" I said.

Li Lu looked at me with amusement. "What part of it don't you understand?" he said. "It's over. When the massacre happened, it was over. Like the story in *Les Misérables*, the revolution is dead! Going to Princeton? to study politics? a naive little brain like yours?"

Li Lu laughed again and left the room.

I was confused. The Li Lu I thought I had known at Tiananmen did not match up with the Li Lu who had just ridiculed me.

If the democracy movement and the bond we shared surviving life and death together aren't lasting and true, what is?

The new, free world had just become more confusing.

Feng joined us for the weekend after running around the country on his own for a few weeks. We all went to the country home of a friend of Mary Daly's, a new acquaintance of ours. It was situated on a beautiful lake.

Almost immediately after we arrived, Li Lu jumped into the water. I soon followed. I had the sensation of utter freedom I'd experienced that day with Wang in The Sea of Good Fortune in Yuan Ming Yuan Park. For a few moments I was able to forget the torment in my mind.

That night, for the first time in a long time, Feng and I were together as husband and wife. The romance of a moonlit night and my celebratory mood at the end of a seven-city speaking tour made me drop my guard.

On the train back to New York City the next day, a deep anger rose within me. Why had I done that with him? Was I too weak to stand the loneliness? Had I fallen once again under the spell of his charm, his sweetness? Had I forgotten how much I'd suffered in Paris—one day happy, the next bereft? Did I want the past to continue into the present? I was only just beginning to learn how to be strong on my own, independent of that painful attachment.

Later, when Feng came into the room where I was staying and began to undress as if everything was fine between us, the sense of reproach I felt toward myself burst out.

"Don't think you can sleep in another woman's bed and then come back to me whenever you want," I said. "It's not going to work."

Before I'd even finished speaking, Feng slapped my face.

"You've insulted me," he said.

Instantly, a red-hot rage rose inside me. "How dare you do that to me after all I've gone through with you!"

All those days and months of patiently waiting, praying, and silently enduring, of giving and hoping to receive, combined into a single resolve. Screaming at Feng, I tried to push him away. But he began pummeling me with his fists. He was still beating me, grabbing my hair, and punching my face when Li Lu came in and pulled us apart.

"Let's go, Old Feng," he said. "You need to sleep in a different room tonight."

As Li Lu steered him away, Feng continued to shout, "She insulted me! She insulted me! I don't care what kind of celebrity she thinks she is, she's still married to me, and I can beat my wife whenever I want."

"This is America," Da Wen said firmly. "You can't hit a woman, even if she is your wife. It's a human rights violation. If you do that again, we'll have to call the police."

Feng stopped shouting and left the room.

Da Wen sat beside me on the bed. "Are you okay?"

I nodded as the tears flowed down my face.

"Can you believe these men?" Da Wen continued. "They fight for democracy during the day and beat their wives at night."

After she left me alone in the pale light of the evening, I curled up on my bed and sobbed. But in my heart I had never felt so calm and settled about this relationship.

As my tears gradually subsided, I looked back at all the key events I'd shared with Feng, as if I were an outsider looking at someone else's life. Moments that had once seemed so bruising no longer bothered me, and I was able to look at the sweet moments with peace.

The monsoon season had ended at last.

———————

I went to stay with a friend in New Mexico. While there I was able to telephone my family in China. That must have been quite a phone bill! After that I went back to Paris to await word from Princeton's China Initiative, where I had applied to be a visiting scholar.

In Paris, while living alone in a hotel, I discovered I was pregnant with Feng's child. This was the baby I had once yearned to have. Yet it was coming at the most vulnerable time in my life. Feng told me that if we had the baby, he would raise it with his French girlfriend. I could not imagine bringing up a child in that kind of arrangement, to suffer the same unpredictable heartbreak I'd experienced with Feng, who one day would tell me he loved me and the next day would ask, "What is love?" In my desperation and despair, I didn't know if either the child or I could survive if I continued to be in any relationship with Feng. Many years later, Feng told me he had wanted me to get pregnant so I wouldn't leave him.

At that point, I still hadn't the slightest idea that a fetus was already a life. I only believed I had no other choice. Some friends in Paris made arrangements for me at the hospital and convinced me it was the best thing to do. I went in, and the doctors gave me full anesthesia. When I woke up, the baby was gone. I felt so empty. As I write about it now, I still feel a deep sadness. That child would be more than twenty years old now.

I was invited to attend an important conference in Oslo, Norway, titled "The Anatomy of Hate." Many world leaders and Nobel laureates were also in attendance.

I had lived in a country so isolated from the rest of the world that when I found myself seated next to former president Jimmy Carter, I wasn't sure who he was.

"What do you do?" I asked him, just to be on the safe side.

"I build houses for homeless people," he replied.

"I mean before that, what did you do?"

"I was president of the United States."

Václav Havel, the newly elected president of the Czech Republic, invited me to visit him in Prague. After all his sacrifice as a young man during the Prague Spring, it was encouraging that twenty years later a new democratic society had been born. It strengthened my hope for China.

Nelson Mandela had recently been released after twenty-seven years in jail, and he spoke eloquently about issues related to race hatred. Later he made remarkable progress in South Africa through the Truth and Reconciliation Commission he initiated.

When it was my turn to speak, I said we are born with a good sense of right and wrong, and as children we know the difference between love and hate. When we are brainwashed, however, and hate takes on a moral justification—for example, "It is right to hate an enemy of the state"—the boundary between love and hate becomes blurred. Violence and hatred accelerate because we aren't equipped with the necessary constraints. This was the essence of the Tiananmen massacre, when the leadership and the army jumped the boundary with the excuse that they were "protecting the country" to cover their wrongdoing. It never would have happened, I said, if the Chinese people had been allowed to listen to the truth instead of government propaganda. I concluded by saying that freedom of speech and freedom of the press are essential foils to the free reign of pure hatred.

THE AMERICAN DREAM MEETS CHINESE REALITY

28

LIFE AFTER TIANANMEN

I WENT TO Princeton at the invitation of the China Initiative program, which had awarded me a visiting scholarship. The China Initiative was the inspiration of a man named John Elliott, who happened to be visiting the celebrated Princeton professor of East Asian Studies Yu Yingshih and his wife on the night of June 4, 1989. Together they witnessed the Tiananmen massacre on TV. The horror of this experience, quickened by the outrage and frustration he witnessed in his Chinese friends, impelled Elliott to donate an initial grant of one million dollars to Princeton to establish a program to provide educational scholarships for student refugees. This fund was administered by Professor Yu, who set up the China Initiative to give refuge to scholars and intellectuals who fled China after Tiananmen. As a refugee who received a China Initiative scholarship, I can attest to the great value it provided its numerous beneficiaries, who could come to Princeton to rest and resettle themselves after the terrible shock of persecution and flight.

Six months after I escaped to freedom, I had an apartment of my own. This was a huge milestone. For sixteen months, I had been living

in other people's houses. Now, at last, I had a key to my own home. Mrs. Yu, who had two daughters of her own, became like a mother to me. Through her love and care, I had a place where I could find the solitude I needed to heal. The feeling I had that first night, when I experienced a sense that once again I was in control of my life, came as a revelation.

I knew I wasn't the only Chinese refugee in America beginning the struggle to recover, but this awareness did not alleviate the long, lonely, difficult process of rebuilding my life in a foreign land and culture. Unlike many of my compatriots who came to this country to start a new life, I had to start by learning to say no to people who continually asked me to give speeches or help organize events. I needed to clear some space in which to grow.

One year after the massacre, the overseas democracy movement had fallen into a state of confusion. Though many Chinese in exile wanted to help the movement forward, this desire became secondary to the pressing business of survival. If you've ever experienced adjusting to a new culture, you know how difficult it can be. For me, almost everything was different—language, culture, politics, grocery shopping. When you can't speak the language, when you have no family or friends to connect you to the community, it undermines your confidence, no matter how strong you are. You perceive the world as a child does—overwhelming, strange, and big—but you must continue to project the image of maturity, confidence, and leadership.

Even though China—our homes, families, people, food, and language—had been stripped from us, we were expected, somehow, to fix our country from overseas. How could anyone lead a movement and win in those circumstances? Still, there were people who argued otherwise.

I kept hearing, "With Chai Ling as your symbol, you can do a lot of good."

Meanwhile, I was also wrestling with survivor's guilt, which made me say no to any activity that seemed difficult. When I visited the Vietnam Veterans Memorial in Washington, DC, I was drawn to the statue of the three soldiers, representing the survivors of war, who gaze, unmoving, at the memorial wall, as if searching for their own names on it. I imagined

how they would feel if they were suddenly airlifted to another planet, without any sense of whom they could trust, even among their own comrades, and then were told, "Now, don't stop to mourn or rebuild, because you have to win another war." That was the type of pressure I felt.

Because I had been nominated for the Nobel Peace Prize, the spotlight was on me to carry the torch for democracy in China; but the foundation, the support, and the organizations were crumbling. I had never seen so much bitterness and enmity among people with whom I was supposedly in alliance, yet I felt it was my responsibility to fill the gaps and accomplish the impossible. Like the ballet dancer in *The Red Shoes*, I couldn't stop dancing, even when I was too exhausted to go on.

Once I was settled at Princeton, I went to see a social worker, who promised to keep everything I said confidential.

"I hate certain people," I said.

"Why?" she said with evident surprise.

"They always ask for more," I said. "No matter how much I give, it's never enough."

I started telling her what I'd been through, and it all poured forth: how I'd lost my family and my home; how the Chinese man holding the baby in Washington, DC, had reacted to me after my speech; how the author of a recent article had called me a traitor because I'd gone to a dance club at the end of my speaking tour.

The social worker listened quietly.

"How about your husband?" she said. "Do you hate him?"

"I don't know," I replied. "It's sort of all the same. No matter how much I gave to him it was never enough." I told her about my marriage and how I had always helped Feng. I told her about his recent act of violence and other things I'd been afraid to tell anyone until that moment.

"In this country," she announced, firmly and clearly, "we call that abuse."

"Abuse." I repeated the word. Her voice was not loud, but to me it sounded like a burst of thunder and echoed back and forth in my mind.

Until that moment I did not know Feng was doing something wrong, even though it did not feel right. In the culture I grew up in, a woman must obey her father, and then her husband when she marries, and then her son if her husband dies. A woman is never given a chance to be her own person.

Feng had even quoted 1 Corinthians 13:4-5—"Love is patient, love is kind. It does not envy, it does not boast, it is not proud. It does not dishonor others, it is not self-seeking, it is not easily angered, it keeps no record of wrongs"—to imply that everything was my fault, that I didn't love enough. It was eye opening for someone to point out that the way he treated me was abusive. The social worker's words altered the way I looked at my past from that time on.

Sometime that first autumn Feng paid a visit to the United States. He wanted to join me at Princeton and start the simple life he'd always wanted. I did not know how to respond. Too much had happened. Was I to believe that Feng had changed, or was this the same old back-and-forth? I had almost forgotten how charming he could be. Mrs. Yu suggested we give it some time. "Let him settle here on his own," she said. "If this turns out to be something he still wants, then you can talk about it again." That was good, motherly advice. I relayed this message to Feng, and the next day he flew back to France. So the decision was made for me. Although part of me still hoped Feng and I could start over again and truly realize our dreams of making it in America, his actions brought clarity and a definitive end to our marriage. He would never change.

I applied to Princeton's Woodrow Wilson School to study politics and international relations. I was determined to find a cure for the ills of modern China. During the application process, I was required to write an essay on why I was qualified to study in the field. I was suddenly unable to put pen to paper. I was blocked.

That evening, as I worked on my application, I happened to be with the director of the China Initiative. She saw I was laboring.

"What's the matter?" she asked. "Why are you having so much trouble with the application?"

I struggled to find an answer. Finally, I broke down and told her.

"It's Li Lu," I said. "He laughed at the idea when I told him I wanted to study politics and international relations. He said, 'With your naive mind, how could you ever expect to understand things like that?'" Tears poured down my cheeks as I spoke. "I felt so naive because I hadn't foreseen the massacre, and so many people died. Maybe I should just give up. Maybe I was never supposed to do this."

The director knelt in front of me, her eyes wide with shock.

"How can you think this way, Chai Ling?" she said. "How could you believe such nonsense? How can you let such lies block your vision? *You* were the one who gave the hunger strike speech, not Li Lu. *You* were the commander in chief at Tiananmen, not Li Lu. *You* were the one who gave testimony on June 8 when you were on the run, not Li Lu. People say all kinds of things out of envy and other motives. Can't you see he was putting you down because you threaten him?

"Don't let anyone take away your confidence," she continued. "You are who you are, and that's why good people love you. I never would have given up a high-paying job to join the Initiative if I had not heard the speech you gave on June 8. I joined because I believe in you. I believe in helping all of you to help China. Now wipe away those tears, and let's finish the application."

Once again, when I was at a low ebb, an angel had appeared to pull me out of my despair and paralysis. I finished the essay quickly and sent my application. Word soon came that I had been accepted. I also received a generous scholarship, as did many other students in the program.

One night as I was just settling in to the discipline and rhythm of my new work as a graduate student, I woke up in horror from a terrible dream in which I saw two coffins burning in a fire.

Instantly I feared for the lives of my mother and grandmother. "It cannot be, it cannot be," I said to myself as I lay in the dark with my heart pounding. "Mom is so young, and so is Grandma. It must be my imagination working overtime."

I turned on the light and called home to China. My father told me in his usual, hesitant voice that everything was fine. He managed to reassure me, and I went back to sleep.

The next night, I visited a friend who had just returned from China. She had brought me some pictures of my family and some that had been taken when I was a child.

"So you know about your mom," she said, unexpectedly.

"What do you mean? I spoke to my dad last night, and he said she was fine."

My friend looked startled. "You'd better talk to him again," she said.

I raced back to Princeton and called home. This time my aunt answered; she told me to call back the next day to talk to my sister.

When I finally got through to my sister, she told me gently that my mother had gotten sick, but they had been able to treat her; she had gotten better and come home from the hospital.

As she continued with a long, drawn-out story about my mother's health, I became impatient. "So what happened?" I asked.

My sister was quiet for a moment and then began to cry. "What happened . . . ? Mom died."

"No—!" I screamed. Despite the premonition from my dream, I was not prepared for the news. Mom had died a month before, and Grandma soon after.

"Why didn't you tell me?" I said, sobbing into the phone.

"What could you have done?" my little sister said.

"I could have flown home, one last time, just to see them."

"That's exactly what Dad was worried about," my sister said. "He was afraid you would do something foolish and get yourself arrested. What good would that do?"

"So my dream was telling the truth," I said. "She was saying good-bye to me, in my dream."

When I hung up the phone, all I could do was pull the covers over my head and scream. In one stroke, I had lost two of my nearest and dearest loved ones.

"Why?" I screamed out to God, though I wasn't sure he existed. "Why? Why? Yes, you gave me freedom, but why did you take *everything else* away from me? What have I done wrong to deserve all this?"

During the midterm break, I moved in with a friend to avoid being alone. But I had no strength to do anything. I just stayed in bed and cried myself to sleep. When I woke up, I cried again.

Finally my friend had had enough. "Are you finished now?" my friend asked me one evening. "Your mom died not because you did anything wrong or because she wanted you to be crushed. She wanted you to be strong, to overcome. So get up and show her that her life was not in vain."

It took a while for the message to sink in; but the next morning, I got out of bed, washed away the tearstains, and was ready to face the day. But one question still lingered in my mind: What would happen to the rest of us who had gone on living? Would we all be crushed?

"No!" I declared. "I will not be crushed. I will not lie down like they hope I will. I will fight back. I will rescue the rest of my family before the government can destroy them. They will not win! I am not giving up. I will not be crushed." From that point on, I became focused and determined. I've always been at my best when I'm in action.

29

AMERICAN DREAM

When I first came to America, I didn't feel like a survivor. I felt more like a dead person having an out-of-body experience. America was a strange, new country, and I felt disconnected, isolated, and overwhelmed. I had learned a bit of English in college, but I'd forgotten most of it. And I couldn't speak it. The way we'd learned to pass tests such as the TOEFL was by memorizing the dictionary.

By the time I graduated from Princeton in 1993, I had learned a great deal. I had purchased a car and driven to Florida and back, participated in a work-study program at the United Nations, and interned on Capitol Hill for Senators Edward Kennedy of Massachusetts and Malcolm Wallop of Wyoming.

In 1992 I attended the Republican convention and the Democratic convention, where Li Lu and I were together at the podium to celebrate and affirm Bill Clinton's support for human rights in China. I later went to the White House Rose Garden to watch President Clinton sign a Most Favored Nation Treaty with China, replete with human rights caveats. I also went to Taiwan, where taxi drivers and

other people recognized me—mostly by my voice—and showed me warmth and love.

By the day of my graduation, I felt confident and whole again. My life in America had become rich with activity, friendships, discovery, and joy. From my experiences at the UN and the Senate, I was already fed up with government bureaucracy, so I pursued opportunities in the private sector. I sent applications to several management consulting and investment banking firms. I was not prepared for some of the responses I received.

More than once I was told, "The partners discussed your qualifications, which are excellent, but they're concerned that hiring you might endanger the Chinese portion of our business. Therefore, we're not able to extend an offer at this time." Despite my hope for freedom and a fresh start, it soon became apparent I could not just leave the past behind. Nevertheless, I eventually received two offers—one in Boston, the other in New York—both starting in the fall.

On the flight back from one of the interviews, with a job offer in hand, I felt a rush of euphoria. After all the years of studying and volunteer work, I was finally worth a decent salary, and I could be independent and self-sufficient. The little black hole of self-doubt disappeared, and I felt accepted in mainstream society. I was no longer a dissident; I was a young professional. Now it was simply a matter of deciding which offer to accept.

Eager to apply my new understanding of public policy, I moved to Washington, DC, for the summer to work with a foundation dedicated to moving China toward a Taiwanese model of democracy, with free media and local elections. The summer passed quickly, and the day soon arrived when I had to decide whether to accept one of the job offers or continue my work for China.

To make the China program work, I needed funding, so I approached the new director of the National Endowment for Democracy and told her my plans. I said, "I have a good job offer in Boston, and I plan to volunteer my time for the China foundation, but I need some grant money to fund the program."

Without hesitation the director replied, "Our programs are focused

inside China now, not with overseas Chinese. There's no funding available. Go take the job."

The next morning I flew to Boston and accepted a junior associate position with a prestigious consulting firm. A few weeks later, I was on my way to a beautiful resort on Cape Cod for intensive training. With five other young professionals from around the world, I went to class from 8:00 to 5:00 each day, followed by a real-life case study after dinner. Our assignment was to work together to figure out the problem and present our solution the next morning to the teaching partners.

Although some complained that the workload was grueling, I instantly felt at home. After years of feeling out of control, the exacting schedule felt routine and normal. I enjoyed the structure and rigor of the program, the challenge to push myself and work hard, and the opportunity to work alongside others with similar talents. As I worked to improve my teamwork, leadership, problem-solving, and organizational abilities, I knew I was made to thrive in this fast-paced, demanding environment.

When the training ended, I flew back to Princeton to prepare for the move to Boston. By then I also needed to update my visa, so I asked for a few weeks off to get everything squared away. On the plane to New Jersey, I felt on top of the world. With a stable job, I had a better chance of getting my father and siblings out of China to join me in the United States, and I was looking forward to writing a book about Tiananmen Square and how to save China. For the first time in a long time, I felt back in control. All the trauma and madness were behind me, and the future looked bright with promise.

When I returned to Boston with my renewed papers, I was ready to get to work. Instead I was greeted by yet another setback. While I was gone, an officer in the company's Hong Kong office had expressed concern about my hiring. He said if I continued working for the firm, he might be arrested on a business trip to Beijing. A few months after I had turned down another job to take the one in Boston, the company wanted to rescind its offer. I was devastated.

During the next six months, as I continued to negotiate with the company in Boston and waited for their final decision, I explored other options in other cities with other firms. But jobs were either not offered or were not what I wanted to pursue. The days dragged on, with my bank account dwindling and rent checks going out every month. I became fearful I'd soon be living on the street. I knew nobody in Boston and had nothing to do during the day except wait for a decision. It was the loneliest time of my life in exile.

When I graduated from Princeton, I thought my journey to freedom was complete. I had the education and the job—I had even done the training and loved it. But now my career was being taken away before it even started. I knew if I missed the opportunity to start consulting at an entry level, I would never have a chance to pursue that career track. I knew it would be hard to find a similar job because these firms are structured to recruit only new graduates. The longer I was without work, the worse my chances became. How would I explain the gap? And how did I know the next company wouldn't also balk at hiring me with my worldwide notoriety?

The worst part was realizing my Tiananmen nightmare wasn't over. If the fear and repression could find me and imprison me in free America, then I would never be truly safe or free anywhere. The persecution hadn't ended when I left China; it had only become more subtle, but every bit as vicious and effective. I had already lost my country, my sense of identity, and my network of friends. If I couldn't hold a job and have a dependable income, I would lose my family, too, because I could never keep the promise I'd made to rescue them from China. I had never realized that freedom was such a hard goal to achieve.

The ultimate irony was that I was rejected because of my involvement in a movement to improve China's overall human rights conditions. In 1997 Hong Kong would be returned to China, and unless the human rights movement continued and succeeded, the people in Hong Kong would suffer too, and the Hong Kong officer's constitutional rights would be deprived by the Chinese regime. Instead of spreading fear, he should have stood with me in solidarity.

The stress during this time was enormous—and it was all on me. Gone was the media spotlight. Gone were the comrades I had rallied

with on the Square. The pressure manifested itself in a sleeping disorder characterized by nightmares in which I relived the horror of the crackdown and the emotions of being hunted down. I awoke feeling cornered, convinced the police were approaching my door to arrest me.

———————

Many years later I learned that my case was no small matter for the Boston company, either. By honoring or dishonoring their offer to a young associate like me, they would set an important precedent defining their important corporate values.

In a high-level meeting at the company's headquarters, the partners discussed the situation. After acknowledging the safety and business concerns expressed by the Hong Kong officer and noting that several of their competitors had not offered me a job for the same reason, they agreed they would not have made me an offer if they had anticipated the problem. Still, they *had* made me an offer, and what was at stake now was the integrity of their corporate values.

One partner said they should let me go since they were the only firm that had hired me. That argument was put to rest by the news that I had turned down an offer from a similar firm in order to take this job. Another partner said it was simply a business decision—and they were in business to make a profit, not to support a cause. "Whatever happened in China is their problem, not ours."

Finally, a partner who had recently returned after several years in Asia, spoke. "Let's think about where we've come from as a country," he said. "All our ancestors came here as refugees like Chai Ling, driven by political, economic, or social pressures. Our founding fathers fought a war to achieve liberty. If we abandon Chai Ling for her courageous work in China, will we be ashamed of our conduct as a company? Is it only business and profit we're pursuing every day and not the core values that define us as a nation? There's no way we can let her go."

The other partners mulled over this latest argument. After further discussion, Barry, the managing director, said, "I agree. We will not give up our principles even in the pursuit of business and profit. We will honor our offer and deal with the China matter in another way."

While I waited for a decision, I met a successful attorney who volunteered to give me advice. He told me to be patient and not talk to the media, as others had suggested.

"The folks in Boston are a successful and powerful group," he said. "If you take your story to the media, it will make some influential people nervous. It's not good to burn bridges. Those things have a way of coming back to bite you. Go back and negotiate with them again. They extended a valid offer and should honor it."

Around this same time, I received word that the Clinton Administration had helped negotiate my family's release from China. Now I really needed to know whether I could have my job back so I could support myself and my family. I went to see the firm's HR director again and sensed the situation had changed. Though it was still a long time before I got a definitive answer, I held on to that glimmer of hope.

Then one day he called and said, "Come in tomorrow and sign the paperwork. You'll work here under a different name."

I was thrilled. This was the end of a long, hard battle. In many ways it reminded me of the experience of going back repeatedly to the campus security department to get my watch back. When I arrived at the office, the HR director had a few conditions to review with me.

"While you're working here," he said, "we don't expect you'll continue your high-profile work for Chinese democracy, for obvious reasons. When your work here is done, we don't expect you'll mention to any media outlet that you've ever worked here."

I looked at him in stunned silence. How could I agree not to speak out on behalf of the Chinese people? It seemed like something that might be imposed on a person being released from a Chinese prison. What I was signing was not a legally enforceable contract, and I'm sure I could have argued for my constitutional right to free speech, but I didn't have the strength to fight another battle. With my family soon to arrive in America, I needed a steady job to provide for them and to spare them the suffering I had undergone as a new immigrant. Swallowing the pain and humiliation, I took the pen and signed "Elizabeth Lee."

The long wait and the struggle for justice made me appreciate the

job even more. But I didn't realize the damage it had done to my spirit. At work I became a different person. Changing one's name is never a casual thing, and burying my passion for China changed who I was. The joy I'd experienced during training had long since evaporated. I sealed up my emotions and immersed myself in the task at hand, like I had in high school when I was preparing to test into college and run away from my parents. I was assigned to a turnaround case at a major computer firm in Massachusetts, which meant I didn't have to travel much. During the day, I enjoyed research and learning the high-tech industry. At night, I worked on my writing. My life was settling into a normal rhythm.

30

CULTURE SHOCK

"I AM COMING TO YOU NOW. I will see you soon." Over the phone came the excited voice of my little sister, whom I had not seen in five years. She was on her way to America.

The night before Little Sister's arrival, I could not fall asleep. It was hard to believe I would finally be reunited with my family. At the airport, many other families were waiting as well. I realized I was looking into the unknown. What would Little Sister look like? Would she be the same sweet, shy, and timid girl I once knew?

The gate for the new arrivals opened, and before I could see anything, I heard a joyful cry.

"Jie Jie—Big Sister!" A little, girlish figure flew out of the gate and into my arms. "Big Sister, I saw you from far away, and I recognized you immediately." We hugged for a long time, our laughter and tears mingling.

When I was able to step back and look at her, I saw she had grown taller—in fact, slightly taller than me—and her face looked more mature. I told her how worried I had been that she would be changed

into a stranger. She laughed and said, "It's me, Big Sister. We've been through a lot, and I may have changed, but touch my face. It's me."

That night we stayed up late, catching up on the past. The next morning, remembering my first impression of America, I took her to a grocery store. Afterward she told me the cashier had overcharged her fifty cents, and she had gone back to get it.

I looked at her with admiration. "You did that? Oh, my goodness, you *have* changed! You are no longer my sweet, shy, and quiet little sister." Believe or not, the Chai family has never liked confrontation. In the past we would have pretended we hadn't noticed the overcharge.

"No," my sister said, "after that event [referring to the June 4 crackdown], we felt our family was like a small boat, completely swept onto an isolated island. Many people gave us the cold shoulder, nasty looks, and a hard time. Our family had to be strong and stick together to endure all that."

After taking another day to catch up on the past five years, we turned our attention to what my sister would do now. She had graduated at the top of her class in medical school, but because of my involvement at Tiananmen, she was not allowed to practice medicine in China. Instead she had worked for a drug company. Now that she was free in America, she wanted to become a doctor. To do that, she would need to pass a medical licensing exam.

With my training as a consultant, in those pre-Internet days, I immediately went to the local library and figured out where and how to apply for the nearest licensing exam. After calling and waiting for hours with no success, we drove to Philadelphia to get the application in person. Within a few days of my sister's arrival, she was registered for a licensing exam two months down the road and had a shared bank account with me and a place to live and study. I even picked up a refugee application from the immigration office and started filling it out for her. There was no way I would let her be sent back to China and risk never seeing her again. As soon as she received her work permit, she would be able to support herself.

Those were intense days with a lot of work, but we did it. It's always good for new immigrants to have a goal. Otherwise they can be com-

pletely crushed by the grim reality of survival and isolation in the land of the free.

A few weeks later, my sister's husband and our little brother arrived in Boston. Now that I had four mouths to feed, plus a dog, on my one-person salary, job security became even more important. After work permits arrived, my sister got a job cleaning houses, my brother-in-law worked as a cashier, and my little brother got a job at Panda Express. I continued my fourteen- to sixteen-hour days at the consulting firm. At night I worked on my book, my sister prepared for her licensing exam, my brother-in-law applied to business schools for an MBA and prepared for the GRE, and my brother studied English. The journey for survival in America was underway.

Just when I would think we were approaching equilibrium, another hurdle would appear. I was working to get the last member of our family—my dad—to come to the United States. What I didn't know was that he had remarried and his new wife had a daughter—and they all wanted to come.

Though I was still struggling to accept my mother's death, I did not object to my father's remarriage, because I felt he deserved companionship. But I couldn't afford to bring three people to America when I had only budgeted for one.

I had to say no. In doing this, I broke a Chai family taboo. We just never did that. If there was a need, we found a way to meet it. Saying no to my father was even more unthinkable.

My dad was silent for a few seconds, and then he responded in a way that was equally unfamiliar. "Ling Ling, our family has suffered so much for what you did, and now I am finally better. This new family likes me and respects me, and they visited me during the most difficult time, when no one in our town would speak to me or your brother. You can't imagine what I've gone through. After your mother and grandma passed away, our home became so lonely. You don't understand what your father was going through. . . . Well, let's not talk about the past. I just need one answer now: Will you or will you not bring her to America?"

A massive dose of guilt broke loose in me. I gathered up my courage and said, "Dad, I am so sorry. It was really hard for me to tell you the truth that I am now stretched to the max. I can't expand any more at this time. My siblings are fighting about wanting to go back to China. We need some time to get stabilized. Why can't she wait for you to come out first? When our situation gets better, we can get her out. I don't even know her. I've never met her . . ."

"Well, you either take all of us or none of us."

"No, Dad. You can't do that to me. You know how important you are to me . . ."

Tears poured down my face. After losing my mother and grandma, was I now going to lose my one last parent?

"I'm going to hang up now," he said. "I'm done talking. Make a decision and let me know."

I sat at my desk and cried, but then I had to get back to work. I had a big assignment to complete on a tight deadline, and my manager was breathing down my neck.

Out of my emotional turmoil, a sober reality emerged. My father had not changed at all. No matter how hard I tried, I would never be good enough for him.

That night I didn't come home from work at all. I stayed in the office to finish my project. By the following morning, I was ready to call my dad again.

"Since the last time we spoke," I said, "I have been working non-stop. I'm trying to keep my job. If I fail here, we will all be living on the street. I need some time to work things out. If that means I won't be able to see you for a while, I am so sorry."

There was a long silence on the other end. Then my dad said, "Let's all give it some time and think about it."

After the difficult exchange with my father, my siblings and I settled into a peaceful routine. My siblings found their own place to live, we all went to work every day, and we were no longer on the roller coaster

of emotions most immigrants feel while assimilating into a new culture. We had the time and space to recover and rebuild.

On April 15, 1995, my twenty-ninth birthday, my family surprised me with a party. My sister and her husband cooked my favorite home-town meals—it was like heaven. For people in exile, the taste of food from home is one of the things we really miss that cannot be replaced by a foreign culture or American Chinese food. When my brother-in-law re-created the old recipes, it brought back a piece of my childhood and quenched the homesickness monster—at least for a while.

As I walked back to my apartment, a long-awaited peace descended on me—as if I had emerged from a long, dark tunnel of struggles. The horror of the massacre, the escape, the heartbreak with Feng, the job crisis, and the feelings of isolation were all in the past. I had persevered and overcome, and my life was now on track.

On Sunday, April 30, I picked up a copy of the *New York Times*. On an inside page, a provocative headline caught my eye: "Six Years After the Tiananmen Massacre, Survivors Clash Anew on Tactics." The article mentioned two documentaries being produced about Tiananmen and the ongoing debate over who was responsible for the massacre. When my eyes settled on my own name, the blood drained from my face, and I felt the way I had when my name first appeared on the most-wanted list after the massacre.

> *Ms. Chai said the hidden strategy of the leadership group she dominated was to provoke the Government to violence against the unarmed students. With statements like "What we are actually hoping for is bloodshed" and "Only when the square is awash with blood will the people of China open their eyes," Ms. Chai denounced those students who sought to bring an end to the occupation of the square.*[1]

I was stunned. I couldn't believe this was an article in the *New York Times*, a paper I held in high regard. A reporter had called me a day or

two earlier to confirm I had taped an interview. When I tried to explain it was not an interview, he ended the call.

Next, a reporter from the *Washington Post* called. He seemed sympathetic, and he gave me a little more time to answer questions, but his article's story line was the same as the one in the *Times*. Then I got a call from a reporter for the local community paper. I told him many details, but his story line was the same as the first two articles. After six years of praising the bravery of the students and condemning the brutality of the Chinese government, these papers apparently felt they had a new angle that would grab the public's attention. Whether it was true did not seem to matter.

I could not believe it. This was the free media we had worshiped and sacrificed our lives for in Tiananmen? What was the difference between these "independent" reports and the stories in the Communist-controlled state newspaper in China? Same story line, same message from the big flagship paper to the small local one.

My education in freedom continued. Once again I was shocked by the realities of America's prized system: First, its politics were not totally dedicated to freedom; then its private companies were not immune to pressure from China; and now the media were marching in lockstep. It was the last place I had expected to be attacked, but there it was. The American media, which had been so instrumental in getting the true story out of China, had now turned its guns on the students and on me. These false accusations shifted responsibility for the massacre onto the students and justified the murders.

The articles in the American newspapers led to an uproar in Chinese overseas media and turmoil in the dissident community. The Chinese reporters took it one step further, accusing me of sending students to die at Tiananmen Square while I left to save my own life.

To my knowledge, there was never a "hidden strategy of the leadership group" to provoke the government to bloodshed so the country would wake up to join the revolution. As I said before, those were slogans I had picked up as a child or heard from Li Lu. Neither had I left the Square while other students were left to make the sacrifices. On the contrary, after I led the orderly withdrawal from the Square, I stepped forward, on June 8, to record an eyewitness report of the massacre, so the world would know the truth and so the students throughout the

nation would maintain peace. That action brought much greater risk and repercussions to my family and me, but I believed it was important to leave a public record so the next movement could be grounded in truth, not based on cover-up lies by the government.

When we were on the Square, we didn't have all the information necessary to make strategic decisions. We were responding to rumors and ideas and pressure from various fronts. All we knew at the time was what we knew at the time. Even looking back over twenty-two years, I'm still not entirely clear about how all the events unfolded. As others will attest, the activity on the Square was in constant flux, with new ideas being put forward, debated, and often put to a vote. There was never complete unity. Even the decision to withdraw from the Square was a split decision, and it was only when Feng took the microphone and said, "Withdraw," that students began to move from the Square. Many students did not even hear that announcement, and it was only by word of mouth that everyone was told to join the line of retreat.

Just as I thought my wounds from Tiananmen had healed, my heart was broken by these inflammatory articles. In the past, I had weathered the attacks because I still believed the world saw the truth, remembered the truth, and stood in solidarity with the truth: The Chinese government had opened fire on unarmed citizens. But now the media and the public had lost track of the truth. The victims were presented as villains, and sacrifices were laughed off as foolishness.

The controversy sent a ripple through the dissident community and divided the already fragile democracy movement into two groups. One group, made up mostly of older dissidents who had fled to exile before my time, attacked and condemned me. The students, meanwhile, especially those who had stayed at the Square, rose up to defend the truth.

The dissident groups knew the facts and didn't believe we'd had a secret strategy to provoke a massacre. But the debate focused on whether we should have left the Square earlier to *prevent* the massacre—implying we should be held responsible for the loss of life throughout Beijing.

The firestorm reignited my survivor's guilt, only this time it hurt even more because it brought back to the surface two questions for which I had no answers: *How could I have not foreseen the massacre?* and *Why was I allowed to live?*

31

TRUE LOVE

By 1996 MY tenure at the consulting firm was quickly approaching its end. The way the business works, after three years junior associates either go on to business school or are let go. Few progress directly to the level of management consultant. I was told I needed an MBA to succeed in the business world, and Bob Maginn, my boss's boss, recommended I apply to the top business schools. Reluctantly I applied to only one school—Harvard—and was accepted.

After I quit my job and took on substantial student loans, my dad finally came out of China. His second marriage had ended, so he had closed down our home and converted his life savings into US currency—two thousand dollars.

A few days after my dad arrived, I started at Harvard Business School and my brother-in-law started at Yale. My sister had passed her medical licensing exam and had a job at Brown University, and my brother was still working at Panda Express and working on his English.

My dad did some volunteer work here and there at places in Chinatown. At one point, he cleaned toilets in a nursing home. That

was a hard transition. When I came home one weekend to be with him, he looked depressed.

"I'm thinking of going back to China," he said. "I did not know how much I would miss it. Before I came, I still had patients chasing after me, 'Please finish one more surgery for us. Please finish one more surgery.' Here, I am nobody; I've become like your grandma. It was fine for her, an old lady from the countryside without much education, but not for me. I want to go home."

This announcement was like a clap of thunder. After I'd tried for years to get my dad out of China, a week later he wanted to go back. I could bring my family to America, but I couldn't provide a sense of identity and accomplishment or build the support network they needed. If I lost my dad back to a country I could no longer visit, I would feel defeated again by China. It was hard for me to concentrate on school.

A week later I saw my dad again.

"I gave it some thought," he said, "and I've decided not to go back just yet. For you and my other children, I will give it a good try to adjust to my life here."

A smile came back to my life.

At the end of my first year at Harvard, I went to New York to start a summer internship at one of the top investment banks. It was a competitive situation, and they worked us hard. But I thrived on the pace and the challenge. Every morning as I walked downtown, I felt I was part of a big life force. I thought if I could master the skills of an investment banker, I could regain control of my life.

Before I left for New York, I had visited the consulting firm to say good-bye to a few friends. We'd been taught never to burn bridges. I saw Bob Maginn and told him about my summer plans.

"I'm going to New York this week," he said. "I'd like to have lunch together."

"That sounds good," I responded politely, not really expecting he would call. But he did. On a Sunday afternoon he met me in Manhattan, and we took a walk through Central Park.

As we strolled along the lakefront, he told me bluntly, "I've been attracted to you ever since we met, but I couldn't ask you out—both because I'm a married man and because we worked at the same place. Now I'm free from both situations. My wife and I are officially separated, and you've left the firm. I would like you to give me a chance to get to you know better."

I was surprised by his directness and by his interest in me. The culture at the consulting company was strictly hierarchical. We were there to work, not to form personal relationships. I was comfortable in that system because I had grown up in the hierarchy of the Chinese military. I had kept a professional distance from everyone in the firm, including Bob Maginn, who was two rungs above me on the ladder. I didn't know him personally, nor had I ever thought about getting to know him.

I couldn't break down the barriers between us on the spot. Besides, after my experiences with Feng, I had not been able to fully trust men. I kept my heart under lock and key. I didn't think I would ever find someone who could truly love me—the real me, with all my imperfections, not the media Chai Ling or an idealized notion of who I am.

Still, there seemed to be no harm in getting to know Bob. As an experienced consultant, he is a master of analysis, even when it comes to romance. "Let's look at the facts," he said. "We come from two cultures, yet we both went to the same kind of school. I think we're compatible intellectually. I sense you have a big and tender heart, even though it's sometimes hard for me to read. But one thing concerns me: Do you believe in God? Because faith is important to me."

I answered honestly, "I don't know much about God. But I'm willing to learn."

"That's good enough for now," Bob said. "We'll both learn."

Just as my personal life began to move in the right direction, my career was struck another devastating blow. At the end of the summer, I was not given an offer. Though it was subtly disguised, it was "the China problem" all over again. Once again, my heart was broken. I loved New York City and the job. I cried all the way back to Boston.

Though the setback in New York made it more difficult to focus on my second year at Harvard Business School, I continued to work and apply for investment banking jobs. I received an offer from another bank in New York. Though the polished and professional senior vice president who made the offer assured me she really liked me and what I stood for, I had been hurt so often by opportunities that hadn't panned out that I wasn't sure whether she would stand by me if she found out that hiring me might negatively affect the bank's China business. I was too afraid to tell her what had happened the past two times.

In the back of my mind, I had always had the idea to start my own company. Now I thought if I started my own business, I would never have to worry about someone deciding not to hire me because of my past. I took a class to learn how to write a business plan, and I soon discovered I loved it. When I was researching my plan, my heart leaped with joy, and I had so much energy. I could stay up all night researching and writing. But whenever I thought about the banking job, my stomach began to ache.

On my birthday in 1998, Bob came to my dorm after I finished class and took me on a tour of Boston. At each stop, he left signs and clues for me to follow—from the Freedom Trail, to Paul Revere's house, to sitting in the pews of the historic Old North Church, and eventually to Bob's new home in Harvard Square. There he held up a ring box, knelt in front of me, and said, "Ling, will you marry me?"

"Do I need to say yes now?" I asked.

A look of disappointment came across his face. "That's usually how it works," he said. "But you can wait if you want."

"Oh—*yes*. I meant to say *yes*." I was overwhelmed by his love and commitment, but I had my fears. Would marriage work this time? Compared to the last time, when I had worked so hard to earn Feng's love only to be left heartbroken, this seemed so easy, undeserved, and unconditional. *Will he wake up tomorrow morning and regret it? Will he still love me once he gets to know the real me? Will I fail again?*

Despite my fears and self-doubt, I reached out my hand to Bob, and he reached out his hand to me. Two people with issues and regrets from

the past made a lifetime commitment to each other and to our ancestors and traditions. Our word became our bond. Out of that bond would come a company, three beautiful little girls, and a home full of love and laughter. As we journeyed together, we would learn something new about each other every day, and every day our love and respect for each other would grow stronger.

———

At the time we got engaged, Bob was running for state treasurer of Massachusetts. He asked me to postpone my move to New York so I could stay in Boston until after the election. The bank graciously allowed me to delay my starting date for a year and keep my signing bonus. While I was waiting, I decided to try my start-up. If it didn't work out, I would join the bank in New York the next year.

I had no experience in starting a business, just as I'd had no experience in leading a protest movement, escaping from China, or surviving in a new country. Little did I know, my start-up Internet business would soon be swept into another revolution—a technological revolution that would transform how we interact across our entire society.

My idea was to build a turnkey intranet portal and learning management system for universities based on an integrated calendar that pulled together course information, lecture schedules, homework assignments, campus news and entertainment, and e-mail—all the must-have information for students, which they could personalize and access from anywhere on campus: the dorms, library, or student union. Unlike most university websites, which tended to serve the interests of the admissions department and alumni groups, my system would create a central hub for students and a pathway for the development of online teaching and learning tools—opening the experience of an elite school, such as Harvard, to a broader audience.

One of the more popular features of the Harvard system was a module like today's Facebook, which included a student's picture, profile, interests, etc. Students could use this feature to find the name of someone they'd seen on campus. The professors tended to use it to identify cold-call targets for their next day's classes.

To make the business work, we wanted to use this must-have content to attract users in the coveted eighteen- to twenty-five-year-old demographic, which accounted for eleven billion dollars in marketing spending each year. If we could direct a small portion of those marketing dollars to sites the students used, it would be a win-win situation: The school and students would have the best learning system, and advertisers could cost-effectively reach this young, affluent demographic. It was an exciting possibility.

My start-up year, 1998, was the front edge of the dot-com boom. Things that could only be imagined in the past were becoming reality as the Internet expanded at lightning speed. The revolution was filled with excitement and creative energy—and everything seemed possible.

With the dot-com boom in full swing, every imaginable name was appended with *.com*. Our first choice, CollegeNet.com, was already in use. Our lawyers suggested we come up with a name that was original and unique and could be trademarked.

Bob and I went skiing one weekend, and as we sat in the lodge in the afternoon, we talked about what this unique name could be. I said that every mother in China hopes her child will grow up in a 尖子. Bob heard what I said and wrote the word *jenza* on a slip of paper.

"Is that what you said?" he asked.

"Close enough."

Then, because we were dealing with higher education, we added the Chinese word for "class of"—*bar*—and it became Jenzabar. We informally tested the name with some people at the ski area and later with friends and investors. It was accepted positively, evoking images of warmth, such as the sun rising over the island of Zanzibar! That was good enough for a girl from the City of Sunshine. The lawyers gave us a big thumbs-up, as this name was easily trademarked and protected so no one could appropriate it. So Jenzabar, our first baby, was born.

At first it was just me working day and night in the loft at Bob's house, with my faithful dog, Tara, under my desk. Then we added more people and moved into the basement. When we hired our nineteenth employee, we outgrew the basement and moved into a space in the back of a church. I interviewed fifteen software development firms before

finding one that would code the first prototype of the system within my small budget. Then I got a few colleges to try the prototype.

It's hard to capture the months of hard work, running a seven-by-sixteen shop in Bob's home with two shifts coming and going—some working full-time and others coming after hours from their day jobs. As the founder, my job description was—*everything*. One minute I was CFO, speaking to potential investors; the next minute, I was administrative assistant, running to Kinko's for business cards and brochures. Someone told me they'd never seen anyone work quite so hard, but I had been working hard my entire life. At Tiananmen Square, we had worked around the clock without much food or sleep. The start-up came close to that level of intensity.

After I used up all my savings, part of my signing bonus, and charged $50,000 of equipment on Bob's credit card, I needed to raise money to sustain our momentum. I talked to Bob about formally investing in the company, but he wisely replied, "I'm fully supportive of what you're doing, but it's not good for me to be your sole investor. If you can find two other people, I will join in."

I accepted Bob's challenge, and through some fortunate breaks I met the CEO of Reebok, Paul Fireman, and Steve Perlman, the founder of WebTV, and they became the first round of angel investors, in addition to Bob.

By 1999, investment bankers were pursuing Jenzabar to go public. Following a two-hour meeting in November about our business strategy with then-Microsoft president Steve Ballmer, we decided to acquire several enterprise software companies that had applications for use on college campuses. Bob stayed up many late nights working through the details of the buyouts. We called these businesses "the pipe" because they connected students, faculty, staff, alumni, and others to the colleges and universities through software systems for admissions, registration, grading, fund-raising, and billing. We had a banker lined up for the initial public offering, and our initial valuation was one billion dollars, but the bank wanted evidence that our business strategy would work and that we were on a good pathway for high growth.

In 2000 Bob officially joined Jenzabar as full-time CEO, and we held fast to our vision. We believed if we could raise a few hundred million

dollars in financing, we could transform the entire higher education industry. With our system, anyone could teach, learn, communicate, and be friends. Physical campuses, requiring billions of dollars each year to operate, would no longer be necessary. The highest level of education could be offered to anyone, anywhere across the globe.

Unfortunately, the dot-com bubble popped in April 2000, just weeks after our closing of a large, private-equity financing and merging of several acquired companies. That and several factors prevented us from going public and raising all the money we needed.

No one believed the game could end so quickly. But it did.

Our East Coast investor group was less interested in the vision and more concerned about getting a bigger stake of the company and turning a bigger profit. In the aftermath of the dot-com bust, we spent a lot of time and money in litigation and refinancing negotiations. We had to adjust our business strategy to focus on earnings, not growth. Still, those years helped me grow into an experienced business manager—from building a team to developing strategies to creating a corporate culture to launching new products.

I also learned true leadership from Bob. Days after 9/11, when our nation was under attack, so was our company. An aggressive investor threatened to force us out so he could sell the company and cash out his position, and our employees came to us in confusion. "What should we do, polish up our résumés or work like we did yesterday?"

Bob said directly and firmly, "I don't know about your blood type, but mine is 'B positive.' That's what I'm going to do: stay focused on running the business. So get back to work." That was inspiring.

It was also critical to the survival of the enterprise. As a CEO friend later pointed out, for any company or organization to be put into a vacuum state for a month or more, it could lead to confusion, chaos, and rapid deterioration of key employees and customers. How close we were to the brink of disaster! But Bob's instinctive response of determination, sharpened by years of playing competitive sports, infused energy and focus into the entire company. We went back to work and turned the business around. Within six months, our pretax profit margins reached 20 percent, and we have never looked back. We have since grown the company by 70 percent, while remaining profitable, building the

strongest balance sheet among our direct competitors. We now employ almost three hundred associates. Through the Jenzabar Foundation, which we created to work with hundreds of colleges and universities on humanitarian efforts both domestically and internationally, we now contribute 10 percent of our corporate pretax earnings, providing more than one million dollars a year for these projects.

Even with our successes, however, I felt I hadn't achieved my dream of freedom. Though I was making money, raising a family, and running a successful company, I thought I should be happier. Instead I felt trapped. I had established a small platform, but my vision was to change the world. Each day I continued my fight. Before I knew it, we'd been in business for more than eleven years, and the twentieth anniversary of the Tiananmen movement was fast approaching.

32

WRESTLING WITH THE PAST

DURING MY ABSENCE from the Chinese democracy movement, attacks against the Tiananmen leaders had taken on a whole new life on the Internet. In February 2007, I googled my name and was linked to selected clips from one of the documentaries and an article saying I should be held responsible for the deaths of three thousand students at Tiananmen.

Tears streamed down my face as I contemplated this latest assault on my character. What would my coworkers and employees think if they googled my name and saw this? Would other parents still want to arrange playdates with my children? Once again I felt overwhelmed by the world. Whoever said truth and justice will prevail? It seemed that politics and power were far more influential. How could I fight against the massive power of evil?

I decided I couldn't deal with the China issue. I wasn't big enough or strong enough. I put it on a back burner and focused on building a great enterprise. Maybe then, with more experience and more money, I would be in a position to help bring justice and freedom to China.

The bottom line for me about Tiananmen Square is that the student leaders never expected, hoped for, or anticipated the Chinese government would actually open fire on its own citizens. Some have suggested the massacre could have been avoided if the students had left the Square sooner. I don't believe that at all. I believe the decision to use force was made by hard-liners in the government on April 25 and 26, when the *dong luan* verdict was announced. By then the protests had engulfed the nation, spreading across the entire society, not just at the epicenter with the students in Beijing. The government wanted to terrorize the people back into submission, and they did everything they could to keep the students on the Square until the crackdown.

Even if we had abandoned the Square before June 4, some other event would have triggered the massacre. The government was determined to retake control of the city and send a message of fear and intimidation to the people—to "kill the chicken to shock the monkey," as the Chinese saying goes. Don't forget, the massacre started on the western side of the city as citizens of Beijing took to the streets in protest. By the time the killing reached Tiananmen Square, hundreds had already died during the army's advance through the streets. As central as Tiananmen Square was to the events of that day, it was only part of the story. In the larger view, it was the Beijing Massacre, in which Tiananmen Square was a key symbol in the push for greater freedom and democracy in China.

One morning in May 2009, as I came out of my daughters' school after dropping them off, I saw an Asian woman taking pictures of the school, my car, and me. She was a reporter from a Hong Kong newspaper who wanted to do a story on what my life had become after twenty years. (They were under the false impression I had gone back to China, gotten rich, and forgotten the victims of Tiananmen.) It was scary to realize someone could find my home address and the school my kids attended and show up with a camera. My first thought was, *What else do they know, and what will they do next?*

That same day, I heard from Feng, with whom I'd had a few polite interactions since our last meeting, that Fang Zheng, the student from

Beijing Sports College who had lost his legs when he was struck by a tank during the withdrawal from Tiananmen Square, had been sponsored out of China by Zhou Fengsuo's organization, Humanitarian China, and was coming to Boston to be part of a rally. I decided to go see him.

When I walked into the hotel, Fang Zheng was waiting in the lobby. A lump formed in my throat at the thought that I could have ended up like him if the tanks had come from the front of the line of retreating students instead of the rear. In twenty years, Fang had overcome his injuries, mastered the wheelchair, and rebuilt his body to the point that he could compete in the Paralympic Games. He was married to a beautiful woman and had a child the same age as one of my daughters, and he was free in America.

As we ate breakfast and I listened to his stories of living in China for the past twenty years, my heart cried out for him and countless others in the same situation. Meeting Fang inspired me to stop focusing on my own struggles and to consider what I could do to bring people hope. Even as I was fighting the big fight and thinking that someday I would have a lot of resources to help many people, I could start right now, with smaller resources, to help one person at a time.

That day, as I joined the rally with the local Chinese community in support of the democracy movement, an invisible mental prison collapsed. The pain of the past no longer had the power to tie me down. As I met some new immigrants, many of whom were in the process of applying for political refugee status, they reminded me of my early days in America—with all the uncertainty, hardship, and hope. I offered encouragement—"Don't give up; you will overcome, and your dream will come true." My heart went out to them. But what could I really do to help? With Bob's encouragement, I pledged to donate one million dollars over five years to help China-related causes. It was a start.

On the eve of the twentieth anniversary of the massacre, as I prepared a speech for a rally in front of the US Capitol, I wondered, *What kind of*

message can I give on this special occasion? What kind of program will help bring reform to China today? And then the words began to flow:

> *Today, those of us who have lived and experienced the freedom and opportunity provided by democracy now appeal to the leaders of China to do the following:*
>
> *It has been twenty years, and the current leadership bears no responsibility for the Tiananmen massacre. Acknowledge the massacre and begin a dialogue with those who suffered; release from prison the political prisoners from June 4, 1989; repeal the blacklist and arrest warrants still in effect; and create an impartial citizens' committee to publish a truthful history of the massacre.*
>
> *Revisit the hard-line approach toward political reform. Studying the successful model of Taiwan and other countries, it is clear that reform does not have to lead to chaos and civil war. Start with permitting freedom of the press, free local elections, and opposition parties.*
>
> *China's current leadership need not fear the well-being of themselves and their families if they embark on reform. The Tiananmen students' beliefs are grounded in nonviolence and rule of law, and the process used in South Africa and Taiwan are models that could easily be followed.*
>
> *In 1989, I hoped the Chinese government would realize and understand that different opinions can exist together peacefully; that transparency and public participation were reasonable and beneficial. My hope, and the hope of my fellow students, was met by tanks and machine guns, death and maiming, blacklists and imprisonment. My hope, twenty years later, is that today's leaders will demonstrate the courage to change. The world is remembering Tiananmen and watching.*

After the rally, I went to a conference where many overseas dissidents gathered to discuss what was working, what wasn't, and how to move forward. There I saw blacklisted writers Su Xiaokang and Zheng Yi, as well as Wang Dan, whom I hadn't seen for more than ten years.

Talking to these comrades from Tiananmen reminded me how I

felt when I first came out of China—confused and overburdened, yet determined to pursue the big cause of reforming China, even with few resources. For the first time I appreciated how far I had come. As they lamented how the overseas democracy movement had fallen prey to the Chinatown syndrome—becoming marginalized from the mainstream of life—I recognized how integrated my life had become. I had an education, spoke English well, and had a wonderful, loving, and supportive husband and family. I owned a company, had some resources, and enjoyed my independence. Now the question was how to have a real impact on the world. My heart burned with a desire to go beyond big words and lofty ideals to make a tangible difference in people's lives.

At the same conference, I met Ms. Jing Zhang, who became a dissident during the Democracy Wall movement in the late 1970s. She was donating time and money to support volunteer work in China to stop forced abortions on women and rescue trafficked children. My heart was drawn to her because of the support Bob and I had given to some Chinese orphanages. I wanted to see what I could do to help.

Then I saw Zhou Fengsuo. In 1989 he managed the broadcast center at the Square, and he was the first student on the most-wanted list to be arrested. He had spent more than a year in jail and had been in the United States for the past ten years. As I got to know him, I learned that at one point he had become so disappointed with the overseas democracy movement and so overwhelmed by his hatred of the Communist system that he could not find a way to overcome it. On the verge of breaking down, he came to faith in Jesus.

Zhou took me to a prayer service at a church, where we spent more than three hours praying for the past, for the victims who died at Tiananmen, and for the future of a peaceful China. There I met Bob Fu, a Chinese Christian who heads a ministry called ChinaAid, which advocates for the persecuted churches in China; and Zhang Boli, who had been one of my three deputy commanders at Tiananmen. Zhang spent two years escaping from China and was now a Christian minister.

During the service, Zhou Fengsuo, Zhang Boli, and Bob Fu prayed for Jesus to enlighten me. My escape experience had made me a firm believer in Buddhism, and I didn't think I needed any other faith. I also

did not want to be disloyal to my original faith. Nevertheless, the prayer service left a lasting impression.

———————

As the summer continued, the attacks on my character—and my mind— continued. On June 5, a local paper published a column portraying my company and me as villains in our effort to stop the documentary film- makers' deceptive use of our corporate trademark to lure users onto their site. I was soon embroiled in depositions, filings, and counter filings. Around the same time, my computer was hacked, and I had a feeling I was being monitored and followed.

My father came back from a visit to China and brought me a mes- sage from the Chinese government: If I continued to push for democ- racy in China, there would be no good results. They didn't specify what the bad results might be, but the warning sparked a heated debate between my father and me. He lashed out about how painful and lonely and difficult the years had been after the Tiananmen massacre, asking how I could be so ignorant to continue. What would I accomplish—one person against a nation? When I turned to my sister for support, she was also against me, calling me self-centered for not taking into consid- eration the whole family's suffering. She worried they would relive the trauma and suffering of twenty years before. Last time they had stood by me and endured with silence and pride. This time I was on my own.

Bob tried to be supportive, but as an American who had lived his entire life in freedom and opportunity, he could never understand the pain and agony my family and I had been through. I looked at my beau- tiful children, busy laughing and giggling in one of their little games. Would I lose them, too?

As summer faded into early autumn, I was in a bad mental state, reliving a lot of fear, agony, anger, and frustration from the past. Several times I tried to complete the manuscript for this book, which I had started twenty years earlier but couldn't finish. But every time I tried to pick up where I'd left off, the pain associated with reliving the events shut me down. I felt an evil, hostile energy swirling around me. After two decades of fighting and not winning, and now facing the risk of

having all my loved ones taken away again, I lost the joy of life. Even though I continued with all my activities, I couldn't focus on my children, my husband, and the beautiful life we'd built together. I went to work, but I couldn't find anything to enjoy or anticipate.

The following Sunday, I made a conscious decision to be with my children, even though my heart felt numb. Our youngest was crying and didn't want to go to church, but I went with her, along with her sisters and my loving husband.

The pastor's sermon was just the medicine I needed. He probed the purpose of our lives and the spiritual legacy we want to leave. Without a clear sense of God's purpose for our lives, he said, we were just chasing money and success, which would never fill the black hole in our hearts. That hole could only be filled by the Spirit of God's love in our hearts. Then he asked, "How do we share God's blessings with others?"

Sitting in the church auditorium, I thought about all the people who had died in Beijing—on the streets, at the Square. By giving their lives to end the violence and repression in China, they were all heroes like Jesus Christ. The tanks had crushed their bodies, and the guns had taken their lives, but the army could not destroy their spirit. *How come they are not remembered and celebrated like Jesus is?*

In October 2009, my downward spiral culminated in the panic attack I had aboard the flight from Boston to Washington, DC, for Fang Zheng's standing-up celebration. Feng picked me up at the airport, and by then I was mostly stabilized, though I still felt weak and nauseated. In the car on our way to the event, Feng's nose began to bleed—further evidence of how emotional a day this was for us. Though in our minds we maintained our composure, deep down we both knew something was wrong with us.

Fang Zheng's event went well. There I saw Bob Fu again. When the music went up and Fang started to dance with his wife, tears came to my eyes. I pictured a day when all the survivors of Tiananmen could stand up like Fang Zheng with their loved ones to celebrate life, love, and triumph over adversity.

FREEDOM CALLING

33

FINDING FREEDOM

THAT NIGHT AFTER Fang Zheng's event, at a dinner hosted by ChinaAid, I met Reggie Littlejohn, president of Women's Rights Without Frontiers, a brave woman fighting to end forced abortions in China. As we talked, Reggie told me how a sudden illness had almost taken her life several years before. One day she was a healthy, high-powered attorney; the next day, she was fighting for her life in a hospital bed, having contracted an aggressive staph infection. For the next three years, she was in and out of the hospital between five surgeries, during which time she became a devoted Christian and committed her life to do the Lord's work.

During her illness and recovery, instead of feeling sorry for herself, she prayed for people less fortunate. Along the way, she became passionate about ending China's forced abortions under the one-child policy. She prayed day and night for Chinese women and their unborn babies. She also wrote an award-winning screenplay, which she was trying to raise money to produce.

Reggie attributed her miraculous recovery and all her success to Jesus

Christ. She was confident the movie project was God's plan for her and that he would open doors for her whenever necessary.

During my ten months in hiding, I met many brave and selfless Buddhists, but I had never met someone like Reggie, who spoke with such humility and confident assurance at the same time. It made me curious about her God—was he for real?

A few days later, when I read a copy of her screenplay, I was deeply moved by the story of women who had to run and hide to avoid a forced abortion, and I could not dismiss the power of Jesus from my mind. I became fired up to help Reggie raise the money to produce the movie. I introduced her to Cindi Leive, editor in chief at *Glamour* magazine, whose Women of the Year awards are an annual event. I knew Cindi had a lot more influence and connections than I did.

In the meantime, I forwarded Jing Zhang's report on China's forced abortion practice to Reggie, and Reggie arranged for Jing to testify before the Tom Lantos Human Rights Commission in Congress about China's one-child policy. She invited me to come as well. As I pondered whether I should return to Washington, my heart broke for all the Chinese women suffering under the one-child policy. Like the decision that led me to Tiananmen Square, I felt compelled to help and support—this time, just as an interpreter. But when I boarded the plane for DC, I had little idea of the transformation awaiting me.

The hearing, chaired by Congressman Chris Smith of New Jersey, a devoted Christian and longtime opponent of China's forced abortion policies and human rights violations, included testimony from Reggie Littlejohn, as well as witnesses such as Harry Wu, who is well known for his fight against *laogai*—the forced-labor system in China; a human rights lawyer from Shandong Province, who testified about ongoing abuse; a leader of the Uighurs, an oppressed minority in China; and Wujian, a victim of forced abortion. I was not prepared for her testimony.

When Wujian became pregnant before she had received a birth permit to have a child, she tried to hide her pregnancy in hopes of avoiding

a forced abortion. But the family planning officials in her county beat and tortured her father, forcing her to choose one life over another—her father's or her baby's. When they discovered her hiding place, she was dragged into a hospital for an abortion. After one shot, the baby stopped moving, but somehow remained inside her, raising Wujian's hopes that her baby might survive the toxic shots and live. But on the third day, before Wujian realized what was happening, she was taken to an operating room and scissors were inserted into her body, cutting her baby to pieces. Above her helpless cries, all she could hear was the sound of the scissors. At last, the doctor pulled out a small baby foot, with five fully formed toes the size of corn kernels. That picture was forever seared into Wujian's mind. At the moment of her baby's death, part of Wujian's life was gone forever.

When she reached this point in her testimony, my heart was broken with pain and sadness, for Wujian and her helpless child and for every mother and unborn baby in China. Her shocking report of cruelty brought back memories of the helplessness and pain I had felt during the June 4 massacre. That night was so brutal, yet we had no strength to stop it, and the rest of the world could not stop it either.

After her forced abortion, Wujian struggled on the edge of life and death. She blamed herself for not protecting her child. She was saved only by finding faith in Jesus Christ. Others were less fortunate. Each day in China, five hundred women commit suicide. Very few news outlets report these untimely deaths.

Though no one could forget the Tiananmen movement, even more than twenty years later, few people seem to realize that three little words—*one-child policy*—have resulted in what amounts to an hourly Tiananmen massacre, for the past thirty years, in broad daylight, right under the world's nose.

Wujian's testimony touched me so deeply that all I could do was cry with her. I had not cried like that since I learned of my mother's death. I wasn't sure what hit me; all I knew was that it touched the deepest part of my heart, the part soaked in pain and sorrow that I had learned to bury under layers of protection. That afternoon, it all broke open. I felt the helplessness of Tiananmen when the tanks moved in on us. I felt the pain and helplessness of that horrible afternoon on the operating

table when they'd performed the abortion on me without anesthesia. I felt a deep-rooted sadness for the baby conceived with Feng when we first came to freedom, the pregnancy I had ended to avoid an ongoing relationship with a husband who had turned abusive. And I remembered the moments when I finally became a mother, how difficult and tiring each pregnancy was with nausea, stress, and sleeplessness, but how, in the end, it was all replaced with the overwhelming joy of holding those wonderful little babies in my arms. As I thought of all the babies who would never feel the embrace of their mothers' arms and all the bereft mothers left with nothing but shame, guilt, terror, self-blame, and despair, the tears poured from my eyes. An overwhelming feeling of helplessness came over me, mixed with rage, and swirled in my heart like hot lava looking for an outlet. Then Congressman Smith's steady voice brought hope into the darkness.

"Words really are inadequate to express my . . . sympathy for what you have lost, but . . . by testifying you not only inform, you inspire us to accelerate and do more for those women who are being persecuted and hurt and you motivate us to unceasingly work and pray for you and for others who have been so horribly victimized."[1]

I soon learned that Congressman Smith has waged a battle against China's forced abortion practices ever since they began in the early 1980s—a battle every bit as heroic as William Wilberforce's opposition to slavery in England two hundred years ago. As lonely as the battle has been at times, his strong faith has sustained him and inspired him to never give up.

As I left the congressional hearing room, two questions burned in my mind: How *can this inhumane crime be stopped?* When *will this inhumane crime be stopped?*

Before I met Reggie, I'd heard bits and pieces about Jesus. I knew he was full of compassion, that when he was slapped on one cheek, he would offer the other. But like many people, my understanding of Jesus was colored with many false pictures as well. And besides, what did Jesus have to do with freedom and democracy in China?

Reggie sent me a book, *The Heavenly Man*, which is the true story of how a young Chinese peasant boy was enlightened by Jesus and became a leader in the house church movement. Because of his faith, Brother Yun was sent to jail and tortured beyond human measure, yet he remained faithful to God. One time prison officials broke his legs to prevent him from trying to escape. But God completely healed him, and he walked out of the prison right in front of the guards. Eventually Yun was able to escape from China and went to Germany. At the end of his book, Brother Yun asked, "Are you ready to walk with Jesus?"

I was deeply touched by the book, but my soul was again thrown into turmoil. To walk with Jesus means to put your love for him before everything—husband, children, family, country—and to potentially suffer more persecutions and torment. I had once been willing to lose everything for the sake of China. Could I ever be ready to lose everything for Jesus?

I called Reggie and said, "If you think anyone who reads this book will become a Christian, you're crazy." Still, I could not get Brother Yun out of my mind.

———

Around Thanksgiving, I went to Park Street Church in Boston, where I met with a group of missionaries to China and Southeast Asia. They told me about a plan to send Chinese missionaries to evangelize the unreached countries between China and Jerusalem. I was concerned about what this meant. If I gave my life to Jesus, would I be asked to drop everything to become a missionary? What did I know about the Middle East?

On December 4, 2009, when I talked to Reggie about all these questions, it was as if the voice of Jesus was speaking through her.

"If I commit myself to Jesus, would I have to join the Back to Jerusalem movement?" I asked.

"No, God has unique plans for each of us," she said. "He has prepared us all our lives to do the work that only we can do."

"Then what is God's purpose for me?" This was the question that had nagged at me for the past twenty years, even before I thought about

the existence of God. *Why am I here? What is my purpose? Why was I allowed to survive Tiananmen when so many others died?*

"God definitely has a special job for you, Chai Ling, because you grew up in China, had an excellent education, ended up in Tiananmen, came here, married an American husband, and started your business— very few people have achieved the level of experience and understanding that you have in so many unique areas."

Reggie explained how God had prepared her for her current work. In addition to law school, she had spent three years in divinity school, learning how to study and interpret the Bible. When she finished, she was good at analyzing and making arguments about this or that point, and she thought she knew God; but she did not truly know him or experience his presence until the moment when she thought she was dying. Then she prayed for God to save her, and he did. Out of her near-death experience was birthed a love for the women of China who were suffering forced abortions. She believed God had given her a vision for exposing this massive crime.

As she was speaking, I gained some clarity, and my heart was filled with a warm desire. I blurted, "If only I could bring God's love to China! All the tragedy could come to an end and what a wonderful place the world would be . . ."

"That's it! Write it down," Reggie said. "Bring God's love to China— that's his plan for you, a job he has prepared for you that only you can accomplish, in a way no one else can."

"Wow, that's a huge job. Where do I even begin?" As I remembered the moment I committed to the Tiananmen movement and all the pain and sacrifice that followed, I asked, "Will I have to endure the pain of losing all my loved ones again?"

"God gives us tasks we can handle," Reggie replied. "When he sees we cannot do it, he will use us in a different way. Like the story of Corrie Ten Boom, who was brave and effective in hiding Jews during World War II. After she was released from the concentration camp and lost so many of her family members, she realized she could no longer go back to save the Jews. God used her after the war to work on reconciliation."

"But what about my children? Would I have to love Jesus before them?"

"Yes, but he's gentle. Even though Jesus was sent to earth to accomplish God's plan, he did not start his ministry until he was over thirty and had fulfilled his duty to raise his other siblings. Chai Ling, Jesus will treat those with young ones gently."

At the end of our conversation, Reggie said, "Chai Ling, remember, if you commit to Jesus, he will treasure your commitment. Because of what you've been through, the pain you've endured, Jesus will know how seriously you have taken this commitment and what you are prepared to do for him. He will dearly cherish your coming to him because you know what it's like to be persecuted and yet you are still willing to commit."

Tears welled in my eyes as I hung up the phone. There is nothing that can describe the feeling of being embraced and understood. In my office on the thirty-fifth floor of the Prudential Building, I got up from my desk, walked to a corner behind the door, and fell to my knees. All my life, I felt I was made to try to help save China. I had tried so hard to do it on my own and gave everything I had for what I believed was right. But I had not succeeded—and my sincere efforts, sacrifice, and devotion were twisted and made to seem evil and self-serving. Yet Jesus would know me and cherish my commitment. I was deeply touched to the core. Looking up, I said, "All my life I have wanted to save China. But I can't do it. If you can, Jesus, I will give my life to you."

A few days after my decision to become a Jesus-follower, God performed a miracle that reinforced my commitment. Jing Zhang's organization, Women's Rights in China, which Bob and I support, had reunited a young woman with her family twenty-five years after she was kidnapped at age seven. When the news came, the entire village, which had witnessed the parents' years of tears and heartbreak, rushed to the train station to greet the lost daughter.

On top of that, Jing, who had been instrumental in supporting the network that rescued the lost girl, was reconciled with her own family. For many years, because of her passion to fight for justice and freedom for China, she had been viewed as the black sheep in her family—

especially when she'd been thrown in jail. But the joyful news of her great deed made her family proud, and they embraced her and welcomed her back into the family.

Zhou Fengsuo, who had prayed for me on the twentieth anniversary of the Tiananmen massacre and whose courage to bring Fang Zheng to the United States started the process that led me to Jesus, told me that when he walked out of his office after hearing about my conversion, the ground was covered with snow—which had not happened in his city in California in thirty years.

When one of my daughters started having nightmares that kept her awake at night, Reggie explained to me the battle in the spirit world, where Satan constantly opposes Christ, and she encouraged me to pray for God's protection for my family.

Then my dad went in for a regular checkup, and it was discovered he had leukemia. Had he not gone in for the test, it might have been too late to treat the disease. After we prayed for him, he learned he had the kind of leukemia that is curable. My sister, whose focus is to find a cure for children's leukemia, could not believe it. She was so sure Dad would have the lethal kind. But God blessed our family with a miracle.

Looking back, I realize how often Bob had tried to witness to me about Jesus. He had taken me to various churches, from the historic Christ Church Cambridge, where George and Martha Washington had worshiped, to the landmark Trinity Church of Boston, to a Catholic church on Cape Cod. He took our girls to Sunday school, put them in the Christmas pageants and church Easter egg hunts, and in the summer sent them to vacation Bible school and a Christian sports/cheerleading camp. But he never pushed me. He was grateful I didn't object to his bringing up the girls in the Christian faith. Later he confessed that he'd tried the soft-sell approach with me and feared a confrontation in which I might object to our daughters being raised to believe in Jesus.

Little did he know that what I needed was a baseball bat over the head—like throwing *The Heavenly Man* at me and then asking me

whether I was ready to give my life to Jesus. I needed to see faith that people were willing to give their lives for, the kind of faith I had seen in the people who had risked their lives to save me in China.

During the years I walked in darkness, Bob was patient, kind, loving, and generous—a shining example of God's love. At the time, I thought he represented the best of the American spirit. Now I know he was reflecting the spirit of Jesus. It was Bob's patience, goodness, and faithfulness that helped to heal me.

My decision to put my faith in Jesus reinvigorated Bob's faith as well. He told me about sitting alone in the giant sanctuary of Trinity Church in the fall of 2009, looking around at others who had their entire families with them and wondering where was the God who would transform my life. Within months, God had answered in a mighty way. We are now surrounded by a wonderful church community and loving brothers and sisters in Christ. What a blessed way to live. And to think I missed the love of God for so many years.

34

ALL GIRLS ALLOWED

A FEW HOURS before I came to Jesus, I finished reading a memoir about coming to America by fellow Tiananmen survivor Su Xiaokang. In 1993 Su and his family were involved in a serious car accident in New York, and his wife sustained a brain injury that kept her hospitalized for an extended time. When Su visited her in the hospital, she talked about an "elder brother" and "the little one" who came to see her at night. It turned out she was having visions of her son's twin, who had died in childbirth, and a third child, whom she had aborted.

Eventually, as her recovery continued and she became firmly anchored in the real world again, the two dead children stopped visiting her. When I read that part, I was shaken to the core. *Does that mean I may have four children who are alive in a different world?*

In March 2010, Reggie and I met again in Boston. She was in town to visit her son at Harvard, and I took her to the launch party for Bob's friend and former boss Mitt Romney's book *No Apology*. There we met Romney's adviser Peter Flaherty, whose brother, Mike, is an amazing film producer. I was hoping to get Reggie's screenplay into Mike's hands.

The next day, Peter called to say that his brother happened to be in town and could meet us. It turned out to be a powerful meeting. Mike told us he was deeply moved by the Tiananmen students in 1989 and had put a white shoelace on his father's car antenna, vowing not to take it down until China was free. Unfortunately, Communist China outlasted his father's car.

During the meeting, Reggie told us about a Chinese girl she'd met who had come to the United States to study. This girl had learned that her mother had had an abortion to avoid a huge fine that would have made it impossible for the girl to get an education. It had finally dawned on the girl that her baby brother's life had paid for her education.

In the car after the meeting, as Reggie and I continued to talk about her work to end China's forced abortions, I suddenly blurted out that I'd had four abortions. Reggie looked at me and said, "Did you confess to God? He will forgive you."

"I did," I said, fighting back tears. We parted ways and I regained my composure on my way to another appointment. I had learned over the years to put aside any strong emotions I couldn't deal with and keep moving on. But that night the pain of the past came back, and I was in deep turmoil.

The next morning was a Saturday, and Bob was busy getting the kids ready to go to Cape Cod for a charity event. Before we left, I could not hold it in any longer. "I need to speak to you," I said.

We went into the living room, and as Bob sat down on the opposite side of the sofa, I told him I'd had abortions before marrying him.

"So I was right," he said, contemplating his words. "When I first met you, I asked whether you had children in China and told you I would be glad to adopt them. You said no. But I sensed you did."

"How would I ever have known they were children?" I said as the tears began to flow. I wrapped my arms tightly across my chest, not knowing what kind of response to expect. "So, do you still love me?"

"Of course I still love you," he said, almost casually.

All the years of pain, shame, and suffering erupted. I could have had four additional children, and they would all be in their twenties now. Four children . . .

"Would you hold me, please?" I managed to choke out. Bob moved to embrace me.

I could not stop sobbing, and I don't think Bob knew quite what to do. At one point I went to the bathroom to get some tissue. When I returned, he had left the sofa. I found him at the dining room table, finishing an e-mail to the board before our trip to Cape Cod. Eventually my young children heard me crying and rushed to my aid and just hugged and hugged me.

On the ride to the cape, my heart burned with anguish. How had I allowed myself to lose four babies?

When I confessed my sin to God, I felt some peace about the time in Paris; but when I thought about the circumstances of the other three, I only felt anger—toward my dad, Qing's dad, and Feng. What could have been done differently? I thought of two immigrant couples I know who aborted their babies in America due to financial insecurity and health concerns. One of the couples, during their time of crisis, was approached by some Christians, but they seemed only concerned about getting my friends to go to church and tithe.

The pain did not begin to subside until that evening. Even though my husband and children still loved me, I felt such turmoil; I felt alone and vulnerable. I felt I had nowhere to turn for help.

On Monday, when I met with my spiritual mentor, Tammy, she told me Bob should have canceled the trip to Cape Cod and given me time to grieve. "The right thing to do was to let you cry and cry until you had cried enough," she said. When I related this message to Bob, he laughed and said, "It would be great to be given an instruction manual next time."

I also realized I had felt judged by Reggie when she told me to confess to God and *he* would forgive me. There was nothing wrong with what she said, except I felt a slight tone of judgment instead of compassion. It's not like women in China skip happily to the abortion clinic.

When I saw Reggie again before she left town, I told her how I felt and suggested that the Chinese women she and other Americans spoke

to in their ministry would need extra care and tenderness. "I would hate to see them hurt again, or turned away again, in the name of God."

Reggie agreed and said, "Ling, I don't think you even realize that your first three abortions were forced abortions."

She was right. The law in China, both then and now, was that a woman could not legally give birth without a birth permit, and permits were not issued to unmarried women or to any woman under twenty-five years old. According to Chinese government statistics for 2009 and 2010, 70 percent of the 16 million abortions each year—that's 11.2 million women and children affected—are for unmarried women. Many of them are driven into the clinics by subtle—yet no less lethal—shame and family and social pressure, not by overt physical attacks such as Wujian endured. These women may not even realize they are also victims of the one-child policy. But God has seen them and heard them, and he has a special message for them.

As I pondered my own deep sadness—and the pain of millions of other Chinese woman and girls—I said to Reggie, "For the Chinese women who will someday come out of their trauma, what they need to hear *first* is not, 'Come to God; he will forgive you,' but, 'Come to God, he will love you, heal you, and free you.'"

In April 2010, I went to Midland, Texas, to visit Bob Fu at the ChinaAid Association, a ministry that supports and defends the persecuted church in China. I liked their ministry so much that I offered to help Bob establish a subgroup to focus on ending forced abortions.

The next month, Bob Fu came to my home with several associates. After spending three days with us, Joe Torres, the chairman of ChinaAid, felt a strong impression from God that I was called to lead this new endeavor. I was not so sure. I had a clear vision to finish writing this book, but I was not prepared to start a ministry.

After taking these guests to the airport, I found a package sent by Reggie at home. It was a taped message by a well-known Christian leader about making your calling true, from Matthew 16:24-26. While I exercised in our basement gym, I listened to the tape. The speaker said

that when God calls you, you had better step out. Don't be so sure that he will call you again. "For whoever wants to save their life will lose it, but whoever loses their life for me will find it" (Matthew 16:25). When God calls, you have to be willing to say good-bye to your home, family, career, etc. As a new Jesus-follower, I listened and obeyed. With fear and trembling, I put away my book plan and my new business plan, and we decided to launch our new ministry, All Girls Allowed, with an announcement on Capitol Hill on June 1, 2010.

Over the past twenty-two years, since the crackdown at Tiananmen, God has breathed life into the Chinese church, creating the largest social movement on earth. An estimated 105 million—almost one in twelve Chinese—are now committed followers of Jesus Christ. When I heard this statistic for the first time, I felt a strong urge to celebrate God's victory. But a few days before our event, someone reminded me that June 1 is Children's Day in China, and I realized that God will not be ready to fully celebrate his victory until *all* his children in China are saved and rescued. Again, I was moved by God's heart of compassion.

Whenever I talk about All Girls Allowed, I'm careful to share about our *whole* vision, which is more than just seeing an end to forced abortions in China. We also want to restore life, value, and dignity to girls and mothers worldwide. In both China and India, families eliminate girls in hopes of raising boys. This crime, called gendercide, is done through prenatal sex selection, infanticide, and abandonment. China's one-child policy makes it worse—with only one baby allowed, who wouldn't choose a boy? Girls cannot carry on the family line and will marry and leave when their parents grow old. For security, every family wants a son. Now in China, six boys are born for every five girls. India, with its dowry system that makes raising a girl expensive, has a similar, terrible gender imbalance problem. A trailer for an upcoming documentary shows an Indian mother who killed eight of her baby girls right after their births.

I knew my father wanted a firstborn son, not a daughter. This knowledge was a painful part of my childhood that began to ease only after I became successful in school and knew he was proud of me. After

having three beautiful daughters, I asked my husband if he wanted me to keep trying for a boy. Bob laughed at the idea and said, "Hey, if having all girls is good enough for the presidents, it's good enough for me!" I was relieved. Here in America, we have examples of successful families raising only girls—the Clintons, George W. Bushes, and Obamas have beautiful daughters who stand strong in their identity as women.

The preference for sons and the one-child policy are a lethal combination. Daily, thousands of baby girls are aborted or killed simply because they are girls. With so many girls now "missing" in China, the surplus of thirty-seven million unmarried young men is bound to cause security and economic problems. With a shortage of available mates for all these eligible bachelors, trafficking of little girls and young women is now out of control in China. All Girls Allowed discovered a city of three million people that has had (over a thirty-year period) as many as six hundred thousand "child brides"—little girls stolen early (so they cannot find their way home), who are then sold to be raised as child brides in strangers' homes.[1]

As the only organization we know of addressing gendercide at a grassroots level, we have started in the rural villages, where the gender imbalance is the worst—in some cases, as many as 130 boys for every 100 girls. We give a financial stipend of twenty dollars per month (which amounts to a substantial subsidy where family incomes are often less than $1,000 per year) to mothers who decide to keep their girls. This allows them to purchase food and clothing for their new babies, and it brings dignity to mothers to help them withstand the pressure to have a son. According to our survey research, women who have participated in our program are most likely to keep their baby (if pregnant again) regardless of gender. This is great progress toward reversing a five-thousand-year tradition. Economist Avraham Ebenstein believes that financial compensation to families in China that give birth to girls can drastically reduce the gendercide.[2]

The movement to end the gendercide of girls is growing. On June 1, 2011, on Capitol Hill, All Girls Allowed launched a bipartisan coalition of Democrats and Republicans, pro-life and pro-choice members of Congress who agree on one thing: killing girls for their gender is wrong and is a crime that has to be stopped. Rather than feeling overwhelmed,

we consider William Wilberforce, who ended the slave trade through his years of prayer and advocacy; and we remember the end of the nine-hundred-year foot-binding movement in China, which was ended in one generation. My grandmother had bound feet. My mother and I did not.

This is where my story joins yours. I encourage you to visit our website—www.allgirlsallowed.org—and ask yourself where you belong in this historic movement. We can end the abortion, infanticide, and abandonment of baby girls in our lifetime.

Shortly after Joe Torres encouraged me to start All Girls Allowed, I lost contact with him for about five months. During that time, I was constantly under attack from unseen forces and constantly questioning my calling.

At one point, Li Lu's name was in the headlines as a possible successor to investment guru Warren Buffet at Berkshire Hathaway. Knowing how hard I had tried to become financially successful, the enemy of my soul whispered in my ear, "Don't you want another chance to prove yourself? Don't you want to go back to the start-up world to execute your new business plan and become successful so you can have the money and resources to do what you want? Do you know what you're doing now? What do you know about running a nonprofit? You've never been good at fund-raising. You haven't trained or prepared for this kind of work." It reminded me of the time when Jesus was tested in the desert and Satan waved the kingdoms of the world in front of him. I had to say, "Go away, Satan. I'm following Jesus!"

Now when I look back at the early days of All Girls Allowed, I am completely at peace. When we resist Satan, it's true that he will eventually flee. As I've continued to grow in my faith and be transformed by the grace of God, my vision for the ministry has come into sharper focus.

With more than four hundred million lives taken in the past thirty years, ending China's one-child policy, the forced and coerced abortion and gendercide of girls, is the most profound social justice cause in the world today. It is one that should unite people on both sides of the abortion issue. Chinese women have no choice, and their babies have no life.

Today about 20 percent of the world's population lives in China under the terror and torment of the one-child policy. The victims are the weakest of society: babies, girls, and women. Every 2.5 seconds, a baby's life is taken by abortion in China. Every day, hundreds of baby girls are abandoned and five hundred women commit suicide. Most of the world does not know about this tragedy. But God knows, and he is working mightily to deliver this nation once and for all into his glorious Kingdom.

When I started All Girls Allowed, I thought of it only as a justice ministry, reflecting God's grieving heart for the more than four hundred million lost children and girls in China, the thirty-five thousand forced abortions taking place every day, and the one million baby girls abandoned each year. As the ministry has grown and I have continued to grow in Christ, I now see that All Girls Allowed is a ministry of hope, a vital step in God's ultimate plan to save China.

The All Girls Allowed movement seeks to restore life, value, and dignity to the most vulnerable members of society—girls and mothers—so that the weak, the orphans, and the widows will truly know and experience the grace of God and the goodness brought by his love. Even though the one-child policy is intended for evil, God is using it for good by mobilizing his church to bring the gospel of Jesus Christ to the rest of the nation.

In the first year after our inception as a ministry, we spent more time praying and studying the Bible than anything else. As a result we've been blessed with miracle after miracle, one amazing encounter after another. God is faithful, and his words are true. There is no doubt this ministry is close to the heart of God, and through his power, grace, and wisdom we will bring this terrible crime against humanity to an end.

———

God has also transformed me through my work at All Girls Allowed. Growing up in China, I had no concept of when life begins. In December 2010, the first time I saw an ultrasound of an eight-week-old fetus, I was shocked by the human likeness of its form. Then a leader who teaches Chinese churches about human development showed me a link

on the Endowment for Human Development website to a *National Geographic* DVD called *The Biology of Prenatal Development.*[3] When I saw the tiny but clearly formed hands and legs, tears started pouring down my face. Only then did I realize that this was how the four little babies of mine had looked before they were sucked away into the pink foam.

Oh, my babies, I am so sorry. I am so sorry. If I had been taught the truth, I would have done everything I could to save you. . . . My God, please forgive me too.

My heart goes out to every young woman or mother who feels ashamed and saddened after her abortion experience. I know the pain and regret. I know the rocky road that lies ahead. How much I desire for you to know the hope and joy I now have and to know that God stands ready to offer forgiveness, healing, and a new life of peace and joy. All you have to do is accept the sacrifice of Jesus on your behalf. He will do the rest. In March 2011, when I read the book *Heaven Is for Real*, my heart leaped for joy when the little boy said he had seen his sister (who had been miscarried) in heaven.

So that's where my four unborn children are, I thought. *That's where the four hundred million murdered Chinese children are—in heaven with Jesus.*

For the first time, I understand why I was kept alive and how God has prepared me each step of the way for this moment of history, for All Girls Allowed and more. Through my journey with God, he has removed my blindfold, showing me a world I never knew existed. I now have a deeper sense of God's passion to save his children and creation, his love for humanity, and his forgiveness for me and for everyone. Not only has he healed me and forgiven me, he has also blessed me with a wonderful husband and three beautiful children. This journey has led me to understand more and more of God's grace and forgiveness. If he can forgive *my* sins, whose sins can he not forgive? Whose sins can *I* not forgive?

35

SACRED SPACES

IN WRITING THIS BOOK, I struggled for weeks to confront this part of my story. Though my journey to faith in Jesus and the founding of All Girls Allowed had brought me a measure of peace about my abortion experience, I still wasn't fully free. At issue was the question of whether this part of my life should remain hidden and private or be shared publically in the hope that other women would come to be set free from the pain and regrets of the past. What I didn't realize was that God had several more steps to take me through to fully heal my heart from the brokenness and shame. With his compassionate care, God was gradually peeling back layers to get to the core of my fear.

At first, I was tentative. The manuscript I submitted to my publisher mentioned the abortion with Feng in Paris and made passing reference to the time when I was eighteen and my father took me. But nobody knew about the others; the secret was still too painful and personal.

As I worked with my editor to develop the final manuscript, we went back and forth, trying to find the best way to include the abortion stories if I decided to share these personal details openly.

On April 15, 2011, I received the edited manuscript to review. Over

the weekend, Bob and I read it and made our notes for corrections and revisions. Finally, on April 18, after we put the kids to bed, we had our first opportunity to sit down together and discuss the book. As Bob and I came to the chapters that talked about the abortions, everything we had been wrestling with over the past few weeks came to the surface.

Bob worried I would be judged harshly by people on both sides of the abortion debate and that the context of my decisions more than twenty years ago in a repressive country like China would be misunderstood in twenty-first-century America. He asked me some questions to prepare me for the responses I might face.

"How could you have so many abortions, especially after the first one was so painful?"

"How could you ever let yourself get pregnant again?"

"What possible benefit could there be of sharing this with the public?"

"What will people think of our children?"

"What will they say about your character?"

"Will our daughters be attacked by mean kids the way you've been attacked about Tiananmen?"

"After this book is published, can you ever go to another meeting at school and look the other parents in the eye?"

"How are you going to feel when heads turn to look at you?"

I'd seen an article in the *Washington Times* about the increasing number of abortions in China and how the demographics are shifting from one-child couples to young, single women.[1] The photo accompanying the article showed a young Chinese woman in the recovery room of an abortion clinic in China. Though only the bottom half of her face was visible in the photo, I could see the sadness and remorse in her expression, and my heart was broken for her. I knew what this woman was going through and what kind of abusive and broken relationships she would continue to face in that society. I hoped that by telling my story, women like her would somehow be led to Jesus, the only one who can give them true hope, freedom, love, and happiness.

"Honey, think about it," I said to Bob. "If we can save even one person by sharing this . . ."

"There might be another way," he said.

Bob is the most loving, kind, compassionate husband I could ever hope for. He has loved me, supported me, and protected me in every way a husband can. When a reporter slammed me with false accusations about Tiananmen, Bob stood up to put forth the truth. This time, though, even he was at the end of his rope.

"I'm only saying these things to protect you and our family," he said.

The same pain I felt when splitting up with Feng washed over me. *Is this the price of freedom? If I tell the truth about what happened to me, will it always lead to friction and fractures with the people I love the most? If I step out to do the work of All Girls Allowed—if I tell the truth about my own abortions so that other women might find hope and healing, will it all come crashing down on my family: my loving, supportive husband and my precious girls?*

What bothered me the most was hearing the same tone from my husband that I recognized from my father, from Feng, and from critics of the Tiananmen movement.

"How could you let it happen?"

It was like the voices I'd heard in the sound of the train on my way home to Rizhao after the incident with the watch: *crush, crush, crush.* I prayed for Jesus to help me and went to bed in anguish.

Early the next morning, I received an e-mail from a woman in my small group at church about the Sacred Spaces the church had set up for people to come and meet with God during the days leading up to Easter. She had personally had a powerful experience there. Before I finished reading the e-mail, I called the office to cancel my morning meeting, took a shower, and drove to the church. If there was ever a time when I needed to meet the Lord, it was now.

The Sacred Spaces were a series of stops around the church campus, each with a particular theme and focus to draw our attention to God. I followed the process to prepare my heart to be quiet and open.

The second stop, in the church basement, was called Confession, based on 1 John 1:9: "If we confess our sins, he is faithful and just and will forgive us our sins and purify us from all unrighteousness."

In a beautifully prepared pamphlet, I read the following description:

In any relationship, unresolved sin will have an impact on the closeness of the relationship. The same is true in our relationship with God. We can't have intimacy with Christ as long as there is ongoing sin in our lives. Confession is necessary for the restoration of the relationship.

As our intimacy with Christ grows, our sins become less like breaking a command and more like betraying a loved one. When you adopt this attitude, confession becomes more like apologizing to a loved one rather than saying a simple prayer. It is not that God wants us to perform some elaborate ritual or jump through some religious hoop. It is that our hearts are broken and we truly desire to make things right.

We are compelled by Christ's forgiveness to forgive others. Sometimes the sin we have in our lives is holding on to hurt or resentment or an unforgiving spirit. Ask the Holy Spirit to show you not only what sins you need to confess, but also whom you need to forgive.[2]

I followed the suggested action, which was to pray Psalm 139:23-24 quietly in my heart: "Search me, O God, and know my heart; test me and know my anxious thoughts. See if there is any offensive way in me, and lead me in the way everlasting." As I read the psalm again, my heart was broken.

Each part of my past was brought up for examination in the presence of Jesus. With tears streaming down my face, I confronted the sex that had led to my abortions.

"Jesus, I am so sorry for doing something offensive to you. I am ashamed that I was not able to be the perfect daughter you wanted me to be, to be blameless in your sight. What does that say about my character? What does that say about my willpower, which was always so strong when it came to scholastic achievement? Now I have a blot on my record that makes me look so weak. Though I didn't know about you for all those years, you know how much my heart was searching for you. I'm so grateful that you found me. But as I move forward to share these stories, the parts I have never shared with anyone, I feel so ashamed. All my

life I thought I was pursuing justice to free my people—like Moses and Esther in the Bible; but now I am so broken before you. I feel more like Mary Magdalene, at risk of being stoned for my sins. How can I finish the work you have called me to with All Girls Allowed? How can anyone have any respect for me? Lord, show me your way. I know you are good. Help me to know the truth!"

As I was soaked in tears and despair, a distinct thought came into my heart: *Child, why are you so filled with fear and despair? In addition to the various circumstances and pressures that led you each time to the moment of consent, there is a part that you were afraid to admit to your husband—that is, the longing in your heart to be connected to and comforted by another being. But those desires and longings are ones that I placed in your heart. To be in awe of another being that I created in my image, the desire to give yourself to another, to be in love—I made you this way before the foundation of the world. I made you in my image to be able to connect and love. I am delighted in you. You are my treasured possession. There is no shame in what I have created in you. What you were searching for was connection to me. But there is a better way to find me and to achieve that everlasting love, which you now know through Jesus . . .*

Like sunshine displacing a dark cloud, I sensed a light had gone on in my heart. It was true; I had been afraid to admit what had led to my consent in those relationships.

Continuing to follow the instructions for the Confession step, I wrote a long list of people I needed to forgive. But my heart was still heavy. I prayed for the Holy Spirit to show me whom else I needed to forgive. The answer brought another torrent of tears. In my heart, I sensed God saying, *The one you really need to forgive is yourself. I have forgiven you and am delighted in you. You should forgive yourself, too.*

In that moment, for the first time in forty years, I felt truly free to just be a child. I felt released from the pressure of all the years when I was expected to be the perfect grown-up, though I was still a young girl, when any small mistake led to severe scolding or punishment. For most of my life—beginning with my father's disappointment when I came

home from the foster home; to the pressure I felt to maintain outstanding scores in school; to the embarrassment of not making it into the physics department at Beida; to the shame and regret I felt for all the abortions; to the attack on my character that grew on a simple twisting and manipulation of one little paragraph in my "last will and testament"; to the misunderstandings I've had over the years, even with Bob, the most loving husband I can imagine, who was now asking me these tough questions—I've felt as if I had to live up to an impossibly high standard if I wanted to be accepted and loved. But now I felt the love of God, who accepts me just as I am and who allows me simply to be his child. As I embraced the freedom that comes with God's forgiveness, I found myself able to let go of the past and forgive others as well.

The next station in the Sacred Spaces was Listening, and a key verse was Hebrews 12:1: "Therefore, since we are surrounded by such a great cloud of witnesses, let us throw off everything that hinders and the sin that so easily entangles. And let us run with perseverance the race marked out for us."

I wanted to embrace this new freedom and continue the race, but my heart was still burdened and my head was bent down. As I closed my eyes to listen and wait for the Lord, a rush came over my body, as if I had just drunk a cup of hot chocolate from heaven—not too sweet, but filled with warmth and a joy beyond my state of sorrow. I felt my head gently lifted, from left to right, and my gaze directed upward. I felt so special, as if the heavenly Father was saying, "*Wipe away your tears; look at me now.*" I felt embraced by light and sunshine. "You, LORD, are a shield around me, my glory, the One who lifts my head high" (Psalm 3:3).

The guidelines for the station instructed me to listen to God and identify anything that was hindering me from following him. Then I was to write that thing on a smooth stone and take the stone with me to a bridge leading out of the Listening station. Before I crossed the bridge—which symbolized determination to follow God with no turn-

ing back—I was to drop the stone by the wayside, leaving all hindrance behind me.

As I listened for God's voice and wisdom, I knew what to write on my stone: *fear of what others may think of me.* That's what was stopping me from following God with my whole heart. I was afraid of other people's opinions. With a desire for freedom welling in my heart, I wrote my fear on the stone, dropped it along the way, and crossed the bridge.

After a while, I went on to the last station—Meditation—where I found many Scripture verses displayed on banners. One verse in particular jumped out at me:

> *Look! God's dwelling place is now among the people, and he will dwell with them. They will be his people, and God himself will be with them and be their God. "He will wipe every tear from their eyes. There will be no more death" or mourning or crying or pain, for the old order of things has passed away. . . . I will be their God and they will be my children. (Revelation 21:3-4, 7)*

Later that afternoon, when I told my friend Tammy what I had experienced at the Listening station, she exclaimed, "Wow, you met the Lord today! That was who was speaking to you, Ling. God has accepted you and embraced you for who you are. And he was doing something very powerful this morning. He was peeling away all the layers of shame that are wrapped around those events. He's breaking them off and setting you free."

Her words were so powerful that I didn't know quite how to digest them.

That night, when I was putting my middle daughter to bed, she wanted me to stay in her room and wait for her to fall asleep. In the quiet darkness, I ran through the events of the day in my mind, asking, "Lord, was that really you? You came, bent down, and lifted my face up from shame to praise." I felt my head lifted up again, this time from left to right and from right to left. I felt the Lord was taking me out through the walls and windows into the open sky, and he was taking me with him, dancing, twirling, and flying. I saw many lights in the darkness—of cities, mountains, and stars. With delight, I experienced beautiful feelings of love and joy, flying freely in the evening sky.

When I shared this experience with Bob and told him what Tammy had said, he was glad but still had reservations about including the abortion stories in the book. I talked to several Christian friends, and they suggested I continue to pray about it. In the meantime, I kept going up and down on the emotional roller coaster.

The day before Easter, Bob and I took our children to the Sacred Spaces stations before they were taken down for the season. There, in the Journaling station, as I read from the book of Ephesians—"Paul, an apostle of Christ Jesus by the will of God"—I felt the Lord speaking to my heart: "*Look at my apostle Paul, who persecuted the church. What do you have to be worried about? I know your desire is to be holy and perfect. But none of my saints has ever been perfect: Abraham, Moses, David, Saul, Peter. There is only one who is holy and blameless; that is my son, Jesus. Don't try to be God. Just be my child.*"

As I read, words and phrases jumped off the page at me, reassuring me of God's love and forgiveness and of his purpose for my life.

He chose us in him before the creation of the world to be holy and blameless *in his sight.*[3]

In him we have redemption through his blood, the forgiveness of sins, in accordance with the riches of God's grace *that he lavished on us. With all wisdom and understanding, he made known to us the mystery of his will according to his good pleasure, which he purposed in Christ, to be put into effect when the times reach their fulfillment—to bring unity to all things in heaven and on earth under Christ.*[4]

For by grace you have been saved through faith. And this is not your own doing; it is the gift of God, not a result of works, so that no one may boast. For we are his workmanship, created in Christ Jesus for good works, which God prepared beforehand, that we should walk in them.[5]

I am simply amazed to know that God and Jesus love me just the way I am—with my past, present, and future. I am God's perfect workmanship, created in Jesus Christ for good works. Despite future challenges, this knowledge has become an anchoring rock in my soul.

At the Journaling station, we were encouraged to write a letter to God. My heart was filled with his love for me and my love for him. I told him I was willing to do whatever he asked me to do—whether that meant telling the story of my abortions or keeping them private. But like Gideon in the Bible, I prayed that God would confirm his will by showing me a sign. Two days later, he did.

36

OVERCOMING DARKNESS (MOVING INTO THE LIGHT)

ON APRIL 25, we received an e-mail on the All Girls Allowed website from a Chinese woman who said she'd had an abortion years ago and now wanted to share some good news. I had a feeling her e-mail had been prompted by God, but I was also afraid her "good news" might be an attack. With fear and trembling, I agreed to speak with her by phone the next day. When she called, she opened her heart and told me her story.

Huang had known of me during the Tiananmen events but was in high school at the time. When she was in her third year of college, she became pregnant. Her boyfriend was a graduate student and told her that keeping the baby might affect her graduation, so she went for an abortion. She and her boyfriend eventually married and came to America, and she became a Jesus-follower. She was ashamed about the abortion, and she didn't want to tell anyone about it. But it was tormenting her.

Then, two years ago, a friend came to visit. While they were having lunch, the friend shared that she'd had an abortion and felt guilty, but

after going to an eight-week Bible study for women suffering over the experience of an abortion, she had been healed by the Lord and now was sharing her story with tears of joy rather than sadness.

Huang said she did not say anything about this at the time, but it began to eat at her. She wanted to call for information about the Bible study, but she was afraid. One day she saw her friend coming out of the library and felt the Lord encouraging her to share the story of her abortion. Her friend was immediately sympathetic and helped Huang secure a spot in the Bible study group.

As she was completing one of the lessons, Huang wept as she felt the full magnitude of her abortion decision, which she had never been willing to face head-on. She said it was as if a tsunami had hit her. But then the Lord began to heal her, just as he restored Saul after his encounter with Jesus on the road to Damascus.

During one of the Bible study sessions, the women were asked to name their babies and offer them to God as a means of letting go. When Huang did this, she felt tremendous peace.

Without revealing the struggle I was experiencing, I told her I knew exactly what she was going through and I would explain why the next time we spoke. She pressed on, saying she felt the Holy Spirit was telling her to tell me he had a big job for me—and she would be part of it too. Then she began to read to me the words of Isaiah 61:

> The Spirit of the Sovereign LORD is on me,
>   because the LORD has anointed me
>   to proclaim good news to the poor.
> He has sent me to bind up the brokenhearted,
>   to proclaim freedom for the captives
>   and release from darkness for the prisoners,
> to proclaim the year of the LORD's favor
>   and the day of vengeance of our God,
> to comfort all who mourn,
>   and provide for those who grieve in Zion—
> to bestow on them a crown of beauty
>   instead of ashes,

the oil of joy
  instead of mourning,
and a garment of praise
  instead of a spirit of despair.
They will be called oaks of righteousness,
  a planting of the LORD
  for the display of his splendor.

I was deeply moved, and I told her these were the very same verses I had used when offering the closing prayer at the National Prayer Breakfast in February 2011. I've learned that those kinds of "coincidences" mean that God is speaking to me about something.

That evening Bob went to bed early after we had stayed up late for several nights working through these issues together. But I could not fall asleep. Finally I called Huang again. I wanted to know the connection between the abortion stories she had told me and the preaching of good news in Isaiah 61.

Huang told me she had learned in the eight-week Bible study that one of the key steps to freedom is for women to share their stories publicly. Because God and Jesus are light, if we bring our hidden shame and pain into the light, we can be set free from the power of darkness. Once the truth is out in the open, the devil no longer has a foothold in our lives. But if we continue to conceal our secrets, we will still be held captive to the past. Jesus wants us to receive and enjoy total freedom.

That was a big challenge for me. The thought of disclosing such personal details made me feel exposed and weak. It made me feel I would be judged and condemned again—as I'd been judged by the saleswoman in 1987—by people who don't even know me and by others who already oppose me because of their perception of my role at Tiananmen Square. Now I risked being misunderstood by both the pro-life and pro-choice sides. I was afraid something I said would trigger an unexpected explosion and condemnation.

Huang did not know what was going through my mind. She was overjoyed to realize that God had begun to prepare her two years ago for this moment when she would share her journey with me. Two years earlier, I wasn't even a Jesus-follower yet. I felt nervous. *God, why would*

you call me, a brand-new believer in Jesus, to do this? It took Sister Huang fourteen years to get to the point where she is able to talk about her experience in public. I haven't even had eight weeks to complete the Bible study!

The next evening, in our small group, I felt God was speaking to me through Philippians 2:5-8: "In your relationships with one another, have the same mindset as Christ Jesus: Who, being in very nature God, did not consider equality with God something to be used to his own advantage; rather, he made himself nothing by taking the very nature of a servant, being made in human likeness. And being found in appearance as a man, he humbled himself by becoming obedient to death—even death on a cross!"

Because of past wounds, I am especially vulnerable to attacks on my reputation—the insults, the judgments behind my back, the silent avoidance. Then I knew God was calling me to humble myself, like Jesus did, to show my brokenness to the world so that he could bring healing to many, even as he brings healing to me.

That evening, as I kept reading Scripture, I felt God speaking to me on every page, encouraging me to press on. He strengthened my conviction that by moving ahead and sharing my stories I would bring good news to the captives—to every woman still suffering in silence, like I had for so long.

On Thursday, I worked up the courage to share my story with my team at All Girls Allowed. Their reactions were amazing. Brian, a recently married Chinese Canadian, told me about his own struggles with sin and how he came to understand the joy of forgiveness and restoration. Though he grew up with a lack of intimacy in his family, he is now experiencing the joy of being loved by his wife, and they look forward to seeing each other every night after work. He said we need to continue to search Isaiah 61 for an understanding of what it means to set the captives free, because he struggled with how to uphold the value of life without further singling out the marginalized: women, minorities, and the poor.

A beautiful young professional woman on my staff was brought to tears by my story. She said her mother had had an abortion and was afraid to tell her husband and children for twenty-six years. When she finally shared with her small group, she felt she was judged by the other women. Now she's so hurt that she's afraid to talk about it anymore. When I said, "The message we need to communicate is not, 'Come to God and he will forgive you,' but, 'Come to God and he will love you, heal you, and free you,'" my staff member's face brightened up. I could see that she already can't wait to bring this book to share with her mom.

After the young woman left the room, I saw tears in the eyes of another woman on my staff. She said her family members were all die-hard Christians and pro-life, and she regretted that one of her sisters has a T-shirt that says, "Abortion is like guns killing babies." I'm glad that God wants to bring truth to the righteous people as well, just so long as they don't try to be God—convicting and condemning others and hoping that will stop the killing. My experience is that God has been most gentle. He teaches us in the most powerful way that a fetus is already a baby, and he turns hearts, but he does not hammer people. We can have the strength of our convictions without condemning those who have had abortions. Our role is to set the captives free, not further enslave them.

While I was testing the waters by sharing my story with trusted friends, Bob was on his own search for peace about sharing this information. I knew that in the back of his mind a single question continued to burn: *How could you let it happen so many times?*

On the evening of April 28, I found him in the library at home, researching abortion in China going back to the 1970s.

"Listen to some of these facts," he said. "More than two hundred million abortions were conducted in China in the 1970s and 1980s, ranging up to fourteen million a year. According to one study, more than 52 percent of women in China, ages twenty to thirty-five, had two or more abortions. Only 14 percent had not had an abortion. A study by Beijing Medical University in 1988 found that the abortion rate in

urban areas was 101 abortions per 100 live births. That's more abortions than births! Another report says that multiple abortions are on the rise again in China as young people choose abortions that are quick, easy, and painless as a means of birth control. China is a culture of abortion, and people even to this day think nothing of it. I'm amazed to find such jarring statistics so readily available from a simple Google search.[1] It's a very well-studied and documented area of sociology."

As I absorbed these statistics, Bob added, "So you were in the majority."

Bob seemed at ease with this information, but something was still wrong. Though he understood that the situation in China is unlike America, he was troubled and distant—which made me sad. I'd been told that following Jesus means you move forward with Jesus even if your family doesn't agree with you, but Bob is also the head of our household, and I did not feel right about disclosing the stories of my abortions without his agreement. I felt it made sense to him intellectually, but in his spirit he was still unsettled.

As the weekend approached, I was worn out, and my heart was aching—this time not for my past but for the tension that had developed between Bob and me. As he flew to New York to attend a retreat hosted by Dr. Tim Keller's City to City ministry, I prayed, "God, help me. If you've called me to share this message of hope for women who have had abortions, you also have to bring unity within my family."

By Monday evening, after struggling to finish the latest round of revisions for the book and send them to my editor, I was physically done. I felt I was coming down with the flu, accompanied by a nasty cough. The thought of flying out on Thursday for a college commencement speech only made me feel worse. By Tuesday I was down for the count, drinking flu remedies and feeling awful. There wasn't a muscle in my body that didn't ache. Whatever burning in hell would be like, it might not be too far from how I was feeling.

On Wednesday morning when I forced myself to get up and go to work, I had no idea what the day would bring. When I checked my e-mail, I found a message from Bob, sent the previous day at the lowest point of my illness. He made reference to a significant breakthrough he'd had at the retreat. I couldn't wait to hear the full story.

On Sunday, May 1, the last day of the retreat, Bob had accompanied some of the City to City staff to hear Tim Keller preach at Redeemer Presbyterian Church. Though sitting in a congregation of thousands, Bob felt as if the sermon—on understanding the meaning of grace—was speaking directly to him.

The key to understanding grace, Dr. Keller said, is recognizing that we were all *dead* in our sins (Ephesians 2:5). If we were merely *sick* in our sins, there would be degrees of illness and degrees of treatment. But dead is dead. When we're dead, we don't need treatment, we need a *resurrection*, and there is nothing we ourselves can do to bring that about. So grace is not only a free gift from God, it is also *indispensable* to our lives. On top of that, even though grace is a free gift to us, it was purchased at the price of Jesus' life—which makes it *infinitely costly*, as well.

If we have received this gift of grace, Dr. Keller continued, which is both indispensable and infinitely costly, on what basis do we look down our noses at others for the sins or wrongs they have committed?

Bob said it took the full length of Dr. Keller's sermon for the message to sink in, but by the end he realized he had been looking down at me for the events of my past. He said, "Tim Keller made me realize I did not understand grace. If I did, I would never have judged anything you did. Now I understand that I am just as guilty as anyone else who has ever done wrong, and I am only made righteous by Jesus—so there's no room for judgment, pride, or boasting. That's why the thief on the cross next to Jesus could be saved at the last minute and it's completely fair to others who have faithfully followed Jesus all their lives. I will do my best not to judge anyone else, remembering that I am saved by God's grace, as are we all. And I will support any decision you make about sharing even the most personal and private portions of your story."

How beautiful God is! He hears our prayers and answers them. He brought unity into my marriage in a powerful way, and he also prepared Bob and me for the road ahead.

I decided to move forward in telling my story because I believe this is how God wants me to share the good news about his healing and his love. When you consider that 86 percent of all Chinese women have had at least one abortion and 52 percent have had two or more, and when more than 40 percent of American women will have an abortion by the age of forty-five, it's clear that hundreds of millions of women are victims of abortion, along with their babies.

I feel heartbroken for women like Wujian, who wanted to be a mother but watched her baby killed and then became a scorned woman, discarded to the lowest levels of Chinese society. I feel compassion for the millions of young women in China who have suffered the same fate I did and are still suffering in silence today. I understand the shattered innocence, the deeply held hurts and shame. I understand crying out for help, yet potentially being betrayed by friends or being marked for ongoing abuse, despair, and violence, both verbal and physical. I was once that girl with the IV in one hand and the other hand covering her face.

I feel compassion for all the American women who live in outward freedom yet are held hostage by the devil for their past. You see, the picture of that young woman in the recovery room is not just a picture of a Chinese girl; it's a picture of every woman who has gone through an abortion and now suffers in silence.

A woman on my staff who read a draft of the manuscript had a great insight. She said, "The biggest villain here is shame. It was shame that led to those abortions. But the victory is to bring all things to light, to not let shame have its way in the darkness." That's powerful. I had never thought of it that way.

I have been set free by God's love, and that's the freedom I want to share. God is doing great things to bring freedom to every woman in bondage to her past. By sharing my stories openly, I hope to create an environment in which all women can feel safe to talk openly about their experiences, without fear of judgment and condemnation, and to be embraced by God's love, acceptance, and delight. "For we are his workmanship, created in Christ Jesus for good works, which God prepared beforehand, that we should walk in them" (Ephesians 2:10, ESV). Only

when we expose the truth about our past experiences can we bring life, value, and dignity to every child, girl, woman, and mother.

If you see yourself in what I've shared, I want you to know that no matter how dark your world may seem, there is one who stands nearby in love and patience, with respect and honor for you. That person is Jesus. He is waiting to save you from your darkness and shame; to give you "a crown of beauty instead of ashes, the oil of joy instead of mourning, and a garment of praise instead of a spirit of despair" (Isaiah 61:3).

THE FACE OF JESUS

IN THE TWENTY-FIRST CENTURY, America will have no relationship more important than its relationship with China. Our leaders must have their eyes wide open and know whom they're dealing with as they build this partnership. The best way to protect America is to help transform China into a peaceful and benevolent society. Respect for basic human rights, the freedom to worship, rule of law, and free media are all part of that necessary transformation. Still, the true transformation of China will not be political or social; it will be a reformation of the heart. The next revolution will not be fought in the streets; it will be won within each individual. As I've learned through my own experience, when we're confronted by the evil inside us and have to ask Jesus to cleanse us so we can receive his grace and forgiveness, then we can truly heal and move on. The same is true for a nation.

Spiritually, there is a great hunger for the gospel in China. Ten percent of the population has come to Jesus over the past sixty years, under the threat of persecution. A friend who recently visited Beijing said, "The Holy Spirit is working overtime in China." In 1983, when

I started at Beida, people had to talk in whispers about secret gatherings in the countryside to worship God. Today, at that same university alone, more than two hundred Bible study groups meet on campus, and an official class on Jesus is offered to seven hundred students.

The Chinese government seems to recognize this spiritual hunger. They even erected a giant statue of Confucius in Tiananmen Square in January 2011. But their efforts to find something to hold the country together will inevitably be undermined by the massive amount of corruption, violence, and crime that results from the people's lack of a transformative belief system.

Even as the spiritual awakening continues, little progress has been made toward democracy. Hu Yaobang, whose death triggered the Tiananmen movement, wanted China to have three reforms: political, economic, and spiritual. Zhao Ziyang, who was dismissed for not approving the massacre, agreed with the first two. But Deng Xiaoping, the leader who ordered the massacre, wanted only one reform—economic reform—and that is what China has had for the past twenty-two years.

Still, as the nation emerges on the world economic scene, the fruits of prosperity are not widely distributed. Five thousand Chinese families control much of the nation's wealth, political power, and military force. There is a growing middle class—certainly more than before 1989—and their lives may be getting better; but for the have-nots in China, the story only gets worse. An estimated 468 million Chinese live on less than two dollars a day.[1] They are forgotten under the shadow of the wealthy few.

I now believe that transforming China into a Jesus-following nation is the key to open democracy in that country. Spiritual reform will be the foundation for the rest of the reforms. Even though the Chinese government may appear bigger and more powerful, and they are continuing to persecute dissidents and faithful Jesus-followers, I feel a strong sense of hope, peace, and joy. I feel victory and freedom are near. For the oppressors, there is hope for them to repent and find true freedom and peace.

In God's timing and in God's way, we will finish the unfinished work we started at Tiananmen, to bring freedom and salvation to China. This time, a new chapter of China's history will be written. Greater things are yet to come. My role today is to help save the hundreds of millions of Chinese women, girls, and unborn children currently under siege from the one-child policy. God wants us to give the oppressed—women, girls, children, the poor, and the weak—a sense of hope, to assure them that Jesus loves them and will never leave them or forsake them, and to let them know that Jesus is preparing a beautiful future for them, as he has done for me.

Recently, God spoke to my heart again and asked me to share the good news about Jesus with men and boys in China as well—to change their hearts of stone into hearts of flesh.

Each night I read a chapter of the Bible with my children. One night, as we read Exodus 3, which picks up the story of Moses after he killed the Egyptian and had to flee to the desert of Midian, I felt God finally answered my long-standing question: Why had we not succeeded at Tiananmen? I could see that just as Moses had tried to bring about justice for his oppressed countrymen by taking matters into his own hands, we had tried to bring freedom and justice to China in our own strength and wisdom. Only later, when Moses was called by God at the burning bush and stepped out in faith and joined God's movement, was he able to lead and free the nation of Israel.

The Tiananmen event was a milestone in God's redemptive plan for China. He allowed evil to happen—the massacre—to kill our belief in the Communist system. This revelation brought an end to my search for an answer to the question I asked during the last hours of the protest: Why do they have to kill us when all we wanted was a dialogue? I believe that God allowed the leaders to harden their hearts, just as he hardened Pharaoh's heart in the time of Moses, so he could reveal the true nature of Communism and kill the false belief and hope the people had in it. God used the massacre to work toward his plan for China.

I remember the moment I was set free from the survivor's guilt I had carried since Tiananmen. Shortly after the twentieth anniversary of the massacre, I decided to confront the past, no matter how painful it might be. I picked up a book called *The Tiananmen Papers*, which is a compilation of internal Chinese government documents and other official documents about the events at Tiananmen in 1989. In a transcript from June 3, President Yang Shangkun says, "We must do everything we possibly can to avoid bloodshed. . . . And let me repeat: No bloodshed within Tiananmen Square—period. What if thousands of students refuse to leave? Then the troops carry away thousands of students on their backs! No one must die in the Square. This is not just my personal view; it is Comrade Xiaoping's view, too."[2]

When I read those words, a chill went down my spine. On the one hand, I was grateful the government had intended to protect the lives of the students. On the other hand, it was now clear the army had decided where and when to kill. Still, I felt the weight of guilt lift from my shoulders. All these years, the truth had been hidden from me and from those who were misled about the massacre. I could now relate to the story of Simba in *The Lion King*, who thought he was responsible for his father's death and did everything he could to run away from the past. But once he learned the truth, he became victorious and brought freedom to his homeland. Now I know that the truth is in Jesus, and he will lead China to freedom.

* * *

God used the Tiananmen events to save me and free me. He used everything that happened afterward to break my dependence on friends, comrades, connections, the media, the public, the legal system, and law enforcement so I could see I'm completely helpless unless I trust and rely only on him. When I thought I was giving my life to Jesus so he would save China, little did I know that the first ones saved would be me and my family.

I no longer live in fear, for I know that God almighty is holding my right hand and watching over me, and my true big brother, Jesus, will be with me until the very end. Even better, it is no longer my battle to fight

or to win—it's *his*. All I have to do is take up my position, stand firm, and watch for God's deliverance.

History will remember the 1989 Tiananmen movement as one vital step forward in China's century-long struggle for true freedom. Beginning with the Boxer Rebellion, China has been through chaos: the warlord era, civil war, the Japanese invasion, the War of Liberation, Communism, the Great Leap Forward, the Cultural Revolution, and the April Fifth Movement to end the rule of the Gang of Four. Then in 1989 came the largest people's movement of the twentieth century. It will not be the last one. I believe greater things will come, and China will be set free.

———

As I finished my review of the edited manuscript, I knew there was still something missing, something without which the book would not be complete. I prayed that God would show me what that was.

On May 9, 2011, he did.

When I opened my e-mail that day, I was surprised to find a message from a long-lost friend and colleague, Li Lanju. She was a Christian student from Hong Kong who was with us at Tiananmen Square in 1989. She had sent me a journal entry she had written in 1999.

On the night of the killings, Li was on the east side of Tiananmen Square, with several other Hong Kong students and Beijing citizens, standing shoulder to shoulder against the army troops. The soldiers on the front line did not open fire, she said, but the ones behind them did. All of a sudden, screams and cries of anguish rose from the crowd behind her. A young boy cried out, "They killed my big brother, they killed my big brother. I am going to fight them, I am going to fight them." She grabbed the boy and held him with all her strength as they cried together. Eventually she was pushed onto a bus and told by the Beijing citizens, "Go back to Hong Kong and tell the world what happened here."

That's what she has been doing for the past twenty years. But like me she has seen the change in people's attitudes, from passion and outrage to coldness, withdrawal, and indifference. And some have even blamed her for the people who were killed. It's lonely to be a survivor and a

fighter when the rest of the world wants to put the past behind them and get on with business.

Over and over throughout the years, she asked God, "Where were you on the day of the massacre? Where were you when all those people were gunned down?"

Ten years ago, she asked the question again. This time, however, rather than questioning God in anger, she quieted her heart and waited for him to answer. At that moment, the image reappeared in her mind that had haunted her for the past ten years: a young student, dying of a gunshot wound, his face covered with blood, but still repeating as he lay on the ground, "Persevere until the end, persevere until the very end. . . ."

Just then, she saw another figure, coming up slowly from far away. He also had blood covering his face, but Li was not afraid or shaken. Even though she could not see him clearly, she recognized him as he walked up calmly, with peace and dignity. Then the picture of the young, dying student and the approaching figure merged into one, and Li heard a gentle voice say, "How could you not know where I was? I was right here."

Li said she instantly burst into tears. A deep wound, which had been open for ten years, was finally healed.

As I read Li's journal entry, I felt my own wounded spirit being healed as well. After twenty-two years, the question of my heart was answered. *Jesus, you were right there with us, on the front line. And you are with my friends in heaven. We will carry on the good work you have prepared for us, persevering until the very end!*

As we wait to see the fulfillment of God's purpose and plan, we will stay firm and hold fast to his promises:

He will wipe every tear from their eyes, and there will be no more death or sorrow or crying or pain. All these things are gone forever. (Revelation 21:4, NLT)

All who are victorious will inherit all these blessings, and I will be their God, and they will be my children. (Revelation 21:7, NLT)

And we pray without ceasing, "Lord Jesus, in your timing, do it swiftly!"

Dear friend, now that you have walked with me through my entire journey, it would not be fair if I left without sharing with you the question Brother Yun once asked me that changed my life forever: *Are you ready to walk with Jesus?*

If you're ready to begin the journey to achieve life-transforming freedom, simply say the following prayer and put your trust in Jesus:

Dear Jesus, I now know that you are my God and my Savior. Please forgive all my sins, known and unknown, and please come into my heart, guide my life, and bring me to freedom. Amen.

If you've decided to take this first step, please feel free to e-mail me at info@allgirlsallowed.org. I would love to hear from you.

NOTES

PRELUDE

1. Mara Hvistendahl, "The Great Forgetting: 20 Years After Tiananmen Square," *Journal of Higher Education*, May 19, 2009, http://chronicle.com/article/The-Great-Forgetting-20-Ye /44267.

CHAPTER 14: THE DONG LUAN VERDICT

1. Zhang Liang, comp., Andrew J. Nathan and Perry Link, eds., *The Tiananmen Papers: The Chinese Leadership's Decision to Use Force against Their Own People—in Their Own Words*, paperback edition (New York: PublicAffairs, 2002), 53–60.
2. Ibid., 73.
3. *People's Daily* editorial, Foreign Broadcast Information Service, April 25, 1989, 23–24.
4. Ren Wanding, *Selected Original Documents from China's Democracy Movement, Big- and Small-Character Posters, Leaflets, Private Newsletters*, part II, 160–163.

CHAPTER 20: DEFENDING TIANANMEN SQUARE

1. Li Lu, *Moving the Mountain* (London: Macmillan, 1990), 193–195.

CHAPTER 21: LAST WILL AND TESTAMENT

1. The English text of this letter can be read online at http://www.64memo.com/d/Default. aspx?tabid=97.

CHAPTER 22: THE LAST STAND

1. Hou Dejian, "Heirs of the Dragon." Translation of Chinese text: http://www.onedayinmay. net/Other/Leehom/HeirsDragon.html.
2. Ibid.

CHAPTER 30: CULTURE SHOCK

1. Patrick E. Tyler, "Six Years After the Tiananmen Massacre, Survivors Clash Anew on Tactics," *New York Times*, April 30, 1995, http://www.nytimes.com/1995/04/30/world /6-years-after-the-tiananmen-massacre-survivors-clash-anew-on-tactics.html.

CHAPTER 33: FINDING FREEDOM

1. *An Evaluation of 30 Years of the One-Child Policy in China*, hearing before the Tom Lantos Human Rights Commission of the United States House of Representatives, 111th Congress, first session, November 10, 2009, official transcript, 38.

CHAPTER 34: ALL GIRLS ALLOWED

1. For an excellent study of the effects of gendercide and gender imbalance, see Mara Hvistendahl, *Unnatural Selection: Choosing Boys over Girls, and the Consequences of a World Full of Men* (New York: PublicAffairs, 2011).

2. See Avraham Y. Ebenstein, "Estimating a Dynamic Model of Sex Selection in China," Population Association of America, 2011; http://pluto.huji.ac.il/~ebenstein/Ebenstein _SexSelection_2011.pdf.

3. Information about *The Biology of Prenatal Development* can be found online at http://www .ehd.org/products_bpd_dvd.php. The "movie clip" I saw from the DVD can be viewed online at http://www.ehd.org/movies.php.

CHAPTER 35: SACRED SPACES

1. Alexa Olesen, "China's Abortion Numbers Grow," *Washington Times*, January 13, 2011; http://www.washingtontimes.com/news/2011/jan/13/chinas-abortion-numbers-grow.

2. These instructions were part of "Sacred Spaces," a self-guided spiritual retreat at Grace Chapel, Lexington, Massachusetts, during Holy Week 2011. The pamphlet was written by Peter Dupre, Grace Chapel's former pastor of worship and the arts.

3. Ephesians 1:4, emphasis added.

4. Ephesians 1:7-10, emphasis added.

5. Ephesians 2:8-10, ESV, emphasis added.

CHAPTER 36: OVERCOMING DARKNESS (MOVING INTO THE LIGHT)

1. Thomas W. Strahan, JD, "Induced Abortion among Chinese Women: I. Sociological Aspects," *Association for Interdisciplinary Research in Values and Social Change*, vol. 14, no. 1, July/August, 1999; http://www.lifeissues.net/writers/air/air_vol14no1_20001.html. Grace Ng, "13 Million Abortions a Year in China," *Straits Times*, February 26, 2011; http://www .straitstimes.com/BreakingNews/Asia/Story/STIStory_639112.html.

CHAPTER 37: THE FACE OF JESUS

1. The number 468 million is based on 36.3 percent of the 1.3 billion population of China living on less than two dollars per day, as reported in *Human Development Report 2009*, "Human and income poverty," http://hdrstats.undp.org/en/indicators/103.html.

2. Zhang Liang, comp., Andrew J. Nathan and Perry Link, eds., *The Tiananmen Papers: The Chinese Leadership's Decision to Use Force against Their Own People—in Their Own Words*, paperback edition (New York: PublicAffairs, 2002), 370. Ellipsis in original.

ACKNOWLEDGMENTS

As I look back at my life to this point, my heart is filled with gratitude. So many people have helped me arrive where I am today. Each one of you has my thanks, even if your name falls beyond the limits of my immediate memory. Please forgive me—and remind me.

First, I want to thank my mom and dad, who gave life to me and taught me service and sacrifice by the way they lived their lives. I thank them for how much they loved me and stood by me. I also thank my grandma, who raised me and taught me hard work and compassion.

Next, I want to thank the countless friends I met and made during the fifty days of the Tiananmen movement. Many of your names I never knew or can't remember, but your faces, your passion, your trust, your boundless courage and devotion will always be part of my life and my memories of those days. You are always my inspiration. I want to especially thank those with whom I worked directly: Feng, Boli, Xiongyan, Fengsuo, Chang Jin, Wang Dan, Li Lu, and the many Hong Kong student leaders who came to support us in Beijing and stood with us until the last hour, including Lanju, another sister.

I am thankful for so many people—Beijing citizens, doctors, news reporters, Chinese government officials, some military soldiers and officers, and friends and supporters around the world—who stood in solidarity with the students. I am very thankful to the friends and supporters from Hong Kong, Taiwan, and overseas, who donated time and resources to support the movement.

I want to acknowledge all who have suffered and all who continue the struggle—especially those who gave their lives and freedom in pursuit of a

better China and a more loving and peaceful world. I particularly want to acknowledge the courage and perseverance of the Tiananmen Mothers, who are continuing the struggle to bring justice on behalf of their loved ones. You are our inspiration.

I want to thank the Western media, especially reporters and correspondents from CNN, CBS, ABC, BBC, VOA, *TIME*, and the *New York Times* for your courageous coverage of the events at Tiananmen Square that shook the world, shaped memories, and helped bring peaceful changes in Eastern Europe and the former Soviet Union. Your work has reached far and beyond—even to the recent revolution in the Middle East, when an Egyptian general declared that the situation there would not be like Beijing and there would not be another Tiananmen-like massacre.

I believe in the power of learning and education to transform the human mind and the human condition. I have been blessed with extraordinary teachers who have shaped my life, and I thank them all. From the beginning, my grade school teachers and math teachers helped me discover my passion for learning; their encouragement and praise set me on the track to future success.

My high school teacher and mentor, Mrs. Qian, taught me about Madame Curie and introduced me to the rich history and heritage of Peking University, our beloved Beida. Her encouragement for me to list Beida as my first school choice was a pivotal moment that shaped my history and affected China's as well. My great teacher Han from high school recognized my abilities early on, encouraged my father, and never wavered in his support, even during the aftermath of the massacre when political pressure weighed upon him. My friends from that period of my life, both girls and boys, were an inspiration to me, and I thank you for being a blessing to me then and in my memories now.

My life blossomed at Beida, thanks to my first-year class director and so many wonderful professors, friends, and schoolmates who helped me come out of my shell of quiet shyness. Special thanks to a long list that includes Qing, Feng, Ping Ping, Xiu Sheng, my young friend from Hunan, my friend at CCTV, my campus newspaper editor, many of my roommates, and the coach of the running team (I will always remember your laughter, your jokes, and your stories). I want to thank the friend who opened the first café at Beida—I had a lot of fun helping you. I also want to thank Beijing Normal University's child psychology director and several roommates and sisters who provided a loving community for me in the time after Beida.

I thank all the brave souls who work for human rights, freedom, and democracy around the world, often at great cost and risk to themselves. I want

to thank Da Ge, Big Brother, and each and every one of the two-hundred-plus-member network that rescued and protected Feng and me during the most dangerous ten months of hiding after the Tiananmen massacre. It is because of your courage and sacrifice that I am still alive—and I am forever grateful. I pray for Jesus to be with you and bless you and your families through a thousand generations. I want to thank Ahong, whom we called Little Brother, who courageously rescued Feng and me out of China. I am thrilled to learn that you came to know Jesus and that the Lord has blessed you with a wonderful family and three beautiful children. I am very thankful to Szeto Wah (Uncle Wah) and other leaders from the Hong Kong Alliance, who rescued Feng and me to the free world after our escape from China, who also helped hundreds of other dissidents escape from China, and who even now continue to courageously and consistently support the democracy movement.

I am thankful for the help provided by Dimon Liu, David Phillips, Mary Daly, Michael Posner, and the leaders of the Chinese student federation in the United States during my first visit to America. I am grateful to Charles and Beth's hospitality in Santa Fe, where I went to rest and recover.

I am very thankful to Jimmy Lai and Teresa Lai, whose generosity enabled me to stay in a hotel during my second time in Paris. I am especially grateful to Teresa, who radiated the love of Jesus during that very lonely and difficult time. She became a precious friend and a wonderful refuge during a time when it seemed the world was going to swallow me up. Teresa has a quiet demeanor, and her spirit is always filled with joy. She was like an angel sent by God. She helped me regain my appreciation for life, from the taste of Japanese noodles to the beautiful design of a perfume bottle. In the valley of life's darkness, Teresa was a ray of sunshine.

I am thankful to those government leaders who were—and are—willing to put the cause of freedom and human rights first when the easy course would be to bow to China's economic power. I am thankful to the French government and diplomats who gave me my first country of refuge and who cared for and protected me during my first few months in the West. Thanks also to Trudie Styler, for her kindness to me; to Congresswoman Nancy Pelosi, who was among the first US government leaders to visit me when I was in Paris; and to Vice President Dan Quayle, who welcomed me to the White House when I first came to the United States.

I thank the late Tom Lantos and the Tom Lantos Human Rights Commission for their tireless work to improve China's human rights situation and for honoring me with their Congressional Human Rights award. Thank you to

Senators Malcolm Wallop and Edward Kennedy and their staffs for hiring me and giving me good insights into democracy at work and to Lianchao, who helped me find a summer residence during my DC internships.

I thank President Bill Clinton for his personal negotiation with the Chinese government to bring my family out from China to be reunited with me; and his trusted adviser (and my friend) Nancy Soderberg, who helped put my family on the list for this negotiation. I thank the people I met in the administrations of Presidents George H. W. Bush, George W. Bush, and Barack Obama, who have continued to press China to reform its terrible record on human rights, religious freedom, and the rule of law. I have seen many leaders in America rise up to defend freedom—from the time of Tiananmen in 1989, when our friend and summer neighbor Ambassador Ray Burghardt and his wife, Susan, searched the hospitals in Beijing for the dead and wounded; to the late Ambassador James R. Lilley, who documented his eyewitness account of Tiananmen in his moving memoir, *China Hands*; to the recent book by our friend Governor Mitt Romney, *No Apology*, calling out the great risk to our own future freedom posed by the Communist government of China.

I applaud Secretary of State Hillary Clinton's criticism of China's human rights record during President Hu Jingtao's visit to Washington, DC, in January 2011. I am thankful to Wenchi Yu, Ambassador Melanne Verveer, and many other leaders for their concern about China's inhuman one-child policy and its devastating consequences in gendercide and a massive gender imbalance. I was deeply moved by Speaker of the House John Boehner's decision not to attend the state banquet in honor of President Hu and his willingness to speak out against China's one-child policy; and we all cheered when House Foreign Affairs Committee Chairwoman Ileana Ros-Lehtinen challenged President Hu about ending forced abortions under the one-child policy. All that President Hu could do was deny that such practices ever existed in China. On behalf of the four hundred million babies lost due to this policy, we pray that God would continue to raise up great leaders who will call China to account for these atrocities and bring to an end to the biggest crime against humanity of our time.

I'm thankful for *The Economist*, the magazine that started global awareness of the one hundred million missing girls and continues to advocate for the cause. Also, thanks to Jamie Dean from *World* magazine and Tim Morgan and his colleague at *Christianity Today* for their work to raise awareness of this cause. I'm thankful for the efforts of the United Nations, through UNFPA, UNICEF, the UN Human Rights Office, UN Women, and the World Health Organization for their joint efforts to end gendercide.

I'm also thankful to Congressman Chris Smith of New Jersey, a great American and champion of freedom, whose constant work for the past thirty-one years to help improve China's human rights conditions and end the one-child policy has been a heroic inspiration for me. His congressional hearings in November 2009 woke me up to the full magnitude of horror inflicted by China's one-child policy. Congressman Smith's integrity, humanity, and humility shine as a light on Capitol Hill as he does his work "as unto the Lord."

As we were finishing the book, we also completed a campaign to build a coalition on Capitol Hill to end gendercide. In addition to Congressman Smith, I am grateful to Congresswoman Vicky Hartzler of Missouri, Congresswoman Sheila Jackson Lee of Texas, Congressman Joe Pitts of Pennsylvania, Congressman Bill Johnson of Ohio, and Congressman Jeff Fortenberry of Nebraska. I also thank Massachusetts Senator Scott Brown for his support, and his beautiful daughter Ayla for signing up for our All Girls Allowed gala.

I thank the Norwegian Parliament, which nominated me unanimously for the Nobel Peace Prize in 1989. I thank the Nobel Committee for courageously granting the 2010 Nobel Peace Prize to our colleague Liu Xiaobo, when many nations were afraid to continue to challenge China on its human rights record. That's what the unprecedented three standing ovations were all about. Though we missed Liu during the ceremony, when the award was presented to an empty chair, we rejoiced at the injection of renewed hope and energy into the free China movement. After all the years of trials and tribulation, this was the first time we were thrown a big party and celebration. I thank the Norwegian people for all the missionaries they have sent to China. Your dedication and sacrifice are bearing fruit in a powerful way today.

I am grateful for the ongoing teaching from churches and others in the body of Christ that supports the transformations taking place in China. I am grateful for Rick Warren's *Purpose Driven Life*, which was instrumental in setting me on the path to find truth and ultimate freedom. Bob and I are grateful for Dr. Tim Keller's books *The Reason for God* and *Counterfeit Gods*, as well as his many teachings on CD and on the Redeemer Presbyterian Church website. I am a great admirer of what their City to City program has accomplished around the world. Jay Kyle and his team are filled with the love of Jesus, as shown by their courageous relief efforts in post-earthquake Japan. I have benefited so much from Bill Hybels's Leadership Summits, and I praise God for Bill's teaching and his willingness to serve other leaders. I am thankful for the amazing ministry of the National Prayer Breakfast and for Mr. and Mrs. Coe, and David and Mimi, and their devoted service and their spirit of love

and teaching. And Maria, you are such a special creation of our dear God. He gifted you with beauty, grace, brilliance, and a huge heart for women and girls. You shine the love of Jesus. Just thinking about you brings a smile into my heart. Thank you for all your prayers for the girls and babies in China. You saw what God saw, and you are so faithful! I am in awe of the number of leaders God has raised up in this country, including some whose names I have chosen to keep private for their ongoing work to share the Good News in dangerous places. All I know is, greater things are yet to come.

I am thankful for Cindi Leive, editor in chief of *Glamour* magazine, for her unique insight and leadership to expand and continue *Glamour*'s twenty-year-long commitment to honor and celebrate women and girls around the world through their inspiring Woman of the Year awards. Every time I attend one of their events, my spirit is lifted up and my heart is broken by the causes they choose to highlight and support—whether it's sex slavery against girls in Cambodia or China or child bride marriage in the Middle East, it inspires me to do more to love the women and children of the world, to raise awareness, and to help the poor and needy. I praise God for equipping Cindi and her excellent team, including Susan Goodall and Ellen Kampinsky, to continue their heroic work to spread the word. Cindi's generous support of the All Girls Allowed orphan program, in her daughter's name, moved us all deeply. Susan Goodall traveled from New York to be at our gala. I am deeply grateful for your generosity and your friendship.

I'm also thankful for our friend Matt Dalio and his family, who founded China Care and Harvard China Care to provide orphanages and surgical care to save and restore children in China, and for Eliza Petrow and Cherry Wan, whose passion and love to aid orphans in China continues to serve as an inspiration.

I am grateful to Mr. John Elliott, whose million-dollar donation enabled the founding of the China Initiative, which housed many exiled dissidents from China and gave me an opportunity to go to Princeton during my first year in America. I am grateful to Professor Yu Ying-shih and Mrs. Yu, who cared for and supported me like parents, with delicious homemade meals, furniture shopping to set up my first apartment, and much wise counsel. I am thankful to Ruan Ming and Mrs. Ruan, who also helped me many times, from driving me to dental appointments to later defending me from defamation. I am thankful to Lorraine Spieces, who sacrificed many years and savings to help people like me—it was with her help and encouragement that I was able to apply to Princeton. I am thankful to many other colleagues such as Zheng

Yi, Xiaokang, and Suwei for everything from their many encouragements to taking care of my dog, Tara.

I am thankful to Professor Lynn White, who advised me to study at Princeton and later recommended me to Harvard. I am thankful to Professor Perry Link, whose shared experience at Tiananmen forms a special bond. I am thankful to many friends at the Woodrow Wilson School who helped my English and sharpened my understanding of democracy and public policy. I am grateful for the full scholarship provided by the Woodrow Wilson School.

I thank Dr. Kim Clark, whose brilliant design of the first-of-its-kind course network inspired my design for Jenzabar.com, and Dr. Jay Light, whose teaching and whose special effort to be kind and supportive to me during my time at Harvard Business School were much appreciated. I thank many of my section mates and professors, with whom I shared debates and friendships. Go Section A, class of 1998! Shake the world to make that positive difference.

I am thankful to the many China scholars whose teaching and personal friendships have been a constant encouragement to me, including Dr. Andrew Nathan, Dr. Jonathan Spence, Dr. Roderick MacFarquhar, Dr. Rowena He, Dr. Orlando Patterson, and Dr. Gene Sharp.

In the commercial and business world, I am grateful to those who were willing to stand with me and support me, notwithstanding any risk to their own business interests in China. We need more like you! I am thankful to my friends at the American Program Bureau, whose service enabled me to earn some speaking honoraria that sustained my early years in America and helped my family in China.

I am thankful to the manager who hired me at the consulting firm, my first paid job in America. I am thankful to the late Barry Harrington, whose decision enabled me to continue to work at the firm and provided vital stability to support my newly reunited siblings after five years of separation. I thank Lynn Stem, whose solid values provided a breakthrough for the HR director to honor the firm's offer to me. I am very thankful to have worked for that firm—because that's where I met Bob, who much later became my husband. I thank the many friends and colleagues I met there.

I thank Paul Fireman and Steve Perlman for being my first two angel investors at Jenzabar. Even though circumstances did not allow us to fully achieve our billion-dollar vision, I would not be here without your courage and support.

I thank my early business colleagues at jenzabar.com—including Joe Malone, who introduced me to Steve Ballmer of Microsoft—and all of our three hundred associates, who work to maximize our customers' success every

day. I am grateful to our board of directors—D. Quinn Mill and Joe San Miguel—for their support and great guidance and to Jamison Barr for his good and faithful work for Jenzabar.

We would not be where we are today without the hundreds of colleges and universities that are loyal Jenzabar customers. I thank them for their service to millions of students, faculty, staff, alumni, friends, and their communities near and far. They inspired us to form The Jenzabar Foundation to support hundreds of student groups that are saving lives by the thousands every year. Among these, I especially thank Dr. Jairy Hunter of Charleston Southern University and his wife, Sissy; Dr. Kim Clark of Brigham Young University—Idaho and his wife, Susan; Dr. Jud Carlberg of Gordon College and his wife, Jan; Dr. Richard Flynn of Springfield University and his wife, Jani; Dr. Doug Hastad of Carroll University and his wife, Nancy; Dr. Jackie Jenkins Scott of Wheelock College and her husband, Jim; Dr. Nancy Blattner of Caldwell College and her husband, Tim; Dr. Pamela Trotman Reid of Saint Joseph College and her husband, Dr. Irvin Reid, president emeritus of Wayne State University; Dr. Stephen Briggs of Berry College and his wife, Brenda; Dr. David Olive of Bluefield College and his wife, Kathryn; Dr. Stephen Pannill of Cecil College and his wife, Pam; Dr. Daniel Carey of Edgewood College and his wife, Terri; Dr. Richard Wylie of Endicott College and his wife, Mary; Dr. William Abare of Flagler College and his wife, Susan; Dr. Kevin Ross of Lynn University and his wife, Kristen; Dr. Dan Martin of Mt. Vernon Nazarene University and his wife, Pam; Dr. Michael Droge of Park University and his wife, Molly; Michael Viollt of Robert Morris University and his wife, Kathleen; Dr. Rita Rice Morris of Shawnee State University and her husband, Jim; Dr. Charles Webb of Spring Arbor University and his wife, Philippa; Sr. Margaret Stallmeyer of Thomas More College; Dr. Donna Carroll of Dominican University; Dr. Elizabeth Stroble of Webster University and her husband, Paul; Dr. Lisa Ryerson of Wells College and her husband, George Farenthold; Dr. William Crouch of Georgetown College and his wife, Jan; Dr. Haywood Strickland of Wiley College; Dr. Helen Sobehart and Sr. Mary Lea Schneider of Cardinal Stritch University; Sr. Kathleen Ross of Heritage University; Dr. Constance Mierendorf, formerly of Sussex Community College; and Dr. Dorothy Cowser Yancy, formerly of Shaw University. Special thanks to Don Oppenheimer, associate dean and chief information officer at Harvard's Kennedy School of Government, who personally supported our Harvard China Care benefit dinner. We are also grateful to our Presidents' Advisory Council and the many advisory and user groups making Jenzabar such a great success. Thank you all.

I have been blessed with great spiritual friends who have changed my life forever and for better. I thank Fengsuo; Fang Zheng; the Rev. John Holt, from the Methodist church on Cape Cod; Jairy Hunter and Jud Carlberg; Reggie Littlejohn, from Women's Rights Without Frontiers; Bob Fu, from ChinaAid; Zhang Boli, pastor of a Chinese church in Virginia; Major Xiong Yan, a US Army chaplain; Sister Tammy McLeod, Park Street minister and chaplain of Campus Crusade at Harvard, and her husband, Pat—their son Zack's heroic commitment to Jesus is a daily inspiration; Dr. Gordon Hugenberger, senior minister at Park Street Church in Boston; John Chung, minister of missions at Park Street Church; Dr. Bryan Wilkerson, senior minister at Grace Chapel; the Honorable Gregory Slaton; Jaeson Ma, hip hop artist and church planter; and the Heavenly Man, Brother Yun—it was your witnessing and help that led me to Jesus.

I am thankful to the many new friends I have met since I started All Girls Allowed: Fred Smith, president of the Gathering; Steve Hass, chief catalyst at World Vision; Wes Anderson; Pastor Jones and his family; Pastor Ron Lewis; Pastor David Hill, Sr., and Pastor David Hill, Jr.; Mac McQuiston, president and CEO of the CEO Forum; Steve South, vice president of the CEO Forum; and many others. Your prayers, teaching, and support are vital to encourage us to focus on finishing the race that has been marked out for us.

I thank Peter Flaherty and Mike Flaherty for their great friendship and spiritual fellowship. Peter came up with the great name All Girls Allowed, helped us get the logo design, and assisted with our first year launch in DC. Mike's life-changing transformation that led to the founding of Walden Media, which brings great movies to our society to teach children the power of love over violence, is a shining inspiration to us all. Mike served as an adviser to All Girls Allowed, offering much of his time, advice, connections, and promotion for the cause. Bob and I are grateful to Mike and his wonderful wife, Kelly, and their children, Christian, Eileen, and Reagan, for their friendship to our family.

I am thankful to Joe Torres for delivering the call to start All Girls Allowed. I am grateful to David Aikman for his faithful prayers, encouragement, and guidance during my first year of spiritual growth and serving through All Girls Allowed. His amazing book *Jesus in Beijing* is a must-read for anyone who wants to know the not-often-told and important modern history of China. I am grateful also to Charlene, Wilfred, and John Quick for their help and contributions to All Girls Allowed.

I am thankful to my Jenzabar team members who walk this spiritual journey with me, and to my All Girls Allowed team: Brian, Sara, Tessa, Val, Katie,

Vicky, Jing, and Yan. I am grateful for all your prayers and support in the past year. You gave me the precious gift of true fellowship.

I am thankful to two dear friends (you know who you are) who encouraged and supported me during the writing of this difficult book project. I am grateful to David Aikman for his generous recommendation to Tyndale. I am grateful to Jan Long Harris and Doug Knox for their decision to publish the book and to publish it so quickly. I am very grateful to my editor, Dave Lindstedt, who did a heroic job to shorten the manuscript to half its size while preserving most of the content and flow. Also for his patience during the final weeks of editing to walk with Bob and me with understanding and grace. I am grateful for the many other team members at Tyndale whose great work has brought this book to print.

I am thankful for my church, my life community, my small group, my brothers and sisters in Christ, including Pastor Bryan, Simone, Steve, Judy, Guiying, Esther, Chengen, Isabella, Mike and Cori, Ken and Kristina, Deb and Chris, Carrie and Mike, Rachel, Yola, Lori, Meghan, and many others. You blessed me with the true American Dream described in Alexis de Tocqueville's *Democracy in America*. The church is truly the foundation of American society.

I could not have done this without my family support. I am thankful to my two faithful nannies, who have been with our family for a decade and supported me and cared deeply for my children.

I am thankful for my mother-in-law, Valerie, who was rooting for me and cheered me on.

I am thankful to my father, who gave up everything to be with us in America and to love us and support us. I am thankful to my brother and my sister, who love me and inspire me every day.

I am grateful for Bob, my husband, who has been and will always be a hero to me for his sacrifice and encouragement over the past two years as I labored on this book. I am thankful to my three girls—Mia, Alicia, and Emma—for their patience and sacrifice and their unconditional love and support.

I am ultimately thankful to God, Jesus Christ, and the Holy Spirit, who knew me before Creation and who gave me life and guided me and protected me. To God be all the glory and thanksgiving.

Visit AHeartforFreedom.com to:

Learn more about Chai Ling and her ministry

Link to an online book discussion guide

Sign up for an online newsletter to receive the latest news about *A Heart for Freedom* and other compelling books from Tyndale

And more!

All Girls Allowed

Join All Girls Allowed in restoring life, value, and dignity to girls and mothers in China:

- **Help End Gendercide**—Educating families against female gendercide and easing the financial burden of having a baby girl.
- **Educate Abandoned Girls**—Providing scholarships for abandoned girls to receive primary, secondary, and post-secondary education.
- **Rescue Trafficked Children**—Equipping parents to find their kidnapped children.
- **Defend Mothers**—Supplying legal defense to victims of forced abortion or sterilization as well as those at risk.

Learn more at www.allgirlsallowed.org.

CP0501

Online Discussion Guide

TAKE YOUR TYNDALE READING EXPERIENCE TO THE NEXT LEVEL

A FREE discussion guide for this book is available at bookclubhub.net, perfect for sparking conversations in your book group or for digging deeper into the text on your own.

www.bookclubhub.net

You'll also find free discussion guides for other Tyndale books, e-newsletters, e-mail devotionals, virtual book tours, and more!

CP0070